# Reviving *the* Reformation

# Reviving *the* Reformation

*A Jewish Believer Peers Backward*
*to Move Biblical Truth Forward*

DANIEL LANG

NORTHLOOP
BOOKS

To

the Jew first

and also to the Greek

(Romans 1:16)

AND

To my *Eyshet Chayil*

# TABLE OF CONTENTS

# Introduction

The Protestant Reformation suffered a premature death. The Reformation attempted to correct some major errors that had crept into the "church" over the previous 1,400 years, but it fell short of the mark. If alive today, the earliest Jewish believers in Jerusalem would have trouble recognizing modern, traditional Christianity as its offspring, including the Protestant churches that reformed. This book is an attempt to continue the reforming process begun in the early 1500s by Luther et al. It will not be an attempt to create something new out of Christianity—the push of liberal theologians to bring Christianity into the modern age. Rather, this book will be an attempt to restore the biblical framework that the God of Abraham, Isaac, and Jacob had planned for His people (Jews and Gentiles) from the beginning.

The above paragraph makes this book sound as if it were written only for Christians. Most observant Jews never belonged to the "church," and they were outsiders to the Protestant Reformation. However, this book was also written for the Jewish community. Through these pages, I will additionally try to correct significant misunderstandings about the authentic Jewish Messianic faith that have been prevalent in the Jewish community for the past 1,900 years.

Imagine that you worked in an airport control tower on September 11, 2001. Pretend that your job, over the radio, was to convince one of the terrorist pilots heading for a target that he was making a wrong choice. Most of us would recognize that this assignment would be futile. That terrorist had fixed his mind on a particular "truth" and, for this reason, no one would be able to shake his faith. All of us to some extent are like that terrorist (including myself). We have accepted faith positions, our own "truths," and there is no shaking us from them.

In this book, I will attempt to rock the foundations of the faith positions held by atheists, traditional Jews, Messianic Jews, and Gentile Christians. Each of these groups traditionally will have different points of conflict with me. I recognize from the start that the writing of this book might be a futile enterprise. Can anyone change 1,900 years of faith-based traditions?* Nevertheless, if I can influence anyone in the smallest way to reconsider some of his or her faith positions, bringing people closer to God, I will have succeeded.

This book is written from a conservative point of view but does not often follow the party line. I have been advised not to question the conventional "truths." I have been told that questioning the traditional faith positions will lead to that slippery slope toward atheism. I think this investigation is like walking on the ridge of a slanted roof. One could easily slip off and never recover his footing. However, truth seeking does not need to be an impossible or an undesirable feat to attempt. In addition, if some of the faith positions we once held dearly are discovered through investigation not to be true, we do not need to cast off other related truths.†

In geometry, one learns that between any two points on a line segment, one can always insert another point. In some ways, this is like the search for the truth. There is an absolute truth out there somewhere, but man's best efforts might only be able to place points

---

\* Few people ever suddenly change their worldview. New ideas that often are shunned initially tend to slowly grow on us over time if they make sense to us.

† The popular author Bart Ehrman seems to be one of those who fell off the roof. He became "born again" in high school, attended Moody Bible Institute and Wheaton College, and then had a radical change in his theology at Princeton Theological Seminary when he discovered some errors in his faith position. (Bart D. Ehrman, *Misquoting Jesus: The Story Behind Who Changed the Bible and Why* [San Francisco: Harper Collins Publishers, 2005], pp. 1–15.)

closer and closer to it over time. In this book, I will attempt to get closer to the truth, but I realize that we will never arrive at our exact destination with our limited knowledge and understanding. As thinking men and women, our responsibility is to get as close to the truth as we possibly can.

In most cases, the truth is easy to defend. Some arguments created to support false faith positions, however, can often be very convincing. Many defenders of "the faith" become contortionists, bending and twisting the evidence to fit their conceptions of the truth. They end up with a Three Stooges plumbing job with pipes running every which way. I hope to take down some of these artificial creations. The responsibility of the follower of God is not to defend the traditional position of the church or the synagogue, but to uphold the truth of God.

Often we take possession of our corner of the world or our life experience and put it in competition with that of others. My school, my football team, my city, my country, my nationality, my religion is better than yours is. Truth seeking should be divorced from competition. We should not be in the business of proving that mine is better than yours, but of striving to find *the* universal truth that belongs to all people.

According to the Torah (the Five Books of Moses), the descendants of Abraham, Isaac, and Jacob are to bring a blessing to the families of the earth:‡ "And in you [Abram] all the families of the earth shall be blessed" (Genesis 12:3). Much of this blessing for the world will involve the promised Jewish Messiah, but there is also a role for the Jewish people themselves. Sha'ul (Paul) seems to say that the acceptance of the promised Jewish Messiah by his own flesh and blood will one day lead to the release of unprecedented supernatural

---

‡   One piece of evidence for the accuracy of this statement is the continued use of the Torah or concepts coming out of the Torah by Gentiles in the two most populous monotheistic religions on Earth, Christianity and Islam. The blessing of the Torah came into the world through the descendants of Abraham, Isaac, and Jacob.

power through the Jewish people. The people of Israel will then be instrumental in bringing the world back to God in a fullness that we have yet to experience: "For if their rejection means the reconciliation of the world, what will their acceptance mean but life from the dead?" (Romans 11:15).

Unfortunately, Messianic Judaism, a movement that started in the 1960s, has not been successful to date in accomplishing this goal. Instead of continuing to blaze a trail that began in the first century, it has veered from the path and lost its way, going toward either Orthodox Judaism or Evangelical Christianity. My hope is that this book can help place the Messianic movement back on track—to form a body that will begin the job of reconciling the world back to God.

Powerful forces have continuously tried to suppress God's voice in the world. The silencing of God's truth, as expressed in Scripture, is accelerating again with the rise of such entities as communism, fascism, scientific materialism, leftist radicalism, and Islamic radicalism. We need to be equipped with the unadulterated "whole armor of God" (Ephesians 6:13–17) to battle these ideologies.

Acquiring head knowledge about God and universal truth is not an end in itself. Our ultimate goal should be to develop an ongoing "trusting"§ relationship with God. Trusting needs to occur even when we are not privileged to see all of the details in which we are trusting: "Trusting is being confident of what we hope for, convinced about things we do not see" (Messianic Jews [Hebrews] 11:1, *Complete Jewish Bible*). Trusting requires submission of our lives into the hands of our Creator: "Trust in the LORD with all your heart, and do not lean on your own understanding. In all your ways acknowledge him, and he will make straight your paths" (Prov-

---

§ David Stern suggests that the New Testament Greek verb for "belief/trust/faith" is better rendered "trusting." (David H. Stern, *Jewish New Testament Commentary* [Clarksville, MD: Jewish New Testament Publications, 1992], p. 329.) Therefore, he translates Romans 1:16: "For I am not ashamed of the Good News, since it is God's powerful means of bringing salvation to everyone who keeps on trusting, to the Jew especially, but equally to the Gentile" (Romans 1:16, *Complete Jewish Bible*).

erbs 3:5–6). It is both the knowledge of the truth and a trusting relationship with God that give our lives meaning. Being light in a dark world gives our lives purpose.

The biblical Messianic faith cannot be understood by reading a Bible verse on a passing sign. It cannot be explained to someone in a thirty-second conversation. Much tangled history needs to be unraveled for proper understanding, and this discussion can often lead to a charged atmosphere. This book, in my opinion, is the type of dialogue required for a correct understanding. It is here for people to digest in the comfort of their homes.

I have an advantage as a writer of theology. My livelihood does not come from "religion." I am not a rabbi, a pastor, or a university professor in a religion department. I do not have to be afraid of offending someone who might be paying my salary. In addition, I am not trying to make money from selling a book. I will say what I think needs to be said. The disadvantage is that I am a layman without formal training. I admit much ignorance in many areas of this topic. I have zero Greek language proficiency and minimal Hebrew language skills. I cannot possibly read everything there is to read. Many academics might say I have not earned the right to be heard. However, understanding God cannot be the purview of only the professionals; it must be the obligation of the laymen, too.

This book is over forty years in the making. Few of the ideas that I discuss in this book are completely original. Where my knowledge is limited, I have used expert researchers from a broad range of Jewish and Christian perspectives. For the first chapter, I have also depended upon theorists from the intelligent design community. I am indebted to those whom I have read or listened to over the years. One could say that I am an editor of ideas. As a writer, I look at my job as making a complex subject simple.

Since we are dealing with truth and reality here, I will start in the first chapter by evaluating the evidence for the existence of the Creator God. At the end of this chapter, I will also begin to hone in on His identity. If God does not exist, any attempt to revive the Reformation would be a useless undertaking.

In the second chapter, I will explore from a Jewish perspective whether Yeshua (Jesus) could be the promised Messiah of Israel. I will do this by evaluating some of the incorrect notions surrounding the messianic idea, including the role of the Messiah as outlined in the Tanach.⁵

The third chapter will characterize the sin nature as it is revealed to us through a classic narrative from the book of Genesis. I will then outline lessons from the Tanach that teach us how to deal with it.

Evidence that supports Torah observance for the follower of God is presented in chapters four through six. This segment includes arguments for keeping a seventh-day Shabbat (Sabbath) and for upholding the Torah's dietary restrictions.

Chapters seven through nine will examine God's holy community composed of both Jews and Gentiles. This portion will look at the relationship between these two entities and make a case for Gentiles also to observe the Torah. The last of these chapters will define the job descriptions of both Jews and Gentiles in the community.

The last three chapters before the summary, chapters ten through twelve, will delve into the concept of the Trinity with a magnifier on the deity of Yeshua. I will first look at the numerous New Testament** texts that contradict a divine Yeshua. Afterward, I will examine prophetic and other "proof texts" in the Hebrew Bible proposed to support Yeshua's deity. Chapter eleven will attempt to identify the descendants of the earliest Jewish believers from Jerusalem and determine what they understood about Yeshua's nature. Lastly, I will investigate the reliability of the New Testament texts that characterize Yeshua as Deity.

---

⁵   TaNaCH is an acronym formed from the three divisions of the Hebrew Bible: *Torah* (the Five Books of Moses), *N'vi'im* (the Prophets), *K'tuvim* (the Writings), commonly known as the Old Testament. The "ch" is pronounce as in the German name Bach.

**   Messianic Jews often shun the name "New Testament" and use instead *B'rit Hadashah* or "New Covenant." The term New Testament suggests that the Old Testament has been replaced or become obsolete. To avoid confusion, however, I have stuck with the familiar name.

The writing of this book is a selfish endeavor. It is a catalog of my personal faith positions. I can use it to help myself stay on track when I am tempted to lose my way. I am hoping it might also be a help like that for others.

## Chapter 1: Evidence for the Existence of God

### YHVH the Creator God

In this first chapter, I am going to be politically incorrect. I am going to argue that there is a God, that He is the "Creator God"[1] described in the Hebrew Bible, and that He is the only one. I am not of the opinion that all religions lead to God or that the story of the same God can be told in many different ways.[2] Because of my understanding of God's reality, I have been told that I join the ranks of those who believe in the tooth fairy. I have no proof for the existence of the tooth fairy, but I do have evidence for the existence of God.

The God of the Tanach identified Himself to Moses in Exodus, chapters 3 and 4, as the Creator God of the patriarchs—Abraham, Isaac, and Jacob. He has a specific name, written by the Hebrew letters *Yod*, *Heh*, *Vov*, and *Heh*, which I will designate as YHVH.[*] (Orthodox

---

[*] Many commentators would say this name is probably derived from the Hebrew verb "to be." Rabbi David Fohrman points out that the three tenses—past, present, and future—of the verb "to be" in the masculine, third person singular form superimposed on one another would spell YHVH. He says the name represents a "simultaneous experience" of time. The Creator God is "outside" of His creation that from the very beginning included the material universe as well as the creation of "space and time." (Rabbi David Fohrman, "Passover: What Does It Mean to Be Chosen?" Segment 4—*What's in a Name*, AlephBeta, accessed June, 14 2015, www.alephbeta.org/course/lecture/whats-in-a-name.) Rabbi Fohrman does not endorse any ideas in this book, here or in later chapters.

Jews do not attempt to pronounce this name; therefore, I will respect that position and not try to do so in this book.) God tells Moses how to reveal His name to the people of Israel: "Say this to the people of Israel, 'The LORD [YHVH], the God of your fathers, the God of Abraham, the God of Isaac, and the God of Jacob, has sent me to you.' This is my name forever, and thus I am to be remembered throughout all generations" (Exodus 3:15). The God of the Hebrew Bible, the true God, has no other name or identity.

The opening words of the Torah in Genesis state: "In the beginning, God created the heavens and the earth" (Genesis 1:1). The book of Genesis is not a scientific textbook but, according to John Sailhamer, is a "historical narrative" ("the re-presentation of past events for the purpose of instruction").[3†] God does not tell us how He did His work, but that He is the One who did it. Naturalists say that religious people often inserted God into the gaps of our scientific knowledge. They say that as our scientific knowledge expands, eventually all men will realize that there is no need for the crutch of God to explain anything. However, just the opposite is true. As science gains more and more information about our universe, it is becoming apparent that it

---

† John Sailhamer's *Genesis Unbound: A Provocative New Look at the Creation Account* is a unique presentation that "opens the door to reconciliation of biblical and scientific world views." Sailhamer argues that the first verse of Genesis is a "merism" declaring that God created the universe and everything in it—including life—over an undetermined amount of time. The rest of Genesis chapters 1–2 tells us that God later "prepared" "the land" (*eretz*—"land" rather than "earth" in this context) in six days for the man and woman to live on and that He created man on the sixth day. This "land" has the same boundaries and theological implications as the Promised Land found later in the text of the Hebrew Bible. When men disobey, they are removed from the "land" like Adam and later Israel (often toward Babylon). As Adam is driven out, cherubim are placed at the east of the Garden. Going back to the "land," Jacob, and later Joshua, meet heavenly beings on the eastern side. The prophets associate the Promised Land with the Garden: Ezekiel 36:35, Joel 2:3, Isaiah 51:3, Zechariah 14:8, and Jeremiah 4:23–26. (John Sailhamer, *Genesis Unbound: A Provocative New Look at the Creation Account* [Sisters, OR: Multnomah Books, 1996].)

was designed.[4] Many of the purely naturalistic explanations for the origins of the universe and life, including neo-Darwinian evolution, no longer satisfy.[‡]

## Origins: A Historical Science

The science of "origins" comes with a particular method of investigation. One fact that is often not appreciated, but is clarified by Stephen Meyer, a popular intelligent design writer, is that the sciences can be broadly divided into two categories: the experimental sciences, such as chemistry, physics, and much of biology; and the historical sciences, such as archeology, forensic medicine, paleontology, and geology.[5] Scientists from both of these scientific categories begin the scientific method by observing the world around them. Afterward, these scientists generate hypotheses to try to explain the observations. The experimental scientists then collect data through experimentation to try to prove or disprove their hypotheses. For example, the scientists who hypothesized that the Earth is round and not flat and that the Earth revolves around the sun, and not the sun around the Earth, could set up the appropriate experiments and eventually prove their point. The historical scientists, however, use a different method, since experimentation is not available for events that happened in the past. As Meyer explains, they use "the method of multiple competing hypotheses or the method of inferring to the best explanation."[6] "Inferring to the best explanation" requires us to use our everyday experience and knowledge to guide us.[7]

Agatha Christie's detective Poirot is the classic "historical scientist."[8] After a crime, which he did not witness, he gathers an immense amount of evidence. During this process, he formulates hypotheses

---

‡   Since this will only be a very cursory presentation of some of the arguments of the scientific discipline of intelligent design, I encourage the interested reader to investigate the books listed in the footnotes and bibliography as well as other books and web sites (http://www.discovery.org/id/) on this topic that are not listed. None of these authors necessarily endorses ideas found in this chapter or in the rest of this book, however.

as to who could have committed the crime and why. By the end of the story, just about every character is a potential suspect. Poirot carefully sifts through the "multiple competing hypotheses" and solves the murder by "inferring to the best explanation."

The science of "origins" falls into the category of a historical science and would use the scientific "method of inferring to the best explanation" to evaluate the generated hypotheses. After evaluating the multiple competing hypotheses to explain the origin of our universe, intelligent design theorists infer that a "designer,"[9] an "intelligent agent,"[10] must have been involved in the "fine-tuning" of our physical universe,[11] as well as the source of the "large amounts of functionally specified information" found in living things.[12]

According to Meyer, our human experience tells us that information always comes from an "intelligent agent." Meyer points out that the United States government SETI project (the Search for Extra-Terrestrial Intelligence), established by NASA, is based on this foundation. Radio telescopes are currently scanning the heavens to find intelligence somewhere in the universe. If those scientists were to receive a signal from deep space that was full of "a complex and specified pattern," they would know that they had found an intelligent source. They would not chalk it up to a material process.[13]

## The Universe Had a Beginning and Is Just Right for Life

Most scientists in the nineteenth and early twentieth centuries believed that the universe did not have a beginning—it was infinite in age.[14] Albert Einstein was such a thinker; he mistakenly modified the equations of his general theory of relativity in 1917 to support his concept of a "static universe."[15] In the early 1930s, however, Vesto Slipher and Edwin Hubble observed that the light from galaxies is shifted to the red portion of the spectrum. Because of the Doppler effect, the stretching of light waves moving away, this red shift suggests that the galaxies are moving away, that the universe is expanding. If the universe is expanding, then, it must have had a beginning. The theory of the big bang was born.[16]

Arno Penzias and Robert Wilson further solidified the big bang theory in the 1960s when they detected remnants of the microwave radiation background left over from the big bang.[17] In addition, the second law of thermodynamics§ supports a beginning to the universe. The energy released by the sun and all the stars will eventually cease, according to this law. The universe could not have remained static forever coming out of the past. It would have met its doom by now.[18] Interestingly, the Bible tells us that the universe had a beginning (Genesis 1:1).¶

Scientists have been studying the fundamental laws of physics for centuries. Modern scientists, more recently, have been able to measure the values of many physical constants of the universe. In *Cosmic Jackpot: Why Our Universe Is Just Right for Life*, Paul Davies names the masses of particles and the strengths of forces as examples.[19] As it turns out, there are about thirty undetermined constants in particle physics and cosmology. Davies says many of these constants (such as the strong and weak nuclear forces, the electromagnetic force, and the force of gravity)[20] had to be "fine-tuned to an accuracy of less than 1 percent" in order for life to exist.

There is no known reason why the constants have been set at the current values. According to Davies, it appears as if a "cosmic

---

§   The second law of thermodynamics states that "an isolated system, free of external influence, will, if it is initially in a state of relative order, always pass to states of relative disorder until it eventually reaches the state of maximum disorder." (Richard T. Weidner and Robert L. Sells, *Elementary Classical Physics*, Volume 1 [Boston: Allyn and Bacon, Inc., 1973], pp. 393–394.)

¶   Richard Dawkins says the Bible had a 50:50 chance of getting the correct answer—either the universe had a beginning or it did not. He suggests that the Bible made a good "guess." (Richard Dawkins, John Lennox, *The God Delusion Debate* [Fixed Point Foundation, 2007].) The brilliant Albert Einstein had the same 50:50 chance of getting the correct answer, but he was wrong. Would Dawkins say he was guessing also? Actually, the same faulty, naturalistic worldview of Richard Dawkins caused Einstein to stumble here.

designer" had been adjusting the knobs for the different constants of a "cosmic designer machine" to make them "just right for life."[21] He calls this "the Goldilocks Enigma"—the conundrum that the physical conditions for life in our universe and on our planet are just right.[22] To push back against the appearance of a designer universe, some scientists have been toying with the idea of a "multiverse." In this concept, our universe is one out of an infinite number of universes, each one having different characteristics.[23] We were the lucky ones who ended up in the universe having the appearance of being designed for life.[24] This idea is certainly a faith position. Our experience would tell us that if it looks like it was designed, then it probably was.[25]**

## Evolution Defined

As we transition to investigate the origin of life, we need first to clarify the meaning of the word "evolution." This word that has multiple meanings has been blurred in the origin of life debates. In *The Design of Life: Discovering Signs of Intelligence in Biological Systems*, William A. Dembski and Jonathan Wells tell us that evolution can mean "that organisms have changed over time, that organisms can adapt to changing environmental conditions, or that gene frequencies may vary in a population."[26] These definitions are often referred to as microevolution. Evolution can also be defined as "universal common descent" or "the creative power of natural selection"[27]—this second definition being called macroevolution.

Often, naturalists do not qualify the meaning of the word

---

** Another fascinating feature of our universe discussed by Guillermo Gonzalez and Jay W. Richards is that it was "designed for discovery." Not only is man capable of discovering, but many features from our vantage point on the Earth lend themselves to effective discovery of the universe—such as "our place in the Milky Way galaxy," the transparent "properties of our atmosphere," "solar eclipses," "sedimentation processes," and many others. (Guillermo Gonzalez and Jay W. Richards, *The Privileged Planet: How Our Place in the Cosmos Is Designed for Discovery* [Washington, DC: Regnery Publishing, Inc., 2004], pp. x, 311, 318–319.)

evolution when used in different contexts, making it seem that microevolution and macroevolution are the same processes. For instance, Meyer writes, they speak much about changes in peppered moth colors, finch beak size, dog breeding, or bacterial antibiotic resistance, assuming that these types of microevolutionary changes can be "extrapolated" into macroevolutionary changes over time.[28] However, even though natural selection does operate in nature to produce "small-scale changes"[29] and can work on a limited supply of potentially advantageous mutations,[30][††] moths remain moths, birds remain birds, dogs remain dogs, and bacteria remain bacteria.[31]

Natural selection is limited in its ability to create.[32] In *The Edge of Evolution: The Search for the Limits of Darwinism*, Michael Behe crunches the numbers to define the limits of natural selection working on random mutations and finds the probability for a creative process to be infinitesimally small.[33] Douglas Axe, another intelligent design theorist, calls this macroevolutionary conjecture, the creative power of natural selection working on random mutations, "Darwin's little engine that couldn't."[34]

## A Primordial Organic Soup?

For years, it had been widely proposed that meaningful organic compounds could have occurred by chance in a "primordial organic 'soup,'" as outlined in one of my college textbooks.[35] A. I. Oparin and J. B. S. Haldane made the first proposals in the 1920s, with later experiments conducted by Stanley Miller in 1953 at the University of

---

†† Mutations, even though sometimes beneficial for an organism, often are breaking down rather than building up. Michael Behe gives the example of the sickle hemoglobin mutation that protects against malaria at the expense of malfunctioning red blood cells. (Michael J. Behe, *The Edge of Evolution: The Search for the Limits of Darwinism* [New York: Free Press, 2007], p. 42.) He also reveals how the mutated chloroquine (antibiotic) resistant malaria organism tends to revert to its original form when chloroquine is removed from the environment. The "original" malaria organism is more fit than the chloroquine resistant strain. (Michael J. Behe, *The Edge of Evolution: The Search for the Limits of Darwinism*, pp. 50–51.)

Chicago.[36] However, the probability of forming meaningful organic compounds by chance from such a "soup" is off the charts.[37]

Richard Dawkins acknowledges that the spontaneous arising of a protein could not have been the key step in the origin of life since proteins cannot make copies of themselves.[38] He also sees the problems encountered by imagining DNA as the original, spontaneous molecule of life since the machinery of DNA requires protein enzymes to make protein enzymes.[39] Dawkins feels that the magic molecule might be RNA as proposed in the RNA world theory, since RNA can replicate and act as an enzyme.[40]

In detail, Meyer points out several problems with the RNA world theory. For instance, RNA is not a stable enough molecule to function in this role. RNA as an enzyme cannot equal the efficacy of protein enzymes. The RNA world theory also does not account for the source of encoded information in the cell.[41] For the record, Dawkins admits, "We know little more than Darwin did about how it got started in the first place."[42] As our knowledge increases in this area, we end up rejecting more and more of the materialistic, "scientific" theories that have been formulated.

## The Source of Biological Information

One of the main features needing to be explained by origin of life researchers today is the source of genetic or biological information. Meyer explores this issue in *Signature in the Cell: DNA and the Evidence for Intelligent Design*.[43] This problem was not well appreciated until James Watson and Francis Crick began unraveling the structure and function of DNA in the 1950s.[44] The DNA machinery is incredibly elaborate, even making the highly structured proteins that are required for its very function,[45] leading to a "chicken and egg" problem.[46]

DNA contains a vast amount of "complex," "specified" information stored in computer-like DNA code.[47] Triplets of four possible nucleotide bases grouped on the DNA backbone encode for all of the amino acids in a protein. This information in DNA is first transcribed into messenger RNA, and then the RNA copy is transported out of the nucleus where the information is translated into a protein. The cell can also replicate DNA to transmit the information to future generations. What is the source of this information stored in computer-like DNA code and the source of the high-tech DNA/RNA machinery? Meyer again reasons that an "intelligent agent" must have designed it.[48]

According to Meyer, the information stored in DNA is turning out to be only part of the information-rich processes governing life. Other "higher-level" sources of information key to building an organism's "body plan" are being investigated,[49] such as "developmental gene regulatory networks" and "epigenetic information" both critical to embryological development.[50] As time goes on, the plot thickens as to the origin of even more layers of information.

## The Junk DNA Fallacy

Shortly after the discovery of DNA, scientists noted that only about 2 percent of DNA was responsible for manufacturing proteins. For many decades, the remaining DNA was regarded as nonfunctional "junk." Neo-Darwinists proposed that this junk DNA was leftover remnants of failed mutations over the course of evolutionary history that pointed away from an intelligent designer who, if he existed, would not logically clutter the genome with junk.[51] As the intelligent design scientist Casey Luskin disclosed, the junk DNA mindset discouraged many scientists from even studying noncoding DNA.[52‡‡]

---

‡‡ Some naturalists are under the impression that belief in God is a "science stopper." John Lennox writes that science historians know this notion is unfounded after studying the lives of men such as Galileo, Bacon, Kepler, Pascal, Boyle, Newton, Faraday, Babbage, Mendel, Pasteur, Kelvin, and Maxwell, who all believed in God. (John C. Lennox, *God's Undertaker: Has Science Buried God?* [Oxford, UK: Lion Books, 2009], pp. 21, 48–51.) Curiously, the opposite is true. Rejection of a designer resulted in Einstein missing big bang cosmology and naturalist researchers missing the importance of noncoding DNA. Intelligent design theorists have the potential to stimulate new paths of research that might have been stifled by naturalist thinking. (Stephen C. Meyer, *Darwin's Doubt: The Explosive Origin of Animal Life and the Case for Intelligent Design* [New York: HarperCollins Publishers, 2013], pp. 402–403.)

Eventually, many scientific papers were published in September of 2012 from the nine-year ENCODE project (Encyclopedia of DNA Elements). As of that date, about 20–50 percent of the noncoding DNA segments were discovered to be involved in regulating genes. It is felt that over time, more and more of the noncoding segments will be found to have a purpose.[53]

## Neo-Darwinian Evolution Cannot Explain Irreducibly Complex Systems

In *Darwin's Black Box: The Biochemical Challenge to Evolution*, Michael Behe informs us that the scientists at the time of Darwin had no clue what was going on inside of cells. It was easy to speculate that cells were simple Jell-O–like forms of life that the process of evolution could readily transform into more sophisticated living organisms.[54] Since the 1950s, though, we have learned that even the "simplest-appearing" cells contain intricate biochemical "machines."[55][§§] Many of these complicated "machines" are "irreducibly complex" systems.[56][¶¶]

Dembski and Wells state that a "functional system is irreducibly complex if it contains a multipart subsystem [the irreducible core] (i.e., a set of two or more interrelated parts) that cannot be simplified

---

§§ Michael Behe relates that when the many branches of biology met to formulate the neo-Darwinian synthesis in the middle of the twentieth century, they did not yet have the information that would shortly spring forth from the discipline of biochemistry—information that now should be changing the neo-Darwinian mindset. (Michael J. Behe, *Darwin's Black Box: The Biochemical Challenge to Evolution* [New York: Free Press, 2006], pp. 24–25.)

¶¶ Michael Behe gives us many examples of irreducibly complex biochemical machines: "the cell cilium (pp. 59–69), the bacterial flagellum (pp. 69–72), the blood clotting system (pp. 74–97), cellular vesicular transport (pp. 98–116), the human immune system (pp. 117–139), "DNA replication, electron transport, telomere synthesis, photosynthesis, transcription regulation" (p. 160), "production of AMP," "biosynthesis of the larger amino acids, lipids, vitamins, heme" (p. 161). (Michael J. Behe, *Darwin's Black Box: The Biochemical Challenge to Evolution* [New York: Free Press, 2006], pp. 160–161.)

without destroying the system's basic function."[57] If you remove one of the components of the "irreducible core," the system will no longer work. By definition, a simpler core does not exist that would allow for the system's essential function.[58]

Behe famously gives the example of a mousetrap as an irreducibly complex system. All of the parts of a mousetrap (platform, hammer, catch, spring, and holding bar) need to be present in the correct relationship for the mousetrap to catch mice.[59] Alternatively, one could think of another type of irreducibly complex system in the favorite board game Mouse Trap. The Mouse Trap game is a "Rube Goldberg"-type machine where in tandem all of the component parts work to produce the desired response[60]—again, that of catching mice.

How could an irreducibly complex system come into existence? Neo-Darwinian evolution proposes a gradual process whereby natural selection works on random mutations to create living systems over time. According to this theory, complex systems do not form all at once, fully made, out of nothing. For this process to construct an irreducibly complex system, it would need to work on some precursor system step-by-step. However, by definition, an irreducibly complex system must be intact for it to provide some function for the cell. Natural selection could not create irreducibly complex machines bit by bit since the precursor machine going through the "building process" would not provide any function for the cell.

If the above mousetraps were living machines, natural selection would be unable to build them in stages since only the finished product could catch mice and provide a function. Since functionless precursors could not offer a survival advantage for the cell, natural selection would be unable to recognize or select them.[61]

Darwin admitted, "If it could be demonstrated that any complex organ existed, which could not possibly have been formed by numerous, successive, slight modifications, my theory would absolutely break down."[62] It appears that with irreducibly complex biochemical machines, Darwin's theory breaks down.***

***    Some naturalist researchers have proposed "indirect" routes for the "creation" of irreducibly complex biochemical machines. Such proposals are always

## The Fossil Record Does Not Tell the Darwinian Story

The fossil record, even though reported to be rather complete, has not revealed the type of evidence for which the neo-Darwinian scientific community would have wished. Darwin himself said:

> The number of intermediate varieties, which have formerly existed, be truly enormous. Why then is not every geological formation and every stratum full of such intermediate links? Geology assuredly does not reveal any such finely-graduated organic chain; and this, perhaps, is the most obvious and serious objection which can be urged against the theory. The explanation lies, as I believe, in the extreme imperfection of the geological record.[63]

Over the 150 years since the time of Darwin, much more exploration has occurred, but the fossil evidence for macroevolution has not changed much.[†††] Since the process of evolution is proposed to have occurred slowly over millions of years, Dembski and Wells assert that the fossil record should demonstrate transition forms that resemble a "color wheel," "blending imperceptibly" from one major group of organisms to another.[64] Rather, what we find in the fossil record is the sudden appearance of "basic body plans"; "stasis" (where organisms remain unchanged in the fossil record over time);

---

speculations, lacking in meaningful details. For instance, what could have been the guiding hand that "co-opted" parts from one biochemical machine to be used in a biochemical machine with a different function? (William A. Dembski and Jonathan Wells, *The Design of Life: Discovering Signs of Intelligence in Biological Systems* [Dallas: The Foundation for Thought and Ethics, 2008], pp. 151–161. Michael J. Behe, *Darwin's Black Box: The Biochemical Challenge to Evolution* [New York: Free Press, 2006], pp. 255–272.)

[†††] Casey Luskin, for instance, reveals that the public voice of evolutionary scientists confidently tells us how "clean" the human evolutionary fossil record is—"clear" transitions without gaps. His review of the scientific literature tells a different story. "There are many gaps and virtually no plausible transitional fossils that are generally accepted, even by evolutionists, to be direct human ancestors" (p. 74). (Casey Luskin, "Human Origins and the Fossil Record," in *Science & Human Origins*, by Ann Gauger, Douglas Axe, and Casey Luskin [Seattle: Discovery Institute Press, 2012], pp. 45–83.)

and "gaps" in the fossil record—where transitional forms would have been expected.[65]

According to Phillip Johnson, professor emeritus of intelligent design, the best evidence for problems in the fossil record often comes from naturalist paleontologists themselves.[66] For instance, Niles Eldredge and Stephen Jay Gould proposed the theory of punctuated equilibrium in 1972 to explain what appears to be rapid periods of evolutionary change (too quick to preserve transitions in the fossil record) among long periods of stasis.[67] Punctuated equilibrium is not the typical neo-Darwinian story line.[68][‡‡‡] In addition, when paleontologists find a new fossil, proposed to be a transition form, the discoverers usually reveal to the media the *real* paucity of data in the fossil record prior to that find.[69] Casey Luskin calls this "retroactive confessions of ignorance."[70]

A profound curiosity in the fossil record is the "Cambrian explosion." Here "about twenty of the roughly twenty-six phyla"[§§§] that are evident in the fossil record suddenly appear together in the fossil record.[71] Gone is Darwin's branching tree representing evolutionary history as gradual change over time. Darwin thought a progression of minor differences among organisms over time would emerge into major differences. As Meyer describes, his would be considered a "bottom-up pattern." Species would progress to genus, to family, to

---

‡‡‡   Dembski and Wells list naturalistic proposals that have been put forth to explain the gaps in the fossil record other than punctuated equilibrium: the fossil record is "imperfect"; there has been incomplete sampling of the fossil record; and there has been "abrupt emergence" of "basic groups of organisms" (p. 69)—"nonbiogenic formation," "symbiogenic reorganization," "biogenic reinvention," and "generative transmutation." (William A. Dembski and Jonathan Wells, *The Design of Life: Discovering Signs of Intelligence in Biological Systems* [Dallas: Foundation for Thought and Ethics, 2008], pp. 69–81.)

§§§   In the classification of living things: "The level below the kingdom is called the phylum (plural: phyla). There are more than twenty different phyla within the animal kingdom. All vertebrates (animals with backbones) belong to the phylum Chordata." (*The Kingfisher Science Encyclopedia* [New York: Kingfisher, 2000], p. 53.)

order, to class, and then to phyla. The Cambrian explosion, however, seems to support a "top-down pattern." Here different phyla occur first and then small differences within the phyla occur later.[72]

Meyer goes into great detail to show that it is no longer reasonable to rely on the hypotheses of incomplete sampling or incomplete preservation of fossils in the Precambrian strata to account for a lack of intermediates leading up to the Cambrian explosion.[73] He also explains that the Precambrian fossils that have been found, the Ediacaran, could not have been the ancestors of the Cambrian animals.[74] Meyer points out that some naturalists have proposed a theory called deep divergence to determine when the common ancestor of the Cambrian animals first appears, using molecular and genetic "molecular clock" evidence. However, this theory "begs the question" for the existence of a common ancestor and has produced inconsistent and conflicting results.[75] Meyer also writes that all attempts to reconstruct an evolutionary tree of life leading up to the Cambrian animals, based on similar molecular, anatomic, or molecular and anatomic data, have been fraught with problems.[76]

Darwin wrote:

> There is another and allied difficulty, which is much more serious. I allude to the manner in which species belonging to several of the main divisions of the animal kingdom suddenly appear in the lowest known fossiliferous rocks.[77]

> Consequently, if the theory be true, it is indisputable that before the lowest Cambrian stratum was deposited long periods elapsed, as long as, or probably far longer than, the whole interval from the Cambrian age to the present day; and that during these vast periods the world swarmed with living creatures.[78]

> To the question why we do not find rich fossiliferous deposits belonging to these assumed earliest periods prior to the Cambrian system, I can give no satisfactory answer.[79]

Darwin could not explain the Cambrian explosion by his theory of evolution in the 1850s, and it appears that no one today can explain this data using his theory either.¶¶¶

---

¶¶¶ Meyer describes a number of newer theories that have all rejected

## Common Design versus Common Ancestry

Attempting to prove a universal common ancestor is of paramount importance to naturalists. Any of the proposed theories of life's origins outside of design, such as through natural selection working on random mutations, could only work through a common descent.[80] Naturalists look at similarities between organisms and equate these with common ancestry. If a designer were involved in the process, however, similarities could be related to common design rather than common descent, or both could be true.[81] Common ancestry is not inconsistent with intelligent design theory,[82] but certainly the arguments given by Meyer concerning the Cambrian explosion point away from a universal common ancestor.[83]****

At this point, no one understands how a designer implemented design into a physical universe. A designer may have used some form of common ancestry, but this determination will need to await future discoveries.[84] However life arose on earth, it was not through a blinded, unguided, purely materialistic process such as that described by neo-Darwinism. Information was built into the system. The creative power of natural selection working on random mutations can

---

one of the three elements of "the neo-Darwinian triad" of "random, minute variation"; "natural selection"; and faithful heritability of "favored variations" (p. 292). These theories include "self-organization," "natural genetic engineering," "neo-Lamarckian epigenetic inheritance," "symbiogenesis," "facilitated variation," "evolutionary developmental biology," and "neutral evolution." If neo-Darwinian evolution is fact, why is there growing dissatisfaction with this theory's power to explain? (Stephen C. Meyer, *Darwin's Doubt: The Explosive Origin of Animal Life and the Case for Intelligent Design* [New York: HarperCollins Publishers, 2013], pp. 291–335.)

**** Michael Behe believes there is strong evidence for common descent. One piece of evidence he gives for common descent comes from pseudogenes (broken genes that resemble working genes but are made nonfunctional by mutations). He gives the examples of similar pseudogenes found in both humans and chimpanzees (pseudogene for vitamin C and pseudogene for beta hemoglobin). (Michael J. Behe, *The Edge of Evolution: The Search for the Limits of Darwinism* [New York: Free Press, 2007], pp. 64–74.)

no longer be considered Richard Dawkins's "blind watchmaker."[85][††††]

## Design That Begs for the Identity of the Designer

Intelligent design theorists have written many excellent books on intelligent design theory. These books build a compelling case for an intelligent designer. Intelligent design theory does not attempt to identify the intelligent designer, nor does it prove that God exists. Nevertheless, the evidence observed in our physical universe is so overwhelming for the role of a designer that it should stimulate a search for the identity of the designer.[86]

This thought was supported by Sha'ul in the first century. He said that men who can see the visible universe have no excuse for not believing in the God of the Bible:

> For the wrath of God is revealed from heaven against all ungodliness and unrighteousness of men, who by their unrighteousness suppress the truth. For what can be known about God is plain to them, because God has shown it to them. For his invisible attributes, namely, his eternal power and divine nature, have been clearly perceived, ever since the creation of the world, in the things that have been made. So they are without excuse. For although they knew God, they did not honor him as God or give thanks to him, but they became futile in their thinking, and their foolish hearts were darkened. Claiming to be wise, they became fools, and exchanged the glory of the immortal God for images resembling mortal man and birds and animals and creeping things (Romans 1:18–23).

---

†††† The website dissentfromdarwin.org has collected the signatures of over 800 PhD scientists from around the world who may not consider themselves intelligent design theorists but do agree with the following statement: "We are skeptical of claims for the ability of random mutation and natural selection to account for the complexity of life. Careful examination of the evidence for Darwinian theory should be encouraged." ("A Scientific Dissent from Darwinism," *Dissent from Darwin*, accessed August 15, 2015, www.dissentfromdarwin.org/index.php.)

## Evidence for God's Existence Also
## Comes from the Tanach

If the evidence displayed in our information-rich universe is not convincing enough to some for the existence of an intelligent designer, the Tanach provides other evidence for the existence of God, whose name is YHVH.

First, the religion of Israel has been observed to be unique among the religions of the world when the comparison is made.‡‡‡‡ It did not evolve from pagan religions.[87] It is like a bolt out of the blue. Some would argue that the genius of the people of Israel developed this new concept of God. I feel that supernatural revelation better explains this phenomenon, as the Bible tells us.

In *The Religion of Israel from Its Beginnings to the Babylonian Exile*, Yehezkel Kaufmann writes:

> The biblical religious idea, visible in the earliest strata, permeating even the "magical" legends, is of a supernal God, above every cosmic law, fate, and compulsion; unborn, unbegetting, knowing no desire, independent of matter and its forces; a God who does not fight other divinities or powers of impurity; who does not sacrifice, divine, prophesy, or practice sorcery; who does not sin and needs no expiation; a God who does not celebrate festivals of his life. An unfettered divine will transcending all being—this is the mark of biblical religion and that which sets it apart from all the religions of the earth.[88]

That the God of the Bible is unique among the gods of mankind gives us more evidence that He is the One.

The accuracy of biblical prophecy also gives us evidence for God's existence. Many believers see future predictions as the primary purpose of biblical prophecy. Usually, however, the "experts" who try to predict the future by using the Bible experience humiliation. A

---

‡‡‡‡   I have minimal knowledge of religions not based on the Tanach and therefore I will not be making any comparisons of concepts presented in this book to other religions. The practitioner of another religion is better able to compare his or her own religion with the concepts here. We would do well to remember that a tree is known by its fruit (Matthew 12:33).

more important function of biblical prophecy is for us to look back on fulfilled prophecy and see the hand of God in the event:

> The former things I declared of old; they went out from my mouth, and I announced them; then suddenly I did them, and they came to pass. Because I know that you are obstinate, and your neck is an iron sinew and your forehead brass, I declared them to you from of old, before they came to pass I announced them to you, lest you should say, "My idol did them, my carved image and my metal image commanded them" (Isaiah 48:3–5).

This value of fulfilled prophecy is true for prophecies related to ancient and modern Israel (see below) as well as prophecies that deal with the coming of the Messiah (see chapter 2).

## Ezekiel's Precise Depiction of a Future Israel

One example of an amazing prophecy that seems to be coming to pass in our own time is from the book of Ezekiel. This prophecy is full of details that could not just be attributed to chance, considering that this prophecy was written about 2,600 years ago:

> The word of the LORD [YHVH] came to me: "Son of man, set your face toward Gog, of the land of Magog, the chief prince of Meshech and Tubal, and prophesy against him and say, Thus says the Lord GOD [YHVH]: Behold, I am against you, O Gog, chief prince of Meshech and Tubal. And I will turn you about and put hooks into your jaws, and I will bring you out, and all your army, horses and horsemen, all of them clothed in full armor, a great host, all of them with buckler and shield, wielding swords. Persia, Cush, and Put are with them, all of them with shield and helmet; Gomer and all his hordes; Beth-togarmah from the uttermost parts of the north with all his hordes—many peoples are with you. Be ready and keep ready, you and all your hosts that are assembled about you, and be a guard for them. After many days you will be mustered. In the latter years you will go against the land that is restored from war, the land whose people were gathered from many peoples upon the mountains of Israel, which had been a continual waste. Its people were brought out from the peoples and now dwell securely, all of them. You will advance, coming on like a storm.

You will be like a cloud covering the land, you and all your hordes, and many peoples with you. Thus says the Lord GOD [YHVH]: On that day, thoughts will come into your mind, and you will devise an evil scheme and say, 'I will go up against the land of unwalled villages. I will fall upon the quiet people who dwell securely, all of them dwelling without walls, and having no bars or gates,' to seize spoil and carry off plunder, to turn your hand against the waste places that are now inhabited, and the people who were gathered from the nations, who have acquired livestock and goods, who dwell at the center of the earth. Sheba and Dedan and the merchants of Tarshish and all its leaders will say to you, 'Have you come to seize spoil? Have you assembled your hosts to carry off plunder, to carry away silver and gold, to take away livestock and goods, to seize great spoil?' Therefore, son of man, prophesy, and say to Gog, Thus says the Lord GOD [YHVH]: On that day when my people Israel are dwelling securely, will you not know it? You will come from your place out of the uttermost parts of the north, you and many peoples with you, all of them riding on horses, a great host, a mighty army. You will come up against my people Israel, like a cloud covering the land. In the latter days I will bring you against my land, that the nations may know me, when through you, O Gog, I vindicate my holiness before their eyes" (Ezekiel 38:1–16).

This prophecy speaks of a confederacy of nations coming against Israel in the last days—some future event. At this time, the prophecy tells us, the people of Israel will be back in their land, which had been a continual waste before they returned. They will be gathered from many nations. Jews from all over the world in the late 1800s began returning to the land of Israel, much of it being a swampy wasteland and desert. Israel became an independent state again in 1948. At this future time, according to the prophecy, they will have acquired cattle and goods. They will be living in a land of unwalled villages, which was not typical of nations 2,600 years ago. It mentions Persia (present-day Iran) for sure and possibly Libya (Put).[89] Could this be an Islamic confederacy? The incredible details of this prophecy speak for themselves—some having already happened. Nevertheless, the specifics of this prophecy's exact fulfillment await a future day.

## Israel's Survival as Proof of God's Existence

The most dramatic prophetic proof of God's existence, however, is the survival of the people of Israel. As the people of Israel were preparing to enter the land of Israel after the Exodus from Egypt, God reestablished His covenant with them. He set before them life and the blessing if they obeyed and death and the curse if they did not obey. Unfortunately, as predicted, they suffered the curses of disobedience and were scattered among the peoples from one end of the earth to the other (Deuteronomy 28–30). Throughout the Hebrew Bible, though, God promised that He would restore the people of Israel back to Himself, and back to their land. Many dramatic prophecies predict this restoration and the continued survival of the people of Israel:

> "And when all these things come upon you, the blessing and the curse, which I have set before you, and you call them to mind among all the nations where the LORD [YHVH] your God has driven you, and return to the LORD [YHVH] your God, you and your children, and obey his voice in all that I command you today, with all your heart and with all your soul, then the LORD [YHVH] your God will restore your fortunes and have mercy on you, and he will gather you again from all the peoples where the LORD [YHVH] your God has scattered you. If your outcasts are in the uttermost parts of heaven, from there the LORD [YHVH] your God will gather you, and from there he will take you. And the LORD [YHVH] your God will bring you into the land that your fathers possessed, that you may possess it. And he will make you more prosperous and numerous than your fathers. And the LORD [YHVH] your God will circumcise your heart and the heart of your offspring, so that you will love the LORD [YHVH] your God with all your heart and with all your soul that you may live" (Deuteronomy 30:1–6).

> In that day the Lord will extend his hand yet a second time to recover the remnant that remains of his people, from Assyria, from Egypt, from Pathros, from Cush, from Elam, from Shinar, from Hamath, and from the coastlands of the sea. He will raise a signal for the nations and will assemble the banished of Israel, and gather the dispersed of Judah from the four corners of the earth (Isaiah 11:11–12).

But Zion said, "The LORD [YHVH] has forsaken me; my Lord has forgotten me." "Can a woman forget her nursing child, that she should have no compassion on the son of her womb? Even these may forget, yet I will not forget you. Behold, I have engraved you on the palms of my hands; your walls are continually before me" (Isaiah 49:14–16).

Thus says the LORD [YHVH], who gives the sun for light by day and the fixed order of the moon and the stars for light by night, who stirs up the sea so that its waves roar—the LORD [YHVH] of hosts is his name: "If this fixed order departs from before me, declares the LORD [YHVH], then shall the offspring of Israel cease from being a nation before me forever." Thus says the LORD [YHVH]: "If the heavens above can be measured, and the foundations of the earth below can be explored, then I will cast off all the offspring of Israel for all that they have done, declares the LORD [YHVH]" (Jeremiah 31:35–37).

Then he said to me, "Son of man, these bones are the whole house of Israel. Behold, they say, 'Our bones are dried up, and our hope is lost; we are indeed cut off.' Therefore prophesy, and say to them, Thus says the Lord GOD [YHVH]: Behold, I will open your graves and raise you from your graves, O my people. And I will bring you into the land of Israel. And you shall know that I am the LORD [YHVH], when I open your graves, and raise you from your graves, O my people. And I will put my Spirit within you, and you shall live, and I will place you in your own land. Then you shall know that I am the LORD [YHVH]; I have spoken, and I will do it, declares the LORD [YHVH]" (Ezekiel 37:11–14).

And the nations shall know that the house of Israel went into captivity for their iniquity, because they dealt so treacherously with me that I hid my face from them and gave them into the hand of their adversaries, and they all fell by the sword. I dealt with them according to their uncleanness and their transgressions, and hid my face from them. "Therefore thus says the Lord GOD [YHVH]: Now I will restore the fortunes of Jacob and have mercy on the whole house of Israel, and I will be jealous for my holy name. They shall forget their shame and all the treachery they have practiced against me, when they dwell securely in their land with none to make them afraid, when I have brought them back from the peoples and gathered them from their enemies' lands, and through them have vindicated my holiness in the sight of many nations. Then they shall know that I am the LORD [YHVH] their God, because I sent them into exile among the nations and then assembled them into their own land. I will leave none of them remaining among the nations anymore. And I will not hide my face anymore from them, when I pour out my Spirit upon the house of Israel, declares the Lord GOD [YHVH]" (Ezekiel 39:23–29).

"I will restore the fortunes of my people Israel, and they shall rebuild the ruined cities and inhabit them; they shall plant vineyards and drink their wine, and they shall make gardens and eat their fruit. I will plant them on their land, and they shall never again be uprooted out of the land that I have given them," says the LORD [YHVH] your God (Amos 9:14–15).

"I will whistle for them and gather them in, for I have redeemed them, and they shall be as many as they were before. Though I scattered them among the nations, yet in far countries they shall remember me, and with their children they shall live and return. I will bring them home from the land of Egypt, and gather them from Assyria, and I will bring them to the land of Gilead and to Lebanon, till there is no room for them. He shall pass through the sea of troubles and strike down the waves of the sea, and all the depths of the Nile shall be dried up. The pride of Assyria shall be laid low, and the scepter of Egypt shall depart. I will make them strong in the LORD [YHVH], and they shall walk in his name," declares the LORD [YHVH] (Zechariah 10:8–12).§§§§

Through a wide-ranging history of suppression, persecution, and annihilation, the Jewish people still endure today in fulfillment of

---

§§§§   Even though Assyria and Egypt have lost their former might on the world stage according to the prophecy, God has promised a special relationship with them in the future: "In that day there will be a highway from Egypt to Assyria, and Assyria will come into Egypt, and Egypt into Assyria, and the Egyptians will worship with the Assyrians. In that day Israel will be the third with Egypt and Assyria, a blessing in the midst of the earth, whom the LORD [YHVH] of hosts has blessed, saying, 'Blessed be Egypt my people, and Assyria the work of my hands, and Israel my inheritance'" (Isaiah 19:23–25). Curiously, the original Egyptians, the Copts, are Christians today and followers of YHVH, as are all Assyrians.

multiple biblical prophecies throughout the Tanach. The survival of the Jewish people is the most convincing proof that the God of the Hebrew Bible exists.

YHVH, the God of the Hebrew Bible, the God of Abraham, Isaac, and Jacob, has revealed Himself through nature as well as through the Scriptures. It does not take a rocket scientist to appreciate the clear evidence. How unfortunate that many people with the minds of rocket scientists have rejected the proof and fought to suppress the truth.

In the next chapter, we will explore the idea of the messianic hope and ask whether Yeshua (Jesus) could be the promised Jewish Messiah.

# (Endnotes)

1  John C. Lennox, *God's Undertaker: Has Science Buried God?* (Oxford, UK: Lion Books, 2009), p. 69. John Sailhamer, "Genesis," in *The Expositor's Bible Commentary*, Vol. 2 (Grand Rapids, MI: Zondervan Publishing House, 1990), pp. 19–20.

2  *The Life of Pi* (the movie), directed by Ang Lee, produced by Gil Netter, Ang Lee, and David Womark, screenplay by David Magee, based on *Life of Pi* by Yann Martel, distributed by 20th Century Fox, 2012.

3  John H. Sailhamer, *The Pentateuch as Narrative* (Grand Rapids, MI: Zondervan Publishing House, 1992), p. 25.

4  John C. Lennox, *God's Undertaker: Has Science Buried God?*, p. 73. Michael J. Behe, *Darwin's Black Box: The Biochemical Challenge to Evolution* (New York: Free Press, 2006), p. 271. Michael J. Behe, *The Edge of Evolution: The Search for the Limits of Darwinism* (New York: Free Press, 2007), pp. 204–205.

5  Stephen C. Meyer, *Signature in the Cell: DNA and the Evidence for Intelligent Design* (New York: HarperCollins Publishers, 2009), p. 150.

6  Stephen C. Meyer, "On Not Reading Signature in the Cell: A Response to Francisco Ayala" in *Signature of Controversy*, ed. by David Klinghoffer (Seattle: Discovery Institute Press, 2010), p. 18.

7  Stephen C. Meyer, *Signature in the Cell: DNA and the Evidence for Intelligent Design*, pp. 159–161.

8  Ibid., pp. 324–325.

9  Michael J. Behe, *Darwin's Black Box: The Biochemical Challenge to Evolution*, p. 196.

10  Stephen C. Meyer, *Signature in the Cell: DNA and the Evidence for Intelligent Design*, pp. 328–329.

11  John C. Lennox, *God's Undertaker: Has Science Buried God?*, pp. 58–77.

12  Stephen C. Meyer, *Signature in the Cell: DNA and the Evidence for Intelligent Design*, p. 372.

13  Ibid., p. 383.

14  John C. Lennox, *God's Undertaker: Has Science Buried God?*, pp. 66–67.

15  Paul Davies, *Cosmic Jackpot: Why Our Universe Is Just Right for Life* (Boston: Houghton Mifflin Company, 2007), p. 58.

16  David Berlinski, *The Devil's Delusion: Atheism and Its Scientific Pretensions* (New York: Basic Books, 2009), pp. 72–74. Paul Davies, *Cosmic Jackpot: Why Our Universe Is Just Right for Life*, pp. 20–21.

17  David Berlinski, *The Devil's Delusion: Atheism and Its Scientific Pretensions*, p. 78. Paul Davies, *Cosmic Jackpot: Why Our Universe Is Just Right for Life*, pp. 21–22.

18  Paul Davies, *Cosmic Jackpot: Why Our Universe Is Just Right for Life*, p. 71.

19  Ibid., pp. 139–140.

20  Ibid., pp. 93–95 and 146.

21  Ibid., pp. 139–140.

22  Ibid., pp. 138, 151.

23  Ibid., pp. 151–190.

24  Ibid., p. 151.

25  Stephen C. Meyer, *Signature in the Cell: DNA and the Evidence for Intelligent Design*, pp. 376–379.

26  William A. Dembski and Jonathan Wells, *The Design of Life: Discovering Signs of Intelligence in Biological Systems* (Dallas: The Foundation for Thought and Ethics, 2008), p. xx.

27  Stephen C. Meyer et al., *Explore Evolution: The Arguments For and Against Neo-Darwinism* (London: Hill House Publishers, 2007), p. 8.

28  Ibid., pp. 87–89.

29  Ibid., p. 90.

30  Michael J. Behe, *The Edge of Evolution: The Search for the Limits of Darwinism*, p. 3.

31  Stephen C. Meyer et al., *Explore Evolution: The Arguments For and Against Neo-Darwinism*, pp. 90–95.

32  Ibid., p. 95.

33  Michael J. Behe, *The Edge of Evolution: The Search for the Limits of Darwinism*.

34  Ann Gauger, Douglas Axe, and Casey Luskin, *Science & Human Origins* (Seattle: Discovery Institute Press, 2013), p. 31.

35  Albert L. Lehninger, *Biochemistry* (New York: WorthPublishers, Inc., 1975), pp. 1031–1056.

36  Ibid., pp. 23–24.

37  Stephen C. Meyer, *Signature in the Cell: DNA and the Evidence for Intelligent Design*, pp. 194–228.

38  Richard Dawkins, *The Greatest Show on Earth* (New York: Free Press, 2009), p. 420.

39  Ibid., p. 420.

40  Ibid., p. 421.

41  Stephen C. Meyer, *Signature in the Cell: DNA and the Evidence for Intelligent Design*, pp.296–323.

42  Richard Dawkins, *The Greatest Show on Earth*, p. 416.

43  Stephen C. Meyer, *Signature in the Cell: DNA and the Evidence for Intelligent Design*.

44  Ibid., pp. 109–110.

45  Ibid., pp. 131–134.

46  Casey Luskin, "Finding Intelligent Design in Nature," in *Intelligent Design 101*, ed. by H. Wayne House (Grand Rapids, MI: Kregel Publications, 2008), p. 82.

47  Stephen C. Meyer, *Signature in the Cell: DNA and the Evidence for Intelligent Design*, pp. 109–110.

48  Ibid., pp. 347–348.

49  Stephen C. Meyer et al., *Explore Evolution: The Arguments For and Against Neo-Darwinism*, pp. 110–111.

50  Stephen C. Meyer, *Signature in the Cell: DNA and the Evidence for Intelligent Design*, pp. 363–366.

51  Daniel James Devine, "Debunking Junk," *World Magazine*, October 6, 2012, pp. 36–37.

52  Casey Luskin, "Gotcha! Stephen Meyer's Spelling & Other Weighty Criticisms" in *Signature of Controversy*, ed. by David Klinghoffer (Seattle: Discovery Institute Press, 2010), p. 122.

53  Daniel James Devine, "Debunking Junk," pp. 36–39. Stephen C. Meyer, *Darwin's Doubt: The Explosive Origin of Animal Life and the Case for Intelligent Design* (New York: Harper One, 2013), pp. 400–402.

54  Michael J. Behe, *Darwin's Black Box: The Biochemical Challenge to Evolution*, p. 24.

55  Ibid., p. 4.

56  William A. Dembski and Jonathan Wells, *The Design of Life: Discovering Signs of Intelligence in Biological Systems*, p. 146.

57  Ibid., p. 146.

58  Ibid., p. 146.

59  Michael J. Behe, *Darwin's Black Box: The Biochemical Challenge to Evolution*, pp. 42–43.

60 Ibid., pp. 74–77.

61 Ibid., p. 39.

62 Charles Darwin, *The Origin of Species* (New York: Signet Classics, 2003), p. 176. Pointed out by Michael Behe.

63 Ibid., p 315. Pointed out by Casey Luskin.

64 William A. Dembski and Jonathan Wells, *The Design of Life: Discovering Signs of Intelligence in Biological Systems*, pp. 60–62.

65 Ibid., pp. 63–64.

66 Phillip E. Johnson, *Darwin on Trial* (Downers Grove, Illinois: InterVarsity Press, 1993), pp. 57–62.

67 William A. Dembski and Jonathan Wells, *The Design of Life: Discovering Signs of Intelligence in Biological Systems*, pp. 73–75.

68 Stephen C. Meyer, *Darwin's Doubt: The Explosive Origin of Animal Life and the Case for Intelligent Design*, pp. 136–152.

69 Casey Luskin, "Finding Intelligent Design in Nature," in *Intelligent Design 101*, pp. 100–104.

70 Ann Gauger, Douglas Axe, and Casey Luskin, *Science of Human Origins*, p. 58.

71 Stephen C. Meyer, *Darwin's Doubt: The Explosive Origin of Animal Life and the Case for Intelligent Design*, p. 31.

72 Ibid., pp. 39–44.

73 Ibid., pp. 50–76.

74 Ibid., pp. 77–97.

75 Ibid., pp. 98–113.

76 Ibid., pp. 114–135.

77 Charles Darwin, *The Origin of Species*, p. 339. Pointed out by Stephen Meyer.

78 Ibid., p 340. Pointed out by Stephen Meyer.

79 Ibid., pp. 340–341. Pointed out by Stephen Meyer.

80 William A. Dembski and Jonathan Wells, *The Design of Life: Discovering Signs of Intelligence in Biological Systems*, p. 140.

81 Ibid., p. 140.

82 Casey Luskin, "Finding Intelligent Design in Nature," p. 89.

83 Stephen C. Meyer, *Darwin's Doubt: The Explosive Origin of Animal Life and the Case for Intelligent Design*.

84   William A. Dembski and Jonathan Wells, *The Design of Life: Discovering Signs of Intelligence in Biological Systems*, pp. 140–142.

85   Richard Dawkins, *The Blind Watchmaker: Why the Evidence of Evolution Reveals a Universe without Design* (New York: W. W. Norton & Company, Inc. 1996).

86   Stephen C. Meyer, *Darwin's Doubt: The Explosive Origin of Animal Life and the Case for Intelligent Design*, p. 413.

87   Yehezkel Kaufmann, *The Religion of Israel from Its Beginnings to the Babylonian Exile,* translated and abridged by Moshe Greenberg (New York: Schocken Books, 1972), p. 2.

88   Ibid., p. 121.

89   *The ESV Study Bible* (Wheaton, IL: Crossway Bibles, 2008), p. 1561.

# Chapter 2: Why Most Jews Do Not Believe Yeshua* Is the Promised Messiah of Israel

## Messiah: A Jewish Concept

The mere mentioning of the name "Jesus" is enough to grate the inner being of most Jews today, for that name carries with it many negative connotations for the Jewish person. A multitude of largely non-Jewish people over the past two thousand years, however, has acclaimed this Yeshua to be the promised Jewish Messiah. Now, the doctrine of the Messiah certainly is central to traditional Judaism, but Yeshua definitely is not. Why do most Jews today not accept Yeshua

---

* Yeshua is the original Hebrew name of Jesus, sounding like the Hebrew word for "he will save"—*yoshia* (from the Hebrew root letters *yod*, *shin*, and *ayin*, meaning help/save/rescue). (David H. Stern, *Jewish New Testament Commentary* [Clarksville, MD: Jewish New Testament Publications, 1992], p. 4.) Jesus is the result of transferring Yeshua from Hebrew to Greek to Latin to English. ("Jesus," *The American Heritage High School Dictionary*, 4th ed. [New York, NY: Houghton Mifflin Company, 2004], p. 744.) Many of the early manuscripts recording Yeshua's name and life history were written in Greek because Greek was a universal language of the Roman Empire in the first century CE, even in Israel. (Louis Harry Feldman, "Hellenism," *Encyclopaedia Judaica*, Vol. 8 [Jerusalem, Israel: Keter Publishing House Ltd., 1971], p. 296.) The historical Yeshua was a Jew. He was born to Jewish parents. He was circumcised on the eighth day (Luke 2:21). As the firstborn son he was redeemed by his parents in the Temple (Luke 2:22–24). He followed the Torah (Matthew 5:17–20). He did not "convert" to Christianity or start a new religion.

as the Messiah?

Messiah is undeniably a Jewish concept. The English word de-
rives from the Hebrew word *mashiach*, meaning "anointed one."[†] The
figure of the Messiah was revealed to the Hebrew people in many
descriptive passages throughout the Tanach. Because of these passages,
traditional Judaism has awaited his arrival for many centuries. The
Passover Seder shows this clearly. During this time, a special cup is
filled with wine for Elijah the prophet and, at one point, the door
is opened for him. According to tradition, Elijah the prophet will
herald in the messianic age (Malachi 3:23). A traditional song sung
at Passover, "Eliahu HaNavi," states: "Elijah, the prophet, Elijah the
Tishbite, Elijah the Gileadite. May he come to us quickly, in our days,
with the Messiah, the son of David." Another example can be found
in the musical *Fiddler on the Roof.* As the Jews are leaving their village,
Anatevka, someone asks, "Rabbi, we've been waiting for the Messiah
all our lives. Wouldn't this be a good time for him to come?" The rabbi
responds by saying that they will have to wait for the coming of the
Messiah someplace else.[1] In addition, in the Thirteen Principles of
Faith drawn up by Moses Maimonides, the twelfth principle states: "I
believe with perfect faith in the coming of the Messiah; and, though
he tarry, I will wait daily for his coming."[2] The concept of Messiah is
deeply rooted in many Jewish traditions, prayers, and thoughts.

## Many Jews throughout History Have
## Believed in the Messiahship of Yeshua

Before we investigate why most Jews today do not believe that Yeshua
is the promised Jewish Messiah, let us first establish the fact that many
Jews in the past have believed, and many Jews today believe, that Yeshua is the Messiah.

All of the first believers (followers of Yeshua) were Jewish and

---

[†]  "Anointed one" (or Messiah) in Greek is *Christos*, from which comes the
English word "Christ." (David H. Stern, *Jewish New Testament Commentary*
[Clarksville, MD: Jewish New Testament Publications, 1992], p. 1.) "Christ"
is not Yeshua's last name.

in the first century existed in large numbers. Hugh Schonfield, the author of *The Passover Plot*, writes: "The New Testament leaves us in no doubt that the early followers of Jesus were Jews, and that they adhered to him from the conviction that he was the expected Messiah. . . . The opposition did not come from the Jewish masses, but from those in the seat of authority responsible to Rome."[3]

The New Testament does support Schonfield's statements.[4] It records that great multitudes of people in Jerusalem (Jewish people) mourned Yeshua's impending death: "And there followed him a great multitude of the people and of women who were mourning and lamenting for him" (Luke 23:27). The New Testament also suggests that the growing number of believers included many Temple priests: "So the word of God continued to spread. The number of *talmidim* in Yerushalayim increased rapidly, and a large crowd of *cohanim* were becoming obedient to the faith" (Acts 6:7, *Complete Jewish Bible*). The New Testament reports that some from the strictly orthodox sect of the Pharisees became believers and demanded the conversion of Gentile believers to Judaism: "But some of those who had come to trust were from the party of the *P'rushim*; and they stood up and said, 'It is necessary to circumcise them and direct them to observe the Torah of Moshe'" (Acts 15:5, *Complete Jewish Bible*). Lastly, in Jerusalem one finds many Jewish believers who remain zealous for the Torah. They remain Jewish. They do not understand their belief in any other way: "You see, brother, how many thousands [myriads or tens of thousands] there are among the Jews of those who have believed. They are all zealous for the law [Torah]" (Acts 21:20).

The fact that all of the writers of the New Testament were Jewish[5] also supports the premise that the vast majority of these early believers were Jewish.‡ One of these writers, Sha'ul, leaves no doubt that he was

---

‡ The author Luke may have been the only Jewish author without Jewish parents (Colossians 4:10–11, 14), i.e., he may have been a convert to Judaism. (*Jewish New Testament*, trans. by David H. Stern [Clarksville, MD: Jewish New Testament Publications, Inc., 1997], p. x.)

raised as a Jew in the finest tradition:

> "Brothers and fathers! Listen to me as I make my defense before you now!" When they heard him speaking to them in Hebrew, they settled down more; so he continued: "I am a Jew, born in Tarsus of Cilicia, but brought up in this city and trained at the feet of Gamli'el in every detail of the Torah of our forefathers. I was a zealot for God, as all of you are today. I persecuted to death the followers of this Way, arresting both men and women and throwing them in prison. The *cohen hagadol* and the whole *Sanhedrin* can also testify to this" (Acts 22:1–5, *Complete Jewish Bible*).

> If anyone else thinks he has grounds for putting confidence in human qualifications, I have better grounds: *b'rit-milah* on the eighth day; by birth belonging to the people of Isra'el; from the tribe of Binyamin; a Hebrew speaker, with Hebrew-speaking parents; in regard to the Torah, a *Parush*; in regard to zeal, a persecutor of the Messianic Community; in regard to the righteousness demanded by legalism, blameless (Philippians 3:4–6, *Complete Jewish Bible*).

Some feel that when Sha'ul became a believer he acquired an attitude of contempt for the Torah of Moses.[6] According to the book of Acts, however, this was not the case. During one of his trips to Jerusalem, Sha'ul purified himself in the Temple to show the Jewish believers there that he also walked orderly, keeping the Torah:

> "Now what they [the Jewish believers in Jerusalem] have been told about you is that you are teaching all the Jews living among the *Goyim* to apostatize from Moshe, telling them not to have a *b'rit-milah* for their sons and not to follow the traditions. What, then, is to be done? They will certainly hear that you have come. So do what we tell you. We have four men who are under a vow. Take them with you, be purified with them, and pay the expenses connected with having their heads shaved. Then everyone will know that there is nothing to these rumors which they have heard about you; but that, on the contrary, you yourself stay in line and keep the Torah" (Acts 21:21–24, *Complete Jewish Bible*).

The next day Sha'ul took the men, purified himself along with them and entered the Temple to give notice of when the period of purification would be finished and the offering would have to be made for each of them (Acts 21:26, *Complete Jewish Bible*).

According to Schonfield, "In Palestine Christianity as a new religion did not exist."[7] All one finds in the early days are many Jews who proclaim Yeshua to be the Messiah, before and after his death.

After this first century of the Messianic faith, Jewish believers slowly begin to drift out of the forefront of the Messianic movement, and as a distinct group almost entirely disappear.[8] Schonfield tells us:

> No sudden and merciful extinction was granted to the ancient communities of Jewish believers; but a slow decay set in which in the course of time reduced their number to a few fragmentary groups who had almost forgotten their own origin.[9]

Even the early history of those first Jewish believers who had established themselves in Jerusalem is not entirely clear after the destruction of the Temple. In *Jewish Christianity Reconsidered*, Matt Jackson-McCabe writes:

> Quite differently than in the case of Paul and his "gospel for the uncircumcised," there are not texts that can be attributed without controversy either to the Jerusalem group itself or to any community resulting directly from its missionary efforts. What is more, the historical fate of the Jerusalem community after the destruction of the city in 70 CE, and thus the relevance for it of reports concerning later groups like the Ebionites and Nazarenes, are not obvious.[10]

In addition to the Roman occupation of Israel in the first and second centuries and the turmoil that came with it,[11] Schonfield reveals two other major factors that contributed to the decline of the early communities of Jewish believers.[12] One factor was due to the opposition directed toward Jewish believers by an evolving "traditional" Judaism after the first (70 CE) and second (135 CE) major Jewish revolts against Rome. Because of religious and political differences at that time, the Jewish believers were eventually ostracized from the traditional synagogue.[13] A second factor was due to the anti-Judaic attitude that sprang up in the growing communities of Gentile believers. This negative attitude toward Judaism spilled over upon Jewish believers who continued to live as Jews.[14]

In *The Jewish People and Jesus Christ: The Relationship between Church and Synagogue*, Jakob Jocz writes that the opposition from both the traditional Jews and the Gentile believers left the Jewish believers of that time with three options. Some drifted back into the traditional synagogue as nonbelievers or secret believers, which eventually caused them to lose their faith.[15] Others cast off their Jewish identity and assimilated into the Gentile church, which led to a type of suicide.[16] A third group tried to maintain their own communities of Jewish believers.[17] This third group failed, according to Schonfield, because of the total isolation;[18] the rise of Islam, which overran their communities;[19] and, most important, the wrong timing in God's predicted plan for large numbers of Jewish believers identifying as Jews to arise.[20]

Although no distinctive communities of Jewish believers existed past the seventh century, and many Jewish believers were lost in the sea of the Gentile church,[21] individual Jewish believers continued to stand out in every period up to the present. Schonfield again says:

> It is a curious kind of history with little of logical sequence; a stepping from century to century and from place to place through all the lands of Israel's dispersion. . . . Occasionally one lights on a family or group that offers a more protracted picture, a beacon that burns a little longer than others before it is swallowed up in the surrounding darkness. Yet a beacon is a static thing, and our chain of believing Israelites is marching with the centuries, a procession of torchbearers.[22]

Jewish believers at no time totally disappear.

Since the nineteenth century, the assimilation of Jewish believers has declined, and believing Jews have again sought to find their place as Jews within the Messianic faith.[23] Many are once again becoming zealous for the Torah. Today, Jewish believers can be located throughout the United States and in many other countries of the world. Their numbers have been growing, but the exact size of this group is unknown. This movement of believing Jews is not one large "cult" as some surmise. The Jewish believers today are divided into various factions—as is the rest of the Jewish community. The number of competing ideas among these Jewish believers concerning the ideal understanding and expression of the Messianic faith is probably as abundant as the number of individuals involved in the movement.

## Why Most Jews Today Reject Yeshua

A number of factors have contributed to modern Judaism's rejection of Yeshua as the Messiah. Since modern Judaism encompasses a diverse population of Jews, these factors have not influenced all Jews equally. Regardless of how these factors may be weighted to affect individuals, the rejection that develops is almost universal.

## Most Jews Reject the Concept of Messiah

One reason most Jews today have rejected Yeshua as the Messiah is because most Jews today, whether they accept the existence of God or not, have rejected the basic scriptural concept of Messiah—any Messiah. Naturally, Jewish atheists who find foolishness in God will find foolishness with the Messiah. The group of Jews that is still seeking a coming Messiah is quite small. According to Rabbi Morris Kertzer in his book *What Is a Jew?*, "Today, only the extreme Orthodox still cling to the literal belief in the coming of a Messiah."[24] It has been estimated that approximately 15–16 percent of Jews in the world today are wholly committed to Orthodoxy.[25] If Rabbi Kertzer is correct, the concept of a messianic figure is dying in modern Judaism.

Most twenty-first–century Jews have intellectualized the concept of Messiah. As Rabbi Kertzer writes:

> Most Jews . . . have reinterpreted the age-old belief in a Messiah, not as an individual Redeemer, but as mankind collectively, who by their own acts can usher in a Kingdom of Heaven. When humanity has reached a level of true enlightenment, kindliness and justice, that will be the Day of the Messiah.[26]§

---

§ Considering the advancement in enlightenment, kindliness, and justice that mankind has made over the past century, this reinterpretation can only lead to despair.

It is the rejection of a Messiah by these modern thinking Jews that has led to their rejection of Yeshua. The rejection by most Jews cannot honestly be over a disagreement as to the Messiah's characteristics and function, because these contemporary Jews no longer honor these messianic criteria.

## Jews Are Not Supposed to Believe in Yeshua

A second reason many Jews today do not accept Yeshua's messiahship is that many Jews are strictly bound by a traditional majority viewpoint that dictates what they should believe. Since the majority of the Jewish people today and throughout history have not accepted the claims of Yeshua, the conclusion is drawn that Yeshua cannot be the Messiah. The majority viewpoint is rarely questioned.

If we survey biblical history, however, the majority viewpoint of the people of Israel is rarely correct in God's eyes. Usually, only a handful of the people of Israel consistently followed God at any one time.[27] The prophet Elijah comes before YHVH with a description of rejection by the children of Israel:

> And it was so, when Elijah heard it, that he wrapped his face in his mantle, and went out, and stood in the entrance of the cave. And, behold, there came a voice unto him, and said: "What doest thou here, Elijah?" And he said: "I have been very jealous for the LORD [YHVH], the God of hosts; for the children of Israel have forsaken Thy covenant, thrown down Thine alters, and slain Thy prophets with the sword; and I, even I only, am left; and they seek my life, to take it away" (1 Kings 19:13–14, Jewish Publication Society, 1917).

The prophet Jeremiah similarly writes how the people rejected him and all of God's prophets before him:

> From the thirteenth year of Josiah the son of Amon, king of Judah, even unto this day, these three and twenty years, the word of the LORD [YHVH] hath come unto me, and I have spoken unto you, speaking betimes and often; but ye have not hearkened. And the LORD [YHVH] hath sent unto you all His servants the prophets, sending them betimes and often—but ye have not hearkened, nor inclined your ear to hear. (Jeremiah 25:3–4, Jewish Publication Society, 1917).

CHAPTER 2: Why Most Jews Do Not Believe Yeshua Is the Promised Messiah

One of the most striking examples of error in the majority viewpoint of the Hebrew people is in the rebellion against, and near stoning of, Moses:

> And all the children of Israel murmured against Moses and against Aaron; and the whole congregation said unto them: "Would that we had died in the land of Egypt! or would we had died in this wilderness! And wherefore doth the LORD [YHVH] bring us unto this land, to fall by the sword? Our wives and our little ones will be a prey; were it not better for us to return into Egypt?" And they said one to another: "Let us make a captain, and let us return into Egypt" (Numbers 14:2–4, Jewish Publication Society, 1917).

> But all the congregation bade stone them with stones (Numbers 14:10, Jewish Publication Society, 1917).

Try to imagine the Passover observance scarred with the stoning of Moses and the returning of the people of Israel to Egypt.

Jewish history tells us that the majority viewpoint of the people of Israel can occasionally be wrong. The fact that most Jews today do not accept a Messianic viewpoint does not automatically dismiss the possibility that Yeshua could be the promised Messiah.

## The Jewish Community Ostracizes Jews Who Believe

A third reason most Jews today are not believers is also closely related to this majority viewpoint. The majority viewpoint does more than passively sway people away from accepting Yeshua's messiahship. Rejection from family and the Jewish community as a whole is quite real and creates a solid partition between most Jews and Yeshua. This rejection stems from the false perception by most nonbelieving Jews that a Jewish believer has turned his back on his people and has divorced himself from his rich heritage. They do not realize that most Jewish believers now feel more fulfilled as Jews by knowing the promised Jewish Messiah. Most Jewish believers seek to gain a better understanding of their Jewishness and their purpose as Jews in God's overall plan for mankind.

One piercing view, which frequently surfaces in the Jewish

community, is that Jews who believe in the messiahship of Yeshua are no longer Jewish. Usually, one is considered a Jew by descent in our society regardless of what he believes—unless he is a Jewish believer. There are atheist Jews and Hare Krishna Jews—but no Messianic Jews. Rabbi Akiva was not expelled from membership in the Jewish community after he proclaimed the secular leader Bar Kochba to be the Messiah during the second major Jewish revolt against Rome (132–135 CE).[28] Ultraorthodox individuals who still recognize the messiahship of the late Rabbi Schneerson have not been excluded from the Jewish people. However, Jewish believers in Yeshua have been socially excommunicated.

Regardless of the hardships, Jewish believers will live the life that God has called them to live. As Daniel Juster, a Messianic Jew, stated, "Truth is a higher value than acceptance, and majority viewpoints do not define truth."[29]

## Judaism Has Not Grasped the Complete Role of the Messiah

For a fourth reason most Jews today have shunned Yeshua, I would humbly put forth that traditional Judaism over at least the past 1,000 years has not understood the full purpose of the Messiah's coming. Messianic prophecies are like pieces of a jigsaw puzzle that God has placed throughout the Hebrew Bible. Traditional Judaism has put together an image of the Messiah's function, but believers feel that a few pieces of the picture were never used. Since the Tanach is the source of the promises about the Messiah, we need to return to it so that all of the available pieces of prophecy can be examined. Only then can we attempt to assemble an accurate portrayal of the Messiah's function in God's plan for humanity.

Traditional Judaism has consistently viewed the Messiah as a descendant of King David, who would deliver the Jewish people from oppression and establish a messianic age. Rabbi Kertzer writes:

> Belief in the coming of the Messiah—a descendant of the House of David who would redeem mankind and establish a Kingdom of God on earth—has been part of the Jewish tradition since the days of the

prophet Isaiah.

As legend pictured him, the Messiah would be a human being of very special gifts: strong leadership, great wisdom, and deep integrity. These he would use to stimulate a social revolution that would usher in an era of perfect peace.[30]

In the eyes of traditional Judaism, if the messianic age did not directly accompany one claiming to be the Messiah, then that claimant was a false messiah. Rabbi Samuel Sandmel, in his book *Anti-Semitism in the New Testament*, states that when Yeshua did not usher in the messianic age and fulfill this Jewish expectation, Judaism had to reject him as being the promised Messiah:

> The Jewish denial of the messiahship of Jesus was simply a denial that the messianic age here on earth had come. The career of Jesus had not brought about what Jews expected of the Messiah. The evil power of Rome had not been broken, no Jewish king had risen to an independent throne, the scattered of Israel had not been miraculously restored to the Holy Land, and the expectation of tranquility and prosperity had not come about.[31]

In the Tanach, it is clear that the Messiah was to be a descendant of King David who would deliver the children of Israel from oppression and establish a messianic age:

> And there shall come forth a shoot out of the stock of Jesse [the father of King David], and a twig shall grow forth out of his roots. And the spirit of the LORD [YHVH] shall rest upon him, the spirit of wisdom and understanding, the spirit of counsel and might, the spirit of knowledge and of the fear of the LORD [YHVH] (Isaiah 11:1–2, Jewish Publication Society, 1917).

> But with righteousness shall he judge the poor, and decide with equity for the meek of the land; and he shall smite the land with the rod of his mouth, and with the breath of his lips shall he slay the wicked. And righteousness shall be the girdle of his loins, and faithfulness the girdle of his reins (Isaiah 11:4–5, Jewish Publication Society, 1917).

> They shall not hurt nor destroy in all My holy mountain; for the earth shall be full of the knowledge of the LORD [YHVH], as the waters

cover the sea. And it shall come to pass in that day, that the root of Jesse, that standeth for an ensign of the peoples, unto him shall the nations seek; and his resting place shall be glorious (Isaiah 11:9–10, Jewish Publication Society, 1917).

Behold, the days come, saith the LORD [YHVH], that I will raise unto David a righteous shoot, and he shall reign as king and prosper, and shall execute justice and righteousness in the land. In his days Judah shall be saved, and Israel shall dwell safely; and this is his name whereby he shall be called, the LORD [YHVH] is our righteousness (Jeremiah 23:5–6, Jewish Publication Society, 1917).

These beautiful passages undoubtedly led to the traditional picture of the Messiah discussed by Rabbi Kertzer, but this is not all that the Tanach has to say about the Messiah.

As one investigates more messianic prophecies, one begins to see a paradox. While some prophecies describe the Messiah as a powerful, ruling, and saving king, other prophecies about the Messiah state that the Messiah will die:

Know therefore and discern, that from the going forth of the word to restore and to build Jerusalem unto one anointed [*mashiach*], a prince, shall be seven weeks; and for threescore and two weeks, it shall be built again, with broad place and moat, but in troublous times. And after the threescore and two weeks shall an anointed one [*mashiach*] be cut off, and be no more; and the people of a prince that shall come shall destroy the city and the sanctuary; but his end shall be with a flood; and unto the end of the war desolations are determined (Daniel 9:25–26, Jewish Publication Society, 1917).

This passage in Daniel reveals that a messiah will come and will be killed during the second Temple period. Soon after his death, the Temple will be destroyed for the second time. The word *mashiach* is not reserved for *the* Messiah; for the priests and kings of the Hebrew people are occasionally characterized by this term[32] (Leviticus 4:3, 1 Samuel 24:7, 2 Samuel 23:1), and even the Persian king Cyrus is referred to as the *mashiach* of YHVH (Isaiah 45:1). This Messiah in Daniel, however, is not an insignificant figure. He is spoken of as "a prince," and this notable prophecy concerning the destruction of the second Temple appears to revolve around him.

In Isaiah, one finds another passage that seems to be talking about the death of the Messiah. This figure described is commonly referred to as the "Suffering Servant":

> Behold, My servant shall prosper, he shall be exalted and lifted up, and shall be very high (Isaiah 52:13, Jewish Publication Society, 1917).

> He was oppressed, though he humbled himself and opened not his mouth; as a lamb that is led to the slaughter, and as a sheep that before her shearers is dumb; yea, he opened not his mouth. By oppression and judgment he was taken away, and with his generation who did reason? For he was cut off out of the land of the living, for the transgression of my people to whom the stroke was due (Isaiah 53:7–8, Jewish Publication Society, 1917).

This servant was oppressed and killed, and his generation did not understand the purpose of his death. A standard Jewish interpretation of this passage over the past 1,000 years states that the "Suffering Servant" is the nation of Israel,[33] and in many ways, this passage does sound as if it could be describing Israel.⁘ In his book *The Messiah Texts*, Raphael Patai writes:

> All the so-called "Servant Songs" (Isaiah 42:1–4; 49:1–6; 50:4–9; and 52:13–53:12) have long been taken to speak of the sufferings of exiled Israel as personified in "the Servant of the Lord." Yet these same passages became in Talmudic times identified with the Messianic theme, and so they have remained in Jewish folk consciousness throughout the ages.

---

⁘ The Jewish believer, Victor Buksbazen, points out that some of the "servant" passages in Isaiah appear to be referring to Israel "collectively" (Isaiah 41:8–16, Isaiah 42:18–21, Isaiah 43:10, Isaiah 44:1–5, 21), whereas others describe a single person separate from Israel (Isaiah 42:1–7, Isaiah 49:1–7, Isaiah 50:4–11, Isaiah 52:13–53:12). Israel "collectively" is not often portrayed as the ideal servant (Isaiah 42:18–25). This blending of the different servants suggests that Israel "collectively" and this individual servant are in a sense one. The individual servant, the Messiah, becomes "the perfect representative of Israel." Where Israel has failed in God's plan to restore mankind, her Messiah will prevail. (Victor Buksbazen, *The Prophet Isaiah*, Vol. II [West Collingswood, N.J.: The Spearhead Press, 1971], pp. 343–349.)

In fact, it is quite probable that the concept of the suffering Messiah, fully developed in the Talmud, the Midrash, and Zohar, has its origin in the Biblical prophecies about the Suffering Servant, as shown by the direct references to Isaiah 53:5 in describing the sufferings of the Messiah in the Talmud, the Midrash Konen (eleventh or twelfth century), and the Zohar (thirteenth century).[34]

It appears that at least some ancient Jewish traditions, for many centuries, saw in Isaiah 53 a portrait of the Messiah. Although these learned men did not accept the messiahship of Yeshua, they did accept some of the messianic characteristics that Yeshua fulfilled. If some of these earlier rabbis recognized a kingly Messiah and a suffering Messiah, who would die, how did they handle this paradox? According to the *Encyclopaedia Judaica*, some of the earlier rabbis developed the concept of two Messiahs. One was the Messiah son of Joseph, who would die, and the other was the Messiah son of David, who would reign as king:[35]

> In rabbinic thought, the Messiah is the king who will redeem and rule Israel at the climax of human history and the instrument by which the kingdom of God will be established.[36]

> A secondary messianic figure is the Messiah son of (i.e., of the tribe of) Joseph (or Ephraim), whose coming precedes that of the Messiah son of David, and who will die in combat with the enemies of God and Israel. Though some (e.g., Torrey, Segal) claim that this figure is described in pre-Christian apocalyptic and apocryphal works, most scholars note that the first unambiguous mentions of this doctrine occur in tannaitic passages of uncertain date (Sukkah 52a) and in the Targums (Pseudo-Jon., Ex. 40:11; Pesh., Song 4:5).[37]

These rabbis reasonably solved the peculiar paradox of the Messiah's function described in the Tanach by creating the concept of two messiahs. The concept of two messiahs, however, is not the only possible interpretation.

If Daniel 9 and Isaiah 53 are talking about *the* Messiah, why was he to die?

> But he was wounded because of our transgressions, he was crushed because of our iniquities: the chastisement of our welfare was upon

him, and with his stripes we were healed. All we like sheep did go astray, we turned every one to his own way; and the LORD [YHVH] hath made to light on him the iniquity of us all (Isaiah 53:5–6, Jewish Publication Society, 1917).

The above verses from the Tanach distinctly state that this "Suffering Servant" or Messiah died because of our transgressions, but is that consistent with Judaism?**

Jews have always been concerned with sin. Rabbi Kertzer writes, "A postscript to every Jew's life, uttered at his graveside, are the words: 'For there liveth no man on earth who is so righteous that he sinneth not.'"[38] Another example of the importance of sin to the Jew is found in Yom Kippur, the Day of Atonement for past sins. This day continues to be the holiest day of the year in Jewish eyes. Sin has attained this level of awareness by the Jew because according to the Scriptures, sin separates man from God:

Behold, the LORD's [YHVH's] hand is not shortened, that it cannot save, neither His ear heavy, that it cannot hear; but your iniquities have separated between you and your God, and your sins have hid His face from you, that He will not hear (Isaiah 59:1–2 - *Jewish Publication Society 1917*).

---

** If the nation of Israel is to be equated with this "Suffering Servant," who by its suffering will atone for the sins of mankind, we need to assume that the nation of Israel is without blemish. Isaiah 53:10 states of this "Suffering Servant": "Yet it pleased the LORD [YHVH] to crush him by disease; to see if his soul would offer itself in restitution [*asham*]" (Isaiah 53:10, Jewish Publication Society, 1917). The word "restitution" here is translated for the Hebrew word *asham*. *Asham* also appears in Leviticus 5, but there it is translated "guilt offering," characterized by a ram without blemish: "And he shall bring a ram without blemish out of the flock, according to thy valuation, for a guilt offering [*asham*], unto the priest; and the priest shall make atonement for him concerning the error which he committed, though he knew it not, and he shall be forgiven" (Leviticus 5:18, Jewish Publication Society, 1917). Could the nation of Israel honestly be characterized as a perfect guilt offering? (Arthur W. Kac, *The Messianic Hope* [Baltimore: Reese Press, Inc., 1975], pp.71–73.)

Jews in every age have sought atonement[††] for their sins. Before the Temple was destroyed for the second time in 70 CE, animal (blood) sacrifices were required to bridge the gap between God and man, along with a changed attitude toward sin: "For the life of the flesh is in the blood; and I have given it to you upon the altar to make atonement for your souls; for it is the blood that maketh atonement by reason of the life" (Leviticus 17:11, Jewish Publication Society, 1917). After the destruction of the Temple, sacrifices could no longer be carried out because they could only be performed in the Temple. Judaism, without the Temple sacrifices, created various formulas that were said to be efficacious in atoning for sin, but these were rabbinic dogmas and not Scriptural (prayer, repentance, charity; suffering; exile and the destruction of the Temple; one's own death).[39]

Johanan ben Zakkai was a rabbi in the first century who developed such an atoning formula:

> "Once when R. Johanan b. Zakkai was leaving Jerusalem, R. Joshua was walking behind him and saw the Temple in ruins. R. Joshua said, 'Woe is us that this has been destroyed, the place where atonement was made for the sins of Israel.' 'No, my son, do you not know that we have a means of making atonement that is like it. And what is it? It is deeds of love, as it is said (Hos. 6:6): "For I desire kindness, and not sacrifice."'"[40]

When the same rabbi was confronted with death, however, he was unable to put much faith into his own atoning formula:

> "When he fell ill, his disciples went to visit him. When R. Johanan b. Zakkai saw them, he began to weep. His disciples said to him: 'Light of Israel, pillar of the right hand, mighty hammer! Why do you weep?' He

---

†† According to the *Encyclopaedia Judaica*: "The English word atonement ("at-one-ment") significantly conveys the underlying Judaic concept of atonement, i.e., reconciliation with God. Both the Bible and rabbinical theology reflect the belief that God is holy, man must be pure in order to remain in communion with Him. Sin and defilement damage the relationship between creature and Creator, and the process of atonement—through repentance and reparation—restores this relationship." ("Atonement," *Encyclopaedia Judaica*, Vol. 3 [Jerusalem, Israel: Keter Publishing House Ltd., 1971], p. 830.)

replied: '. . . when there are two ways before me, one leading to Paradise and the other to Gehinnom, and I do not know by which I shall be taken, shall I not weep?'"[41]

He was unsure where he stood before God.[42]

Believers understand that Yeshua is the promised Messiah. They believe that he appeared as the "Suffering Servant" once before the second Temple was destroyed, and according to the prophet Isaiah, "The LORD [YHVH] hath made to light on him the iniquity of us all" (Isaiah 53:6, Jewish Publication Society, 1917). This concept is very much in keeping with the Judaism of the Tanach. The animal sacrifices of the early Hebrews prospectively pointed to this very function of the Messiah.[43] In the book of Jeremiah, God promises to establish a new covenant with the descendants of Israel. A fundamental feature of this covenant is that our sins will be forgiven and remembered no more:

> Behold, the days come, saith the LORD [YHVH], that I will make a new covenant with the house of Israel, and with the house of Judah; not according to the covenant that I made with their fathers in the day that I took them by the hand to bring them out of the land of Egypt; forasmuch as they broke My covenant, although I was a lord over them, saith the LORD [YHVH]. But this is the covenant that I will make with the house of Israel after those days, saith the LORD [YHVH], I will put My law in their inward parts, and in their heart will I write it; and I will be their God, and they shall be My people; and they shall teach no more every man his neighbour, and every man his brother, saying: "Know the LORD [YHVH]"; for they shall all know Me, from the least of them unto the greatest of them, saith the LORD [YHVH]; for I will forgive their iniquity, and their sin will I remember no more (Jeremiah 31:31–34, Jewish Publication Society, 1917).

Through the Messiah's atoning death, we no longer need to be unsure of our standing before God.‡‡ We can have this new covenant

---

‡‡ Believers feel that salvation has always been an undeserved gift given to us by God through our trusting in His provision for us. Yeshua's atoning death is God's provision for us. God never intended us to earn our own salvation by legalistically following a set of rules. None of us can reach the perfection required

relationship with God where He is our God, and we are His people according to His promises. Believers feel that the Messiah Yeshua, once killed, came back to life, and will return a second time in the future to set up the messianic age, solving the problem of the seeming paradox in the Scriptures.

## Jews Reject a Divine Messiah

A fifth reason why most Jews have rejected the messiahship of Yeshua is that Judaism has always strongly dismissed the idea that the Messiah will have characteristics that extend beyond humanity. Rabbi Kertzer, again speaking of the Messiah, states, "There was never any suggestion of divine power brought to bear. The Messiah was envisioned as a great leader, a moulder of men and society, but, for all that, a human being, not a God."[44]

The Christian church, divorced from its Jewish roots, eventually developed the incomprehensible doctrine of the Trinity, a word interestingly never found in the New Testament. Here is a succinct definition of the Trinity from James White: "Within the one Being that is God, there exists eternally three coequal and coeternal persons, namely, the Father, the Son, and the Holy Spirit."[45] Contradictions abound in this concept.

Clearly, the Messiah was to be a unique human being. In disagreement with Rabbi Kertzer's statement about the Messiah, previously quoted, I would submit that God's Spirit (divine power) was to come upon the Messiah, and considerable authority was to be given to him by God. Still, the Messiah was never envisioned as God. I agree with Anthony Buzzard and Charles Hunting, former Trinitarians, who view the doctrine of the Trinity to be "Christianity's self-inflicted wound."[46] Much more will be written about the Trinity and the deity of Yeshua in the coming chapters. Undoubtedly, this has been an

---

by God. Having said this, however, many Jewish believers understand that the written Torah remains a guidebook as to how the followers of God should live their lives before men and God. It is a special instruction to us as to how to live our lives to the fullest, how to live holy lives (see chapter 4).

unnecessary stumbling block to the Jewish people in recognizing their Messiah.

## Christians Have Stripped Yeshua of His Jewishness

A sixth reason most Jews have rejected Yeshua is that Jews are unable to recognize Yeshua as the promised Jewish Messiah after he has been removed from the context of Judaism. Earlier, I established that the Messianic faith was a Jewish faith, understood by its earliest followers as a fulfillment of Judaism, not something new or contrary to Judaism. Not long after its beginnings, however, a significant metamorphosis occurred in the Messianic faith, mainly because of the political turmoil in Israel during the first and second centuries CE, as discussed previously. The upheaval in Israel in the first century led to the destruction of the second Temple in 70 CE, during the first major Jewish revolt against Rome (66–70 CE).[47] (The Jewish stronghold at Masada fell shortly afterward.) In the second century, as discussed by Samuele Bacchiocchi in *From Sabbath to Sunday*, oppressive decrees were issued by Emperor Hadrian after the second major Jewish revolt (132–135 CE), according to which the Jews, including the Jewish believers, were no longer allowed to enter Jerusalem or freely allowed "to practice their religion."[48]

According to Bacchiocchi, in order for the growing and eventually dominant number of Gentile believers, "primarily of pagan descent," to avoid these "repressive and punitive measures" aimed at the Jews, they distanced themselves from Judaism:[49]

> Both external pressures and internal needs encouraged many Christians at that time to break radically with the Jews. Externally, the existing conflict between the Jews and the empire made it necessary for Christians to develop a new identity in order to avoid the repressive and punitive measures (fiscal, military, political, and literary) aimed at the Jews. Internally, the influence of the synagogue and of Judaeo-Christians who insisted on the literal observance of certain Mosaic regulations, prompted Christians to sever their ties with Judaism. To develop this new identity, many Christians not only assumed a negative attitude toward the Jews as a people, but also substituted characteristic

*56*

Jewish religious observances such as Passover and the Sabbath with Easter-Sunday and the weekly Sunday. This action apparently would serve to make the Roman authorities aware that Christians liberated from Jewish religious ties represented for the empire irreproachable subjects.[50]

The disease of anti-Semitism also broke out in the early church, causing many Gentile and probably some Jewish believers to reject their Jewish roots and minimize the importance of the Torah.

The Messianic faith is a Jewish faith, even though the Gentile church has transformed it over the years into something that is unrecognizable. Originally, the Gentiles, who wished to participate and also serve the God of Abraham, Isaac, and Jacob, were to be grafted into the Jewish olive tree (Romans 11:17–24). They were to become partakers in the commonwealth of Israel (Ephesians 2:11–22). They were not to replace the physical Jewish nation but to serve and worship God side by side with them (see chapter 7).

Throughout the centuries, most of the traditional Gentile church has continued to perpetuate most of the anti-Judaic culture and traditions established by the early Gentile church (although today often unknowingly). Today, even traces of a Jewish flavor are difficult to find in the traditional Christian church. In fact, few Gentile Christians have a clear understanding that Yeshua is the promised Messiah spoken of by the Hebrew prophets.

A Messianic Jewish man in Chicago told me a story many years ago. He had been showing a Protestant, church-going woman around his home. When they came to a painting of a bearded, Orthodox Jewish man on his wall traditionally dressed with *tallit* and *tefillin*, he pointed jokingly to the portrait and said, "This is Jesus." The woman became solemn and said, "I'm sorry, but you must be mistaken. This can't be a picture of Jesus." "Why not?" the man asked. "Because this man looks Jewish!" the woman replied. Since most Gentiles who call themselves Christians do not see or portray Yeshua as the promised Jewish Messiah, Jews certainly have not seen him as such either, but as a foreign, Gentile god.

Even though the Gentile church missed the mark by rejecting their Jewish roots and the Torah, still, over one billion Christians in almost every country in the world have been exposed to the Hebrew Scriptures and the God of Abraham, Isaac, and Jacob. This fact is amazing! As was revealed previously in Isaiah 11, one of the responsibilities of the Messiah will be for him to bring the knowledge of God to all of mankind. He will bring the nations to God:

> They shall not hurt nor destroy in all My holy mountain; for the earth shall be full of the knowledge of the LORD [YHVH], as the waters cover the sea. And it shall come to pass in that day, that the root of Jesse [the father of King David], that standeth for an ensign of the peoples, unto him shall the nations seek; and his resting place shall be glorious (Isaiah 11:9–10, Jewish Publication Society, 1917).

If Yeshua is not the Messiah, then the Messiah, who will come, will need to perform a similar miraculous act among the nations in teaching them a]bout God.§§

## Christian Anti-Semitism

A seventh reason most Jews do not accept Yeshua as the Messiah is because Jews have been persecuted in the name of "Christ" and by people who have affiliated with the Christian church in almost every period of history since the first century CE.[51] To understand how a person who claims to be a follower of the Jewish Messiah could persecute the Jewish people, one must understand that many claim to be believers in name, but few live as true believers. It is important to recognize that few Gentiles are true believers, even though they may

---

§§ Some nonbelieving Jews have suggested that Yeshua is the savior for the Gentiles but not for the Jews (p. 20). Pinchas Lapide writes that even Maimonides in *Mishneh Torah* (Hilkhot Melakhim XI, 4) understood that Yeshua's life caused the knowledge of the Messiah, the Torah, and the commandments to be spread throughout the world. According to Maimonides, even though the ideas coming from Christianity are false, they will pave the way for the real Messiah when he comes (pp. 142–143). (Pinchas Lapide, *The Resurrection of Jesus: A Jewish Perspective* [Minneapolis: Augsburg Publishing House, 1983].)

identify culturally with a particular Christian group. In the movie *The Hiding Place*, Casper ten Boom says, "If a mouse lives in the cookie jar, that doesn't necessarily make him a cookie."[52] Similarly, the person who categorizes himself as a Christian but opposes the life that God has called him to live is masquerading under a false label. Many sincere Gentile believers love the Jewish people, and a number died during World War II trying to save Jewish lives.[53]

## Predicted Jewish Blindness for a Time

An eighth reason most Jews have not become followers of Yeshua is because God has allowed a temporary and partial blindness to come upon the people of Israel (Isaiah 6:8–13, Isaiah 29:9–14; Hosea 3:4–5; Romans 11:7–10, 11:25–29). Various forces, some already discussed, are preventing the Jewish people from recognizing and following the promised Messiah. The prophet Isaiah declares that this blindness is at least partially a result of an insincere attitude toward God:

> And the LORD [YHVH] said: Forasmuch as this people draw near, and with their mouth and with their lips do honour Me, but have removed their heart far from Me, and their fear of Me is a commandment of men learned by rote; therefore, behold, I will again do a marvellous work among this people, even a marvellous work and a wonder; and the wisdom of their wise men shall perish, and the prudence of their prudent men shall be hid (Isaiah 29:13–14, Jewish Publication Society, 1917).

The following two prophecies describe the rejection of the Messiah that has resulted from this blindness:

> He was despised, and forsaken of men, a man of pains, and acquainted with disease, and as one from whom men hide their face: he was despised, and we esteemed him not. Surely our diseases he did bear, and our pains he carried; whereas we did esteem him stricken, smitten of God, and afflicted (Isaiah 53:3–4, Jewish Publication Society, 1917).

> This is the gate of the LORD [YHVH]; the righteous shall enter into it. I will give thanks unto Thee, for Thou hast answered me, and art become my salvation. The stone which the builders rejected is become

the chief corner-stone. This is the LORD's [YHVH's] doing; it is marvellous in our eyes (Psalm 118:20–23, Jewish Publication Society, 1917).

YHVH, however, will not allow this blindness of Israel to go unchecked much longer. The prophet Zechariah writes that one day the Jewish people will come to accept the Messiah and mourn over their past rejection:

> And it shall come to pass in that day, that I will seek to destroy all the nations that come against Jerusalem. And I will pour upon the house of David, and upon the inhabitants of Jerusalem, the spirit of grace and of supplication; and they shall look unto Me because they have thrust him through; and they shall mourn for him, as one mourneth for his only son, and shall be in bitterness for him, as one that is in bitterness for his first-born. In that day shall there be a great mourning in Jerusalem, as the mourning of Hadadrimmon in the valley of Megiddon (Zechariah 12:9–11, Jewish Publication Society, 1917).

Even though most of the nation of Israel has sat for many years with a neutral attitude toward God, they will soon come back to His goodness, and find *HaMashiach ben David* (the Messiah son of David):[54]

> For the children of Israel shall sit solitary many days without king, and without prince, and without sacrifice, and without pillar, and without ephod or teraphim; afterward shall the children of Israel return, and seek the LORD [YHVH] their God, and David their king; and shall come trembling unto the LORD [YHVH] and to His goodness in the end of days (Hosea 3:4–5, Jewish Publication Society, 1917).

This future time will be the day when the Jewish people will finally find shalom while holding fast to their God.⁋⁋

---

⁋⁋   The story of Joseph and his brothers foreshadows the history of Yeshua and the Jewish people. Joseph is portrayed as being perfect without sin. His brothers turn against him. He is sold to a foreign people for silver. His brothers eat a meal before betraying him. He is placed down in a pit, taken down to Egypt, and again placed in a pit (prison) in Egypt as if he were dead. He is accused falsely by his brothers and Potiphar's wife and is silent before his accusers. He in a sense comes back to life (comes out of prison), puts on new clothing,

"Yeshua" is not a household word in most Jewish homes today. The numerous misconceptions about the Messianic faith and the person Yeshua have contributed to this Jewish rejection of Yeshua as the promised Messiah of Israel. The Messianic faith, however, is a Jewish faith and appears to be based solidly in the Tanach. May the God of Israel soon restore vision to His people.

Defining and dealing with the sin nature is the next topic that needs reforming.

---

is presented before the king/pharaoh, and is made second in command to the king/pharaoh. He is thirty years old when he enters the service of the king/pharaoh. He is said to have the spirit of God and is able to discern between good and evil. By finding a solution to the famine he first saves Gentiles from death and later also saves his brothers. His brothers do not recognize him for a time as the one who could save them from death. They eventually mourn over their onetime rejection of him (Genesis 37–50).

## (Endnotes)

1    *Fiddler on the Roof*, directed by Norman Jewison (1971; United States: Metro-Goldwyn-Mayer Studios, Inc., 2007), DVD.

2    *The Authorized Daily Prayer Book*, translated by Dr. Joseph H. Hertz, revised ed. (New York: Bloch Publishing Company, 1975), p. 255.

3    Hugh J. Schonfield, *The Passover Plot* (New York: Bantam Books, 1967), p. 188.

4    John Fischer, *Sharing Israel's Messiah* (Highland Park, IL: The Watchman Association, 1978), p. 12.

5    William F. Albright, "Toward a More Conservative View," *Christianity Today*, VII (January 18, 1963), p. 3.

6    Samuel Sandmel, *Anti-Semitism in the New Testament?* (Philadelphia: Fortress Press, 1978), p. 8.

7    Schonfield, *The Passover Plot*, p. 188.

8    Thanks to Lawrence Rich who directed much of my thinking in the present discussion.

9    Hugh J. Schonfield, *The History of Jewish Christianity: From the First to the Twentieth Century* (London: Duckworth, 1936), p. 119.

10   Matt Jackson-McCabe, "What's in a Name? The Problem of 'Jewish Christianity,'" in *Jewish Christianity Reconsidered*, ed. by Matt Jackson-McCabe (Minneapolis: Fortress Press, 2007), p. 32.

11   Paul Johnson, *A History of the Jews* (New York: Harper Perennial, 1987), pp. 137–150.

12   Hugh J. Schonfield, *The History of Jewish Christianity: From the First to the Twentieth Century*, p. 113.

13   Ibid., pp. 62–63.

14   Samuele Bacchiocchi, *From Sabbath to Sunday: A Historical Investigation of the Rise of Sunday Observance in Early Christianity* (Rome: The Pontifical Gregorian University Press, 1977), pp. 169–185. Hugh J. Schonfield, *The History of Jewish Christianity: From the First to the Twentieth Century*, p. 62.

15   Jakob Jocz, *The Jewish People and Jesus Christ: The Relationship Between Church and Synagogue* (3rd ed.; Grand Rapids, MI: Baker Book House, 1979), pp. 190, 200.

16   Ibid., pp. 190, 200.

17   Ibid., p. 200.

18  Hugh J. Schonfield, *The History of Jewish Christianity: From the First to the Twentieth Century*, p. 113.

19  Ibid., p. 120.

20  Ibid., p. 120.

21  Ibid., p. 120.

22  Ibid., p. 124.

23  David A. Rausch, *Messianic Judaism: Its History, Theology, and Polity* (New York: The Edwin Mellen Press, 1982), pp. 21–43.

24  Rabbi Morris N. Kertzer, *What Is a Jew?* (New York: Collier Books, 1978), p. 20.

25  Daniel J. Elazar, "How Strong is Orthodox Judaism—Really? The Demographics of Jewish Religious Identification," *Jerusalem Center for Public Affairs*, accessed May 30, 2015, http://www.jcpa.org/dje/articles2/demographics.htm.

26  Rabbi Morris N. Kertzer, *What Is a Jew?* p. 20.

27  John Fischer, *Sharing Israel's Messiah*, pp. 141–142.

28  Harry Freedman, "Akiva," *Encyclopaedia Judaica*, Vol. 2 (Jerusalem, Israel: Keter Publishing House Ltd., 1971), p. 489.

29  Daniel C. Juster, "Letter to a Rabbi," *The American Messianic Jew* (Spring 1980), p. 11.

30  Rabbi Morris N. Kertzer, *What Is a Jew?* pp. 19–20.

31  Samuel Sandmel, *Anti-Semitism in the New Testament?* p. 131.

32  David L. Cooper, *The 70 Weeks of Daniel* (Los Angeles: Biblical Research Society, 1941), pp. 43–44.

33  Victor Buksbazen, *The Prophet Isaiah*, Vol. II (West Collingswood, NJ: The Spearhead Press, 1971), p. 404.

34  Raphael Patai, *The Messiah Texts* (Detroit: Wayne State University Press, 1988), pp. 1–2.

35  Victor Buksbazen, *The Prophet Isaiah*, p. 403.

36  Gerald J. Blidstein, "Messiah," *Encyclopaedia Judaica*, vol. 11 (Jerusalem, Israel: Keter Publishing House Ltd., 1971), pp. 1410.

37  Ibid., pp. 1410–1411.

38  Rabbi Morris N. Kertzer, *What Is a Jew?* p. 11.

39  "Atonement," *Encyclopaedia Judaica*, Vol. 3 (Jerusalem, Israel: Keter Publishing House Ltd., 1971), p. 830–831.

40  Quoted in "Johanan ben Zakkai," *Encyclopaedia Judaica,* Vol. 10 (Jerusalem, Israel: Keter Publishing House Ltd., 1971), p.153.

41    Quoted in "Johanan ben Zakkai," *Encyclopaedia Judaica*, p. 154 (from Berachot 28b.).

42    Thanks to Louis Goldberg for this idea.

43    Charles Lee Feinberg, *The Prophecy of Ezekiel: The Glory of the Lord* (Chicago: Moody Press, 1969), p. 254.

44    Rabbi Morris N. Kertzer, *What Is a Jew?* p. 20.

45    James R. White, *The Forgotten Trinity: Recovering the Heart of Christian Belief* (Minneapolis: Bethany House Publishers, 1998), p.26.

46    Anthony F. Buzzard and Charles F. Hunting, *The Doctrine of the Trinity—Christianity's Self-Inflicted Wound* (New York: International Scholars Publications, 1998), p. 1.

47    Menahem Stern, "History," *Encyclopaedia Judaica*, Vol. 8 (Jerusalem, Israel: Keter Publishing House Ltd., 1971), pp. 641–642.

48    Samuele Bacchiocchi, *From Sabbath to Sunday: A Historical Investigation of the Rise of Sunday Observance in Early Christianity*, pp. 159–161.

49    Ibid., pp. 167, 305.

50    Ibid., p. 305.

51    John Fischer, *Sharing Israel's Messiah*, pp. 33–35.

52    *The Hiding Place*, directed by James F. Collier (1975; United States: World Wide Pictures, Inc., 1990), VCR.

53    Corrie ten Boom with John and Elizabeth Sherrill, *The Hiding Place* (Washington Depot, CT: Chosen Books, 1971).

54    Arthur W. Kac, *The Rebirth of the State of Israel: Is it of God or of Men?* revised edition (Grand Rapids, MI: Baker Book House, 1976), pp. 149–151.

# Chapter 3: Dealing with the Sin Nature

## Dr. Jekyll and Mr. Hyde and the Sin Nature

In 1886, Robert Louis Stevenson published the short novel *The Strange Case of Dr. Jekyll and Mr. Hyde.* In the novel, the character Dr. Jekyll is a physician/scientist who understands that all men have a dual nature. To Dr. Jekyll, this dual nature consists of a good and evil nature bound together in every person. He realizes that there is a continuous struggle between the good nature and the evil nature. His desire is to separate these two natures, and he does this by concocting a chemical potion. When he drinks the potion, Dr. Jekyll changes into his pure evil nature, which he names Mr. Hyde. Mr. Hyde seeks out every pleasurable experience without restraint. His only concern is for himself, and to achieve his goals he steps on others. Mr. Hyde is a beast of instinct like an animal. In the beginning, whenever Mr. Hyde drinks the potion again, he changes back into Dr. Jekyll. However, eventually, Dr. Jekyll is transformed into Mr. Hyde without the potion. In the end, Dr. Jekyll is entirely ruled by Mr. Hyde. The novel gives us a glimpse of the sin nature that plagues us all.

## Jacob and Esau and the Sin Nature

Thousands of years before Stevenson penned this novel there was a narrative recorded in the Torah with a similar theme. This narrative could be entitled *The Strange Case of Jacob and Esau.*

Starting with the birth of Jacob and Esau in Genesis 25:24, we read:

> When her days to give birth were completed, behold, there were twins
> in her womb. The first came out red, all his body like a hairy cloak, so
> they called his name Esau. Afterward his brother came out with his
> hand holding Esau's heel, so his name was called Jacob. Isaac was sixty
> years old when she bore them (Genesis 25:24–26).

The first point that we should notice is that Rebekah has twins.
Even though Esau comes out before Jacob, they are twins nonetheless.
They have been developing together in the same womb. Twins are
different from other siblings born to the same mother. It is as if they
are two separate individuals bound up as one.

Notice the description given of Esau in verse 25. Not only is he
reddish, but he is covered all over with hair. The description is more
like that of a bear cub than of a human baby. So begins the portrayal
of Esau's animal characteristics as outlined by Nahum Sarna[1] and
Robert Alter.[2]

"When the boys grew up, Esau was a skillful hunter, a man of
the field, while Jacob was a quiet man, dwelling in tents" (Genesis
25:27). The Hebrew here tells us that Esau is a man who knows
hunting and a man of the field. Hunting was not a highly respected
profession in the Bible. The only other hunter mentioned in the
Bible is Nimrod.[3] Animals are usually hunters. Esau is also a man
of the field in contrast to Jacob, who seems to be more civilized,
or more human, living in tents. Jacob is called an *eesh tam* in the
Hebrew. *Eesh tam* is translated in various ways but could mean that
he was a complete man, or better, a blameless man. Unlike Esau,
Jacob is described as the perfect man.

> One day when Ya'akov [Jacob] had cooked some stew, 'Esav [Esau]
> came in from the open country, exhausted, and said to Ya'akov [Jacob],
> "Please! Let me gulp down some of that red stuff—that red stuff! I'm
> exhausted!" (This is why he was called Edom [red].) (Genesis 25:29–
> 30, *Complete Jewish Bible*).

Here we have Esau coming in from the field exhausted and hungry. He asks Jacob if he could swallow some of his lentil stew. This
Hebrew word for swallow, however, is peculiar and only used here in

the Bible. According to Sarna, rabbinic Hebrew uses the verb later to describe feeding animals.[4] Therefore, Esau is saying something like "let me wolf down some of that red stuff." Notice also that Esau is rather inarticulate here. He cannot come up with the word for lentil stew and asks for the red stuff. Speaking is a human characteristic that Esau does not seem to have mastered. The last point in this verse is that Esau asks for the red, red stuff. He repeats the word red twice. Red, red stuff sounds like blood. Maybe Esau also thought the cooking stuff was blood. Animals eat blood.

In summary, we see that Esau has animal characteristics. He is red and hairy. He hunts and lives in the field. He is inarticulate and wolfs down his food. He likes to eat blood.

Esau becomes the representative example of a man with animal-like instincts. Jacob becomes the representative example of a man who is blameless. Yet, the real Esau was not totally depraved, nor was the real Jacob perfect.*

Now, let us skip ahead to Genesis chapter 27 which recounts Jacob's deception of his father to get the blessing. Thinking he will die

---

* Ancient rabbinic thought considers Jacob and the other patriarchs to be men without fault. As pointed out by Alter, however, Jacob received just punishments for cheating his blind father in the dark with the garment of Esau and a goat. First, Jacob's uncle Laban cheats him in the dark when he gives him the older daughter Leah as a wife instead of the loved, younger daughter Rachel (Genesis 29:15-30). Later, Jacob's sons deceive him with Joseph's coat of many colors, the garment, dipped it in the blood of a goat (Genesis 37:12-36). (Robert Alter, *The Art of Biblical Narrative* [New York: Basic Books, 1981], pp. 45, 181.) According to John Sailhamer, by dishonoring his father, Jacob also suffered the consequences of violating the fifth of the Ten Commandments: "Honor your father and your mother, as the LORD [YHVH] your God commanded you, that your days may be long, and that it may go well with you in the land that the LORD [YHVH] your God is giving you" (Deuteronomy 5:16). Jacob at the end of his life told Pharaoh how short and hard his life had been (Genesis 47:8-9). He also died in the land of Egypt, outside of the Land of Promise. (John Sailhamer, "Genesis," Vol. 2 of *The Expositor's Bible Commentary*, ed. by Frank E. Gaebelein, 12 vols. [Grand Rapids, MI: Zondervan Publishing House, 1990], p. 264.) The biblical text informs us that Jacob was not the model son, nor was he the ideal husband or father.

soon, the old and blind Isaac calls for his firstborn son, Esau, so he can confer the patriarchal blessing upon him. He first asks Esau to hunt for and prepare his favorite dish. While Esau is gone, Rebekah devises a strategy for her Jacob to get the blessing of the firstborn before it is given to Esau. Isaac is missing one out of five senses, he cannot see, but his other senses are intact. The scheme here is to change Jacob into Esau. She makes Jacob feel like Esau, by placing goatskins on his hands and neck. She makes him smell like Esau, by dressing him in Esau's clothing. She makes him taste like Esau, by using Esau's recipe for goat meat to prepare tasty food that Isaac loves. Since Isaac is blind, Rebekah does not need to alter Jacob's appearance. She cannot modify Jacob's voice.

Do you see what is happening here? Just before Jacob sins against his father, he is transformed into Esau. He becomes a man of the field and is no longer a complete, blameless man. The transformation is complete when Jacob tells his father in chapter 27, verse 19, "I am Esau." Jacob, too, becomes animal like, similar to his brother Esau, and then he sins against his father. Even though Jacob represents the perfect man, in reality, he, like the rest of us, is not so perfect.

Being animal like is being a "creature of appetite," as Alter would say.[5] Animals operate by instinct. They do whatever makes them feel good at the moment. Many in our culture seek to satisfy their animal appetites and teach others to do the same. We are often told, "If it feels good, do it." An animal can only focus on the physical, not the spiritual. Esau was like this. He spurned the sacred responsibility of being in the line of Abraham for a bowl of stew.

## The Origin of Sin

Even though the first man was created perfect and without sin, in the image of God, man fell away from God. All of us seem to have the brothers Jacob and Esau bound together inside of us. They are struggling within us as they were struggling in Rebekah's womb. Our God-given free will allows this scenario to play out.

The Esau inside of us is what could be referred to as the sin nature. Sha'ul seems to be characterizing this sin nature somewhat in

Romans 7:19–24:

> For I do not do the good I want, but the evil I do not want is what I
> keep on doing. Now if I do what I do not want, it is no longer I who
> do it, but sin that dwells within me. So I find it to be a law that when I
> want to do right, evil lies close at hand. For I delight in the law of God,
> in my inner being, but I see in my members another law waging war
> against the law of my mind and making me captive to the law of sin
> that dwells in my members. Wretched man that I am! Who will deliver
> me from this body of death?

Rabbinic thought has a similar concept. They would say that all
men are born with the *Yetzer HaRah*, or the evil inclination, and later
develop the *Yetzer HaTov*, or the good inclination, as they study the
Torah. This concept comes from Genesis 6:5 and 8:21, where God is
describing men before and after the flood:[6]

> The LORD [YHVH] saw that the wickedness of man was great in the
> earth, and that every intention [*yetzer*] of the thoughts of his heart was
> only evil continually (Genesis 6:5).

> And when the LORD [YHVH] smelled the pleasing aroma, the LORD
> [YHVH] said in his heart, "I will never again curse the ground because
> of man, for the intention [*yetzer*] of man's heart is evil from his youth.
> Neither will I ever again strike down every living creature as I have
> done" (Genesis 8:21).

Traditional Judaism rejects the idea of an inherited sin nature.[7]

Traditional Christianity developed the concept of original sin
where, in its extreme form, all men inherit from Adam the guilt of his
sin as well as a sinful state.[†] This idea seems to have been developed,
however, from a misunderstanding of the line of reasoning that Sha'ul
offers in Romans 5:12–21. David Stern points out that Sha'ul makes
a rabbinic *kal v'chomer* (light and heavy) argument here, comparing

---

† David Stern gives a summary of this topic in his *Jewish New Testament
Commentary* for those interested. "Are we sinners because we sin or do we sin because we are sinners?" (David Stern, *Jewish New Testament Commentary* [Clarks-
ville, MD: Jewish New Testament Publications, 1992], pp. 359–373.)

Adam to Yeshua:[8]

> Therefore, just as sin came into the world through one man, and death through sin, and so death spread to all men because all sinned (Romans 5:12).

> Therefore, as one trespass led to condemnation for all men, so one act of righteousness leads to justification and life for all men (Romans 5:18).

Sha'ul seems to be saying that since Adam was the first man to have sinned, sin entered the world through one man. Since God then removed Adam from the source of life, found only in the garden, all men after him also lost access to this life-giving source. Therefore, Adam dies, and all men after him. Verse 12 tells us, however, that all men sin, thus each person is responsible for his or her own death.[9]

Regardless of where this sin nature comes from, it appears that men universally are unable to live perfectly righteous lives by their own power.‡ All men sin. Ecclesiastes 7:20 tells us: "Surely there is not a righteous man on earth who does good and never sins." All of us know what it is like to start growing hair on the smooth parts of our necks and the back of our hands. Nevertheless, we should not be content to be animal like. We were made different from animals. We were created in the image of God. We should continue to be like Jacob, the ideal representation of the perfect man in our narrative, but

---

‡   According to John Sailhamer, Enoch was an example of someone in the Torah who found the way to life by walking with God: "Enoch walked with God, and he was not, for God took him" (Genesis 5:24). There is the suggestion that he lived a perfectly righteous life and therefore did not die. Enoch is probably a type of Yeshua. Noah also walked with God and lived a perfectly righteous life (Genesis 6:9). It appears that Noah also would not have died if it had not been for his drunkenness. The flood narrative interrupts Noah's genealogy that begins in Genesis 5:32, but in Genesis 9:28–29 we get the conclusion of his genealogy, after his drunkenness, which includes his death. (John H. Sailhamer, "Genesis," Vol. 2, in *The Expositor's Bible Commentary*, ed. by Frank E. Gaebelein [Grand Rapids, MI: Zondervan Publishing House, 1990], pp. 74–75.) If Noah, the one man saved from the flood, could not maintain total righteousness in his life, there is not much hope that another Enoch will appear on planet Earth, except for the occasion of the Messiah.

how do we accomplish this feat?

## God's Provision for Our Sin

Before we can answer this question, we need to deal with a more pressing issue. Because all of us sin, and none of us now is perfect, we all reside in bodies "bound for death" (Romans 7:24, *Complete Jewish Bible*). Our depravity requires a remedy. None of us can earn our own salvation before a holy God. We must accept the provision of God as revealed to us in Isaiah 52:13–53:12—the atoning death of Yeshua the Messiah. It is common to hear from Christian circles that those who do not believe in Jesus will go to hell, as if unbelief in Yeshua was the transgression. It is our personal sins, however, that have already compromised our relationship with God. Yeshua's atonement, already accomplished in history, must be accepted to restore our relationship with our Creator. Once our relationship has been restored, the struggle is not over. God expects us to live holy lives (lives set apart) because He is holy.

## Believers Continue to Sin after Acts Chapter 2

When it comes to living perfectly righteous lives, men and women are like toy cars without batteries. They do not have the power to always do the right thing. Throughout the Tanach we observe certain men accomplishing great acts because God's Spirit was upon them—Joseph (Genesis 41:38), Moses (Deuteronomy 34:9–12), Bezalel (Exodus 31:2–5), Joshua (Numbers 27:18), Gideon (Judges 6:34), Samson (Judges 14:6), David (1 Samuel 16:13), and probably all of the prophets.

After Yeshua's death, believers were promised a similar power through God's Spirit to help them live righteously. Kefa (Peter) said the phenomenon of God's Spirit coming upon believers on the Shavuot/Pentecost recorded in Acts chapters 1 and 2 was a fulfillment of a prophecy in Joel: "And it shall come to pass afterward, that I will pour out my Spirit on all flesh; your sons and your daughters shall prophesy, your old men shall dream dreams, and your young men shall see visions" (Joel 2:28). The prophecy says more, however: "And I will show wonders in the heavens and on the earth, blood and fire and columns of smoke. The sun shall be turned to darkness, and the moon to blood, before the great and awesome day of the LORD [YHVH] comes" (Joel 2:30–31). It is clear that the prophecy was only partially fulfilled at the time of Acts. This prophecy awaits a further fulfillment.

I would suggest that the fullness of God's Spirit did not come upon believers at that time, nor has it come upon believers today. We still have free will. The Spirit of God is not now driving our lives down the highway of righteousness, as many believers assume. Believers continue to sin. With the measure of God's Spirit that we have been given for now, however, we can pursue the steps for righteous living outlined below.

## The Three Steps for Righteous Living

Living holy lives involves three steps.

1) We need to fear YHVH.
2) We need to keep the Torah.
3) We need to separate ourselves.

Abraham's life becomes our model for living out these three actions. First, Abraham feared God. The angel of YHVH called to Abraham in Genesis 22:12: "He said, 'Do not lay your hand on the boy or do anything to him, for now I know that you fear God, seeing you have not withheld your son, your only son, from me.'" Abraham feared God to the point that he was even willing to sacrifice his only son at God's command.

Abraham also kept the Torah. YHVH revealed this to Isaac as He extended the blessing to him:

"I will multiply your offspring as the stars of heaven and will give to your offspring all these lands. And in your offspring all the nations of the earth shall be blessed, because Abraham obeyed my voice and kept my charge [*mishmeret*], my commandments [*mitzvah*], my statutes [*chukah*], and my laws [*torah*]" (Genesis 26:4–5).

Thirdly, Abraham separated himself. Sailhamer points out that every time Abraham separated himself God reconfirmed the covenant promises.[10] He separated himself from his country, his kindred, and his father's house. He then separated himself from his nephew Lot. Finally, Abraham separated himself from his only son, Isaac, by nearly sacrificing him on Mount Moriah at God's command. Like Abraham, we need to fear YHVH, keep the Torah, and separate ourselves.

Another biblical figure who incorporated these three actions was Job. Like Jacob, Job is called an *eesh tam*—a blameless man: "There was a man in the land of Uz whose name was Job, and that man was blameless and upright, one who feared God and turned away from evil" (Job 1:1). Job feared God. He evidently kept the Torah since he was described as blameless and upright. Also, by turning away from evil he was separating himself.

## Fearing God

Proverbs tells us that the fear of YHVH is the beginning of knowledge and the beginning of wisdom (Proverbs 1:7 and Proverbs 9:10). Without this fear, we will never be truly knowledgeable or wise. Head knowledge about the right thing to do often is not converted to action without fear of YHVH.§ Fearing YHVH is having an overwhelming awe of Him. It is the sense of being dwarfed by His infinite power. Those who have experienced mighty natural events might have a small clue as to what it would be like to be dwarfed by God's infinite power. When people truly experience this fear of YHVH, it causes them to fall on their faces.

## Keeping the Torah

Fearing God motivates us to do the second action—keeping the Torah.¶ "Moses said to the people, 'Do not fear, for God has come to

---

§ Government-run abstinence training programs in public schools have not led to a culture of abstinence. These programs can teach about the benefits of abstinence, but they are forbidden to teach about the fear of YHVH.

¶ Love and respect for this infinite God who is our creator also motivate us test you, that the fear of him may be before you, that you may not sin'" (Exodus 20:20). Keeping the Torah—or instructions of God—is called righteous living. Contrary to a common teaching in the church, the written Torah is still in force (more about this in chapter 4). We do not keep the Torah so we can gain our own salvation before a holy God. Salvation comes to us by grace through Yeshua's atoning death. Since salvation comes to us through grace, however, "What shall we say then? Are we to continue in sin that grace may abound? By no means! How can we who died to sin still live in it?" (Romans 6:1–2). Now that we have been made righteous by Yeshua's atonement, we need to live righteously.** The real example of an *eesh tam*, a blameless man, is not Jacob, but Jacob's future son Yeshua the Messiah. Yeshua kept the Torah perfectly. Yeshua becomes our example to follow for righteous living.††

---

to obey Him, but love and respect are offshoots of fear.

** Clearly one of the greatest struggles for righteous living is in the area of human sexuality. The Torah instructions have much to say about proper sexual conduct and relationships. Unfortunately, we often hear about God-fearing men who fall over ungodly sexual conduct. The primary moral battle raging in our culture today between Jacob and Esau is over sex. Atheist haters of religion and God become inflamed by those promoting sexual restraint. (David Berlinski, *The Devil's Delusion: Atheism and Its Scientific Pretensions* [New York: Basic Books, 2009], p.18.) Enormous amounts of political and financial capital are expended to ensure the rights of people to have unrestricted sex without guilt, without shame, without responsibility, and without consequences (from abortion rights, the morning after pill, condoms and condemnation of abstinence in schools; to HPV, Hepatitis B, and HIV vaccines; to no fault divorce, the crusade for shacking up, the LGBT agenda, and pushes for polygamy). Esau does not want to hear about sin.

†† A number of figures in the Tanach are "types" of Yeshua. "Types" of Yeshua are typically ordinary people who walk with God and become extraordinary—Enoch, Melchizedek, Joseph, Judah, Esther. They then foreshadow the life of Yeshua. Maybe those of us who walk with God today can also become "types" of Yeshua.

## Separating Ourselves

Just as fear of YHVH motivates us to keep the Torah, keeping the Torah is one of the principal means of performing the third action, that of separating ourselves. Several Jewish blessings start with "Blessed are You, Lord [YHVH] our God, King of the universe, who has sanctified us with Your commandments." The Hebrew root for "sanctify" means "to set apart." This blessing tells us that God is setting us apart or separating us with His commandments.

Separating ourselves is the last action required for us to avoid sin. Separation requires us to hang around the right people. It means avoiding sinful behaviors, especially those things that can lead to addictions. It means fleeing from temptation. Sin can be very pleasurable for a time, but it always leads to misery and, in the end, to death. Joseph is one of the best examples of a man who knew how to deal with temptation. When Potiphar's wife came to Joseph with desire in her heart, he took off, not even stopping to get his coat. Drug abusers know that treating a drug addiction usually requires them to move out of the neighborhood, out of the city, out of the state. They know that separation from the old environment and "friends" is the only way for them to attempt a fresh start.

Separating ourselves does not mean removing ourselves from the world. We do not need to set up a community in the wilderness of Alaska to live righteously. Messianic Jews Ariel and D'vorah Berkowitz suggest that we can safely live in the world and go out into the world to do good, as long as we have a safe Torah community to work out of as our home base. However, it is critical that everyone in our believing community is wrestling with the instructions of God.[11]

## Losing Our Free Will to Do Good

As mentioned previously, our God-given free will allows the internal struggle between Jacob and Esau. It is clear in the Tanach, however, that our free will can be take away. The narrative in the Torah concerning the Exodus from Egypt describes a pharaoh, who lost his free will by having his heart "hardened" by God. Rabbi David Fohrman points out that Pharaoh hardened his own heart up until the plague of hail. After that plague, Pharaoh continued to rebel, even though he realized that YHVH is God. At that point, God hardened Pharaoh's heart permanently, and he lost his free will.[12‡‡] Similarly, the more Dr. Jekyll chose to become Mr. Hyde, the more Mr. Hyde began to dominate over him until Mr. Hyde eventually consumed him.

This principle undoubtedly also works in the opposite direction. Imagine the story of Dr. Jekyll and Mr. Hyde told in reverse. Suppose an evil Mr. Hyde started drinking a potion that changed him into the righteous Dr. Jekyll. Imagine that he continued to do this over time until Mr. Hyde was transformed into Dr. Jekyll without drinking the potion, and eventually the righteous Dr. Jekyll consumed Mr. Hyde.

There is evidence in the Tanach that those who accept the atoning death of Yeshua and who try to live righteously by their free will shall in the end have their free will overpowered by God's Spirit. Their instinct then shall be to follow the Torah automatically. Jeremiah 31:31–34 seems to describe this concept. Eventually, the Torah will be written on the believer's heart. Ezekiel 36:26–27 describes a future time when God will change a heart of stone into a heart of flesh:

> And I will give you a new heart, and a new spirit I will put within you. And I will remove the heart of stone from your flesh and give you a

---

‡‡ Rabbi Fohrman shows that there are mainly two Hebrew words describing the hardening of Pharaoh's heart. One describes the strengthening of the heart, or giving the heart courage. The other term suggests a stubborn heart. Pharaoh gives his heart courage and causes his heart to be stubborn throughout the narrative. God mainly gives Pharaoh's heart courage—He enhances his free will up until the plague of hail. After this plague in Exodus 10:1, God makes Pharaoh's heart stubborn and Pharaoh loses his free will. (Rabbi David Fohrman, "Passover: What Does It Mean to Be Chosen?," Segment 2—*With a Heavy Heart,* AlephBeta, accessed June 14, 2015, www. alephbeta.org/course/lecture/with-a-heavy-heart/autoplay; Segment 5—*God Against the "Gods"?,* AlephBeta, accessed June 14, 2015, www.alephbeta.org/ course/lecture/god-against-the-gods/autoplay; Segment 7—*Through Pharaoh's Eyes,* AlephBeta, accessed June 14, 2015, www. alephbeta.org/course/lecture/ through-pharaohs-eyes/autoplay.)

heart of flesh. And I will put my Spirit within you, and cause you to walk in my statutes and be careful to obey my rules.

We will shake off our struggle with the sin nature in that day.

Men like Esau and Pharaoh reject God, and they become gods unto themselves. They often lose their free will to their sinful nature over time. Alternately, men who struggle to emulate the ideal Jacob, but fail, learn the lesson God has been trying to teach mankind throughout history. They discover that men and women are unable to live wholly righteous lives apart from God. Sailhamer tells us that this was the mistake of Eve. She thought she could "see" the "good" for herself instead of allowing God to "see" the "good" for her.[13] Once people surrender their lives to God and attempt to use God's power to live more righteously, their free wills shall be consumed by righteousness in time.

Dr. Jekyll, describing the dual nature of man, writes: "It was the curse of mankind that these incongruous faggots were thus bound together—that in the agonized womb of consciousness, these polar twins should be continuously struggling."[14] It appears the author, Stevenson, was aware of the biblical narrative in Genesis that seems to be describing the struggle between Jacob and Esau in all of us. In our lives, let us continue to force the older brother to serve the younger. Sin is crouching at the door, and its desire is for us, but we must rule over it (Genesis 4:7). With God's help, I believe we can rule over Esau by fearing God, keeping the Torah, and separating ourselves. Eventually God will change our hearts of stone back into hearts of flesh.

In the upcoming chapters, we will deal with the long-standing question of whether believers should continue to keep the Torah.

## (Endnotes)

1   Nahum M. Sarna, *The JPS Torah Commentary: Genesis* (Philadelphia: The Jewish Publication Society, 1989), pp. 180–182.

2   Robert Alter, *The Art of Biblical Narrative* (New York: Basic Books, 1981), pp. 42–45.

3   Nahum M. Sarna, *The JPS Torah Commentary: Genesis*, p. 181.

4   Ibid., p. 182.

5   Robert Alter, *The Art of Biblical Narrative*, p. 44.

6   Samuel Rosenblatt, "Inclination, Good and Evil," *Encyclopaedia Judaica*, Vol. 8 (Jerusalem, Israel: Keter Publishing House Ltd., 1971), pp. 1318–1319.

7   Louis Jacobs, "Sin," *Encyclopaedia Judaica*, Vol. 14 (Jerusalem, Israel: Keter Publishing House Ltd., 1971), p. 1593.

8   David H. Stern, *Jewish New Testament Commentary* (Clarksville, MD: Jewish New Testament Publications, 1992), pp. 358–359.

9   Ibid., p. 358.

10  John Sailhamer, "Genesis," Vol. 2 of *The Expositor's Bible Commentary*, ed. by Frank E. Gaebelein, 12 vols. (Grand Rapids, MI: Zondervan Publishing House, 1990), p. 118.

11  Ariel and D'vorah Berkowitz, *Take Hold: Embracing Our Divine Inheritance with Israel* (Littleton, CO: First Fruits of Zion, 1998), pp. 150–153.

12  Rabbi David Fohrman, "Passover: What Does It Mean to Be Chosen?," Segment 2—*With a Heavy Heart*, AlephBeta, accessed June 14, 2015, www.alephbeta.org/course/lecture/with-a-heavy-heart/autoplay; Segment 5—*God Against the "Gods"?*, AlephBeta, accessed June 14, 2015, www.alephbeta.org/course/lecture/god-against-the-gods/autoplay; Segment 7—*Through Pharaoh's Eyes*, AlephBeta, accessed June 14, 2015, www.alephbeta.org/course/lecture/through-pharaohs-eyes/autoplay.

13  John Sailhamer, "Genesis," *The Expositor's Bible Commentary*, pp. 51–52.

14  Robert Louis Stevenson, *Dr. Jekyll and Mr. Hyde* (New York: Oxford University Press, 1998), p. 61.

## Chapter 4: Law versus Grace – A Case for Torah* Observance

### Characterizing the Torah

The traditional church teaches that law and grace are at opposite poles.[1] They usually point to passages such as Romans 6:14, where Sha'ul says, "You are not under law but under grace." Fallen men who are "under grace" accept God's undeserved favor. They believe God lifts them up by providing for their atonement and salvation. Fallen men who are "under law" attempt to gain standing before God through their own efforts by obeying a set of rules. Believers understand that salvation is through grace and not through law. The traditional church early on, therefore, deduced that the law, identified as the Torah, was abrogated. I argued in the last chapter that keeping the Torah is one of the steps required to deal with the sin nature. How can I explain this paradox?

The confusion about the Torah lies in the fact that there has been a misunderstanding as to what the Torah is. Being under grace is the opposite of being under law. However, the kicker is—keeping the Torah does not equal being under law. Keeping the Torah does not oppose grace.

---

\*    By the word "Torah," I am mainly focusing on the instructions, commandments, statutes, and judgments given to us by God in the Five Books of Moses.

The Hebrew word *Torah* does not exactly mean "law."† It is better translated as "direction, instruction, or teaching." It comes from the Hebrew root letters *yod, resh,* and *hey*—"to shoot an arrow, to point out/show." Therefore, it can mean "to teach." The word *moreh*—"teacher"—comes from the same root.[2]

The Torah is God's special instruction to us as to how to live life to the fullest. The Torah is not a set of rules that we are required to follow in order for us to obtain our salvation. To get an even better feel for the Torah, let us look at some passages from the Scriptures that talk about the Torah. Let us also examine how Yeshua and Sha'ul dealt with the Torah in their lives and what they said about it.

## The Portrayal of the Torah in the Tanach

First, let us look at how the Tanach speaks of the Torah. Two psalms speak much of the Torah—Psalm 19 and Psalm 119. These passages are as valid today as when they were written:

> The law [Torah] of the LORD [YHVH] is perfect, reviving the soul; the testimony of the LORD [YHVH] is sure, making wise the simple; the precepts of the LORD [YHVH] are right, rejoicing the heart; the commandment of the LORD [YHVH] is pure, enlightening the eyes; the fear of the LORD [YHVH] is clean, enduring forever; the rules of the LORD [YHVH] are true, and righteous altogether. More to be desired are they than gold, even much fine gold; sweeter also than honey and drippings of the honeycomb. Moreover, by them is your servant warned; in keeping them there is great reward (Psalm 19:7–11).

> Blessed are those whose way is blameless, who walk in the law [Torah] of the LORD [YHVH]! Blessed are those who keep his testimonies,

---

† According to David Stern, the Septuagint (the Greek translation of the Tanach) and the New Testament translated the Hebrew word *Torah* by the Greek word *nomos*. *Nomos* has the meaning of "law" rather than "instruction." This translation probably influenced the thinking of the early traditional church. (David H. Stern, *Jewish New Testament Commentary* [Clarksville, MD: Jewish New Testament Publications, 1992], p. 25.)

who seek him with their whole heart, who also do no wrong, but walk in his ways! You have commanded your precepts to be kept diligently. Oh that my ways may be steadfast in keeping your statutes! Then I shall not be put to shame, having my eyes fixed on all your commandments. I will praise you with an upright heart, when I learn your righteous rules. I will keep your statutes; do not utterly forsake me! (Psalm 119:1–8).

These psalms seem to say that if we follow the instructions in the Torah we will be blessed, refreshed, made wise, and made happy.

Other passages in the Tanach seem to say that in the last days the Torah of YHVH will still be in force, that it will not be abolished. One of these passages is Isaiah 2:2–3:

It shall come to pass in the latter days that the mountain of the house of the LORD [YHVH] shall be established as the highest of the mountains, and shall be lifted up above the hills; and all the nations shall flow to it, and many peoples shall come, and say: "Come, let us go up to the mountain of the LORD [YHVH], to the house of the God of Jacob, that he may teach us his ways and that we may walk in his paths." For out of Zion shall go the law [Torah], and the word of the LORD [YHVH] from Jerusalem.

Here we see the Torah going forth from Zion in the last days. It is our instruction manual to learn about God's ways.

Another passage is Jeremiah 31:31–33:

"Behold, the days are coming, declares the LORD [YHVH], when I will make a new covenant with the house of Israel and the house of Judah, not like the covenant that I made with their fathers on the day when I took them by the hand to bring them out of the land of Egypt, my covenant that they broke, though I was their husband, declares the LORD [YHVH]. For this is the covenant that I will make with the house of Israel after those days, declares the LORD [YHVH]: I will put my law [Torah] within them, and I will write it on their hearts. And I will be their God, and they shall be my people.

As part of the new covenant, YHVH will put His Torah in our hearts. How can we, then, who claim to be partakers of the new covenant, minimize the importance of the Torah in our lives?

## Yeshua and the Torah

How did Yeshua view the Torah? First, he affirmed the Torah:

> Do not think that I have come to abolish the Law or the Prophets;
> I have not come to abolish them but to fulfill them. For truly, I say
> to you, until heaven and earth pass away, not an iota, not a dot, will
> pass from the Law until all is accomplished. Therefore whoever relaxes
> one of the least of these commandments and teaches others to do the
> same will be called least in the kingdom of heaven, but whoever does
> them and teaches them will be called great in the kingdom of heaven
> (Matthew 5:17–19).

He seemed to say that the Torah will be in force for some time to
come (until heaven and earth pass away), and he encouraged us to follow the Torah and to teach it. He suggested that the Torah continues
to be God's standard of righteousness. Did he say we will not enter
the kingdom of heaven if we do not follow the Torah? No, he did not,
because our salvation is a free, undeserved gift from God. Our salvation does not rest upon our Torah observance. Yeshua did say, though,
that those of us who do not follow the Torah will be called least in the
kingdom of heaven.

Secondly, Yeshua himself lived by the Torah. He observed the
Torah faultlessly. He did not do this for our sakes so that we do not
have to.

One action we see that confirms Yeshua's Torah observance was
his wearing of the memory device fringes or *tzitziyot* on his garment:

> And behold, a woman who had suffered from a discharge of blood
> for twelve years came up behind him and touched the fringe of his
> garment, for she said to herself, "If I only touch his garment, I will be
> made well" (Matthew 9:20–21).

The Greek word for "fringe" here also can mean "tassel" or "border."[3]
The same Greek word is used in Matthew 23:5 where Yeshua criticized
the Pharisees for lengthening the tassels on their garments, which is
an obvious reference to *tzitziyot*: "They do all their deeds to be seen by

others. For they make their phylacteries broad and their fringes long" (Matthew 23:5). Keep in mind that Yeshua did not wear *tzitziyot* to show that he was Jewish. He wore the fringes or *tzitziyot* on his garment to remember all the commandments of YHVH, to do them, according to Numbers 15:37–40:

> The LORD [YHVH] said to Moses, "Speak to the people of Israel, and tell them to make tassels [*tzitzit*] on the corners of their garments throughout their generations, and to put a cord of blue on the tassel [*tzitzit*] of each corner. And it shall be a tassel [*tzitzit*] for you to look at and remember all the commandments of the LORD [YHVH], to do them, not to follow after your own heart and your own eyes, which you are inclined to whore after. So you shall remember and do all my commandments, and be holy to your God.

Yeshua's participation in the Torah festivals offers further evidence of his personal Torah observance. Yeshua observed the seventh day Sabbath or Shabbat and taught about the proper observance of the Shabbat (see Mark 2:23–28). Luke 6:16 says that he entered the synagogue on the Shabbat, as was his custom. He also observed Passover, which probably involved a sacrificed lamb. Mark 14:12–16 suggests this as they prepare for the "Last Supper":

> And on the first day of Unleavened Bread, when they sacrificed the Passover lamb, his disciples said to him, "Where will you have us go and prepare for you to eat the Passover?" And he sent two of his disciples and said to them, "Go into the city, and a man carrying a jar of water will meet you. Follow him, and wherever he enters, say to the master of the house, 'The Teacher says, Where is my guest room, where I may eat the Passover with my disciples?' And he will show you a large upper room furnished and ready; there prepare for us." And the disciples set out and went to the city and found it just as he had told them, and they prepared the Passover.

Thirdly, Yeshua taught the Torah. After affirming the Torah in Matthew 5:17–19, Yeshua set a high standard for the way his followers should live by following the Torah: "For I tell you, unless your righteousness exceeds that of the scribes and Pharisees, you will never enter the kingdom of heaven" (Matthew 5:20). Keep in mind that the first-century scribes and Pharisees were zealous for the Torah and were practicing a relatively high standard of righteousness.

In Matthew 5:21–48, Yeshua went on to give examples of God's high benchmark of righteousness. He did not change the Torah instruction in these cases but gave the Torah's original intended meaning. At the same time, he corrected misunderstandings that the religious community had about the Torah. He raised the bar of righteousness:

> You have heard that it was said to those of old, "You shall not murder; and whoever murders will be liable to judgment." But I say to you that everyone who is angry with his brother will be liable to judgment; whoever insults his brother will be liable to the council; and whoever says, "You fool!" will be liable to the hell of fire (Matthew 5:21–22).

> You have heard that it was said, "You shall not commit adultery." But I say to you that everyone who looks at a woman with lustful intent has already committed adultery with her in his heart (Matthew 5:27–28).

> It was also said, "Whoever divorces his wife, let him give her a certificate of divorce." But I say to you that everyone who divorces his wife, except on the ground of sexual immorality, makes her commit adultery, and whoever marries a divorced woman commits adultery (Matthew 5:31–32).

Admittedly, the level of Torah observance taught by Yeshua was out of reach for people (Matthew 19:23–26), but this was never made an excuse for individuals to give up reaching for the goal.

Fourthly, Yeshua criticized the Pharisees for not following the Torah:

> Then Pharisees and scribes came to Jesus [Yeshua] from Jerusalem and said, "Why do your disciples break the tradition of the elders? For they do not wash their hands when they eat." He answered them, "And why do you break the commandment of God for the sake of your tradition? For God commanded, 'Honor your father and your mother,' and, 'Whoever reviles father or mother must surely die.' But you say, 'If anyone tells his father or his mother, "What you would have gained from me is given to God," he need not honor his father.' So for the sake of your tradition you have made void the word of God" (Matthew 15:1–6).

At first glance, it appears that Yeshua was criticizing the Pharisees for not following the fifth of the Ten Commandments—"Honor your father and your mother." The traditional church does not have a problem with this, for they have separated out the Ten Commandments from the rest of the Torah as rules they should follow. If you look carefully here, however, you see that Yeshua was quoting from more than the Ten Commandments. He also quoted from Exodus 21:17 which is not part of the Ten Commandments: "Whoever curses his father or his mother shall be put to death." Yeshua criticized the Pharisees for not following a section of the Torah that is outside of the Ten Commandments.

What about the woman in John 7:53–8:11 who was caught in the act of adultery and brought before Yeshua? She was condemned to be stoned to death according to the Torah instruction (Leviticus 20:10), but Yeshua went against the Torah and pardoned her. Remarkably, this story is not found in the earliest and most reliable manuscripts of John and appears to be a later addition to the text. Therefore, this narrative seems to be fiction. Even some conservative scholars feel this story should not be a part of the Bible.[4]

The picture of the Torah outlined so far is that of a wonderful gift given to us by God. It appears to be instruction to us that was not to be annulled when Yeshua died. It was to continue to have importance for our lives.

## Sha'ul and the Torah

Then we come to the writings of Sha'ul. Occasionally he wrote passages that affirmed Torah:

> Now we know that the law is good, if one uses it lawfully (1 Timothy 1:8).

> All Scripture is breathed out by God and profitable for teaching, for reproof, for correction, and for training in righteousness, that the man of God may be complete, equipped for every good work (2 Timothy 3:16–17).

So the law is holy, and the commandment is holy and righteous and good (Romans 7:12).

At other times, however, Sha'ul seems to be condemning the Torah. His teaching on the Torah looks to have a different twist:

For sin will have no dominion over you, since you are not under law but under grace (Romans 6:14).

For Christ [Messiah] is the end of the law for righteousness to everyone who believes (Romans 10:4).

Look: I, Paul [Sha'ul], say to you that if you accept circumcision, Christ [Messiah] will be of no advantage to you (Galatians 5:2).

You are severed from Christ [Messiah], you who would be justified by the law; you have fallen away from grace (Galatians 5:4).

But if you are led by the Spirit, you are not under the law (Galatians 5:18).

Since Sha'ul was writing after the death of Yeshua, was he telling us that we are now in a new dispensation and that the role of the Torah has changed?

The key to solving the seeming problem with Sha'ul is knowing that he also walked orderly—keeping the Torah:[5]

On the following day Paul [Sha'ul] went in with us to James [Ya'akov], and all the elders were present. After greeting them, he related one by one the things that God had done among the Gentiles through his ministry. And when they heard it, they glorified God. And they said to him, "You see, brother, how many thousands there are among the Jews of those who have believed. They are all zealous for the law, and they have been told about you that you teach all the Jews who are among the Gentiles to forsake Moses, telling them not to circumcise their children or walk according to our customs. What then is to be done? They will certainly hear that you have come. Do therefore what we tell you. We have four men who are under a vow; take these men and purify yourself along with them and pay their expenses, so that they may shave their heads. Thus all will know that there is nothing in what they have been told about you, but that you yourself also live in observance of the law.

But as for the Gentiles who have believed, we have sent a letter with our judgment that they should abstain from what has been sacrificed to idols, and from blood, and from what has been strangled, and from sexual immorality." Then Paul [Sha'ul] took the men, and the next day he purified himself along with them and went into the temple, giving notice when the days of purification would be fulfilled and the offering presented for each one of them (Acts 21:18–26).

Since Sha'ul himself (along with thousands of Jewish believers in Jerusalem) followed God's instructions in the Torah, it does not make sense that he would then condemn the Torah in his writings. Any passages written by Sha'ul that seem to condemn the Torah must be saying something different from what we find in the usual English translations.

Many New Testament scholars say that Sha'ul was like a chameleon, conforming to the culture of whatever group of people he found himself in so that he could win converts:

For though I am free from all, I have made myself a servant to all, that I might win more of them. To the Jews I became as a Jew, in order to win Jews. To those under the law I became as one under the law (though not being myself under the law), that I might win those under the law. To those outside the law I became as one outside the law (not being outside the law of God but under the law of Christ [Messiah], that I might win those outside the law. To the weak I became weak, that I might win the weak. I have become all things to all people, that by all means I might save some (1 Corinthians 9:19–22).

They would say, for instance, if Sha'ul were among Jews in Jerusalem he would keep the Torah, but for their sake only—not because he felt compelled to keep the Torah. What a small view of Sha'ul this is! I believe Sha'ul tried to get into the mindset of the people he was interacting with, to deal with them at their level. It is unlikely that Sha'ul had no convictions of his own.[6]

The seeming problem with Sha'ul is that those who have translated his writings have approached the text with an anti-Torah bias, and they have misunderstood him. For instance, David Stern gives the example of Romans 10:4 previously quoted: "For Messiah is the end of the Law for righteousness to everyone who believes." According to Stern, the Greek word *telos* means "goal" here rather than "end." According to Stern, Messiah is not the end of the "Law" but "the goal at which the Torah aims." This translation is much different from the traditional translations. This understanding is much more consistent with the Scriptures as a whole, however.[7]

A number of difficult passages are found in Galatians and Romans. Here Sha'ul was not hostile to the Torah but was teaching against a legalistic perversion of the Torah. He was teaching in opposition to the concept held by some that salvation was dependent upon obedience to the Torah. A legalistic obedience to the Torah, however, was never meant to be the means for us to obtain salvation. Salvation has always been an undeserved gift given to us by God through our trusting in His provision for us, even before Yeshua. Sha'ul rightfully should have condemned this position.

At the time of Sha'ul's writings, there was no way to adequately express the concepts of legalism, legalist, or legalistic in Greek (see the quote from Cranfield following). When writing about the legalistic perversion of the Torah, Stern writes, Sha'ul often had to resort to using two phrases—"under law" and "works of law." In these instances, Sha'ul was not condemning the Torah, but he was denouncing the legalistic perversion of the Torah that was apparently common at that time.[8] Christian commentator C. E. B. Cranfield writes:

> *For Paul, the law is not abrogated by Christ.* This thesis is stated in full awareness of the widespread tendency today, observable not only in popular writing but also in serious works of scholarship, to regard it as an assured result that Paul believed that the law had been abrogated by Christ. This "assured result," like so many others, needs to be reexamined.
>
> There are, of course, a number of passages in the epistles which, at first sight, seem to provide support for the view we are opposing, and these we must now consider. In doing so, it will be well to bear in mind the fact . . . that the Greek language of Paul's day possessed no word-group corresponding to our "legalism," "legalist," and "legalistic." This means that he lacked a convenient terminology for expressing a

vital distinction, and so was surely seriously hampered in the work of clarifying the Christian position with regard to the law. In view of this, we should always, we think, be ready to reckon with the possibility that Pauline statements, which at first sight seem to disparage the law, are really directed not against the law itself but against that misunderstanding and misuse of it for which we now have a convenient terminology. In this very difficult terrain Paul was pioneering. If we make due allowance for these circumstances, we shall not be so easily baffled or misled by a certain impreciseness of statement which we shall sometimes encounter.[9]

## The Book of Hebrews and the Torah

The book of Hebrews is another document that is used to try to show that the Torah has been done away with. The following verses are often cited:

> For if that first covenant had been faultless, there would have been no occasion to look for a second (Hebrews 8:7).

> In speaking of a new covenant, he makes the first one obsolete. And what is becoming obsolete and growing old is ready to vanish away (Hebrews 8:13).

> For since the law has but a shadow of the good things to come instead of the true form of these realities, it can never, by the same sacrifices that are continually offered every year, make perfect those who draw near (Hebrews 10:1).

However, the middle of the book of Hebrews is addressing the sacrificial system. These verses sit in this context. The author was not writing that the whole Torah has now been terminated after the death of Yeshua. He was showing that the current system of priests and sacrifices, the older system, was to be filled full by the death of Yeshua.[10] In fact, the older system, which was imperfect in itself, always anticipated the death of Yeshua, just as it appears that sacrifices in a rebuilt Temple in the future messianic age will point back to the once-and-for-all sacrifice of Yeshua (Ezekiel 40–46).[11] Atonement by sacrifice is still in force, the sacrifice of Yeshua the Messiah.

## What Is the Torah? A Summary

To summarize:

1) Being under law is the opposite of being under grace. However, by "under law" here, we are speaking of a legalistic perversion of the Torah, holding the concept that salvation is dependent on obedience to the Torah. Sha'ul attacked this legalistic perversion of the Torah vigorously. He often used the phrases "under law" and "works of law" to express this concept.

2) "Torah" does not equal "law." The Torah is God's instruction to us. It was not abrogated after Yeshua's death. Our salvation is not dependent upon following it.

3) "Torah" is not the opposite of "grace." In fact, these terms are not necessarily connected. Our salvation comes only through grace—trusting in Yeshua's atoning death for us. However, the Torah is a guidebook for how the followers of God should live their lives. If God has given us special instructions as to how to live our lives to the fullest, how to live holy lives, and how to live useful lives for service, should we follow these instructions, or should we reject them? Is it wrong to obey God? If God were to come to any of us in a vision and give us a specific instruction to follow, would we object, saying that we are not under law? In the same way, we should not reject written instructions given to us by God thousands of years ago.

## The Torah Was Written on the Heart from the Beginning

As mentioned previously, in the messianic age, prophecy suggests that the Torah will be written on hearts (Jeremiah 31:31–33). Since the Garden of Eden seems to foreshadow the future messianic age (Ezekiel 36:35, Isaiah 51:3, and Zechariah 14.8),[12] one could speculate that God wrote the Torah on the hearts of men from the beginning, just as he will write it on the hearts of men in the future. Maybe eating from the tree of the knowledge of good and evil began this process of changing a heart of flesh into a heart of stone. A heart that was only perfused by God's good became a heart that could discern for itself between good and evil.[13] Having the Torah written on hearts from the beginning perhaps explains why Abraham knew what the Torah required before the Torah had been given to Israel at Sinai (Genesis 26:5).[14] Sha'ul spoke to this also:

> For when Gentiles, who do not have the law, by nature do what the law requires, they are a law to themselves, even though they do not have the law. They show that the work of the law is written on their hearts, while their conscience also bears witness, and their conflicting thoughts accuse or even excuse them (Romans 2:14–15).

Sailhamer calls attention to the intermittent addition of new "laws" given to Israel seemingly every time they failed God.[15] I suspect that because of man's progressive rebellion against God, the Torah instructions written on the heart from the beginning became less accessible to the mind. Over time, man required more of these instructions to be written down. Whether engraved in stone or written on the heart, the Torah instructions remain the same.

## Without the Torah, No Standard for Righteousness

Without the Torah, many believers begin doing what is right in their own eyes, like the nation of Israel in the period of the judges. Many believers begin tracking the world's standard of righteousness rather than God's. They stay just one step above the norm of the world. As the world moves downhill, the believer typically is not far behind. Believers continue to feel that they are living righteous lives because they have their eyes on the rest of the world, but down they go just the same. Unfortunately, often not much distinguishes the believer from the world.

## Wrestling with the Torah

In Matthew 5, Yeshua declared that the least of the Torah commandments are important. Which Torah commandments are we going to follow, however? Some of the Torah commandments seem silly to our "modern" society. Are we really going to avoid mixing two types of material together in our clothing (Leviticus 19:19, Deuteronomy 22:11)? Should we build a fence around the roofs of our houses (Deuteronomy 22:8)? Some of the Torah commandments we cannot do since the Tabernacle and Temple are not currently standing, for example, having the wife of a jealous husband drink a cocktail made up of dust from the Tabernacle floor (Numbers 5:12–31). Some of the Torah commandments we could not do without violating the laws of our society nor could we bring ourselves to do them, such as putting to death our children who curse us (Leviticus 20:9).

We need to continue the age-old process of wrestling with the Torah instructions as well as with the teachings in other areas of the Scriptures. What do they mean? How can we apply them to our lives? Our goal is not to follow the precepts of Rabbinic Judaism but the precepts of God.‡ Nevertheless, believers do not need to reinvent the wheel and cast off rabbinic traditions that are consistent with the Torah instructions.

A community that is Torah observant is protected and strengthened within. It is then in a better position to reach out to the rest of the world.[16] We are to be light to the world by showing forth our good works:

> You are the light of the world. A city set on a hill cannot be hidden. Nor do people light a lamp and put it under a basket, but on a stand, and it gives light to all in the house. In the same way, let your light shine before others, so that they may see your good works and give glory to your Father who is in heaven (Matthew 5:14–16).

I am convinced that when we begin to wrestle with the Torah and the other Scriptural instructions and apply them to our lives, we will become a capable, spiritual army for God.

---

‡ Rabbinic Judaism has strayed away from the biblical concept that it is God who saves. Instead, it has developed a works-righteousness form of salvation. The sense is that man can atone for his sinful nature by righteous deeds. This works-righteousness form of salvation has led to self-deception and a yoke of man-made rules. Yeshua, the Jewish Messiah, addresses these issues in loving correction with the Pharisees back in the first century (Matthew 15:1–9, Matthew 23:1–39, Luke 18:9–14).

Observing the commandments in the Torah will never justify us before a holy God. We are only made righteous by trusting in Yeshua's atoning death. After we have been made righteous, however, with the help of God's spirit, we need to live righteously. God has given us an instruction manual to help guide us into righteous living: "All Scripture [including the Torah] is breathed out by God and profitable for teaching, for reproof, for correction, and for training in righteousness" (2 Timothy 3:16). Let us not reject the wonderful gift that God has given to us:

> And when Moses had finished speaking all these words to all Israel, he said to them, "Take to heart all the words by which I am warning you today, that you may command them to your children, that they may be careful to do all the words of this law [Torah]. For it is no empty word for you, but your very life, and by this word you shall live long in the land that you are going over the Jordan to possess" (Deuteronomy 32:45–47).

The next two chapters will focus on two sets of Torah instructions that need to be revived.

# (Endnotes)

1   Ron Moseley, *Yeshua: A Guide to the Real Jesus and the Original Church* (Hagerstown, MD: Ebed Publications, 1996), p. 30.

2   Ron Moseley, *Yeshua: A Guide to the Real Jesus and the Original Church*, p. 54.

3   James Strong, *A Concise Dictionary of the Words in the Greek Testament; with Their Renderings in the Authorized English Version* in *The New Strong's Exhaustive Concordance of the Bible* (Nashville: Thomas Nelson Publishers, 1984), p. 43.

4   Darrell L. Bock and Daniel B. Wallace, *Dethroning Jesus: Exposing Popular Culture's Quest to Unseat the Biblical Christ* (Nashville: Thomas Nelson, 2007), pp. 62–64.

5   Ariel and D'vorah Berkowitz, *Torah Rediscovered: Challenging Centuries of Misinterpretation and Neglect* (Littleton, CO: First Fruits of Zion, Inc., 1996), pp. 117–120. Daniel Juster, *Jewish Roots: A Foundation of Biblical Theology* (Gaithersburg, MD: DAVAR Publishing Co., 1986).

6   Daniel Juster, *Jewish Roots: A Foundation of Biblical Theology*, pp. 107–110.

7   David H. Stern, *Jewish New Testament Commentary* (Clarksville, MD: Jewish New Testament Publications, 1992), pp. 395–396.

8   Ibid., pp. 535–538.

9   C. E. B. Cranfield, *A Critical and Exegetical Commentary of the Epistle to the Romans*, Vol. II (New York: T & T Clark LTD, 1979), pp. 852–853. Thanks to David Stern for introducing this quote.

10  Ariel and D'vorah Berkowitz, *Torah Rediscovered: Challenging Centuries of Misinterpretation and Neglect*, pp. 54–57.

11  Charles Lee Feinberg, *The Prophecy of Ezekiel: The Glory of the Lord* (Chicago: Moody Press, 1969), p.254.

12  John Sailhamer, *Genesis Unbound: A Provocative New Look at the Creation Account* (Sisters, OR: Multnomah Books, 1996), p. 110. John Sailhamer, *The Pentateuch as Narrative: A Biblical-Theological Commentary* (Grand Rapids, MI: Zondervan Publishing House, 1992), p. 37.

13  John Sailhamer, *The Pentateuch as Narrative: A Biblical-Theological Commentary*, pp. 103–104.

14  Ibid., pp. 66–71.

15  Ibid., pp. 44–59.

16  Ariel and D'vorah Berkowitz, *Take Hold: Embracing Our Divine Inheritance with Israel* (Littleton, CO: First Fruits of Zion, 1998), pp. 150–153.

## Chapter 5: *Whatever Happened to the Seventh Day Shabbat?**

### From Decalogue to Nonalogue

It is common to hear in the news these days about groups of believers who are fighting to have the Ten Commandments posted in our schools or courtrooms. Among all of the Torah instructions, the Ten Commandments are still honored by those in the traditional church. When we look through the various commandments, however, it is clear that the traditional church has sandblasted the fourth commandment off the tablets of stone. Instead of Ten Commandments, they have reduced the number to nine.†

The fourth of the Ten Commandments is about the seventh day Sabbath, or in Hebrew, *Shabbat*. This commandment clearly states that the Shabbat is to be on the seventh day:

---

\* The English word "Sabbath" comes from the Hebrew word *Shabbat*. "Shabbat" most likely comes from the Hebrew root letters *shin*, *bet*, and *tav*, meaning "cease" or "desist." The verbal form is used in Genesis 2:2–3 twice in relationship to the seventh day. (Nahum M. Sarna, *The JPS Torah Commentary: Exodus* [Philadelphia: The Jewish Publication Society, 1991] pp. 111–112.)

† In Hebrew, the Ten Commandments are *Aseret haD'vareem*—literally the "ten words" (Exodus 34:28, Deuteronomy 4:13). The Jewish counting is different from the Catholic and Protestant counting. The first word (or commandment) according to Jewish reckoning is "I am the LORD [YHVH] your God, who brought you out of the land of Egypt, out of the house of slavery." (Exodus 20:2)

Remember the Sabbath day, to keep it holy. Six days you shall labor, and do all your work, but the seventh day is a Sabbath to the LORD [YHVH] your God. On it you shall not do any work, you, or your son, or your daughter, your male servant, or your female servant, or your livestock, or the sojourner who is within your gates. For in six days the LORD [YHVH] made heaven and earth, the sea, and all that is in them, and rested on the seventh day. Therefore the LORD [YHVH] blessed the Sabbath day and made it holy (Exodus 20:8–11) [see also Deuteronomy 5:12–15].

We are commanded to remember and to keep or observe the seventh day as the Shabbat. The Exodus passage explains that the seventh day was chosen because God rested on the seventh day after preparing the land for man to dwell on (John Sailhamer's interpretation)[1]. At the conclusion of making the sky, the land, the sea, and all that is in them, He blessed the seventh day and made it holy or set apart (Genesis 2:1–3). The discussion should end here.

Most authorities in the traditional church would say that the Shabbat was changed from the seventh day of the week to the first day of the week after Yeshua died. We still have Shabbat, but it is now on the first day of the week.‡

Other authorities would say that the Shabbat was not actually changed to another day but was replaced by a new day, "the Lord's day."[2]

---

‡ It is interesting that in about one hundred modern and ancient languages, the word for the seventh day of the week (our Saturday) is derived from the Hebrew word *Shabbat*—for instance Armenian: *Shabat*; Greek: *Savvato*; Indonesian: *Sabtu*; Polish: *Sobota*; Romanian: *Sambata*; Russian: *Subbota*; Spanish: *Sabado*. At some point, these cultures must have understood that the Shabbat was on the seventh day of the week. (United Church of God, "Names for Saturday in Many Languages Prove Which Day Is the True Sabbath," in *Sunset to Sunset: God's Sabbath Rest*, posted on February 10, 2011, www.ucg. org/bible-study-tools/booklets/sunset-to-sunset-gods-sabbath-rest/names-for-saturday-in-many-languages.) In English, one can get away with saying that the Sabbath changed from Saturday to Sunday, but in these other languages one cannot as easily say that the Sabbath changed from Sabbath (meaning the seventh day) to Sunday.

Regardless of which theory is professed, the traditional church must have considerable evidence available somewhere to justify such a profound change, for it is not a trivial matter to cancel out one of the Ten Commandments.

## The Church's Arguments against a Seventh Day Shabbat

To give me assistance in reviewing this subject, I have brought in Professor Gleason Archer.§ I will be referencing to and quoting from a taped message Dr. Archer delivered in 1991 at a John Ankerberg apologetics conference entitled "Is the Sabbath Saturday or Sunday according to the Bible?" Dr. Archer is the author of *Encyclopedia of Bible Difficulties*, was a pastor for some years, taught at the university level, and is fluent in a number of languages including Hebrew. He is a bright man who represents a traditional Christian view of the Sabbath.

There are three main arguments against the seventh day Shabbat put forth by those in the traditional church:

1) Out of all the Ten Commandments, the fourth commandment is the only one not restated in the New Testament. Therefore, it is no longer valid.

2) The evidence from the New Testament and extrabiblical writings proves that the early church chose Sunday as the new Christian holy day immediately after Yeshua's death.

3) The New Testament abrogates the seventh day Shabbat along with the rest of the Torah instructions.

---

§ Actually, the real assistance I will be receiving in this chapter is from the book written by Dr. Samuele Bacchiocchi, *From Sabbath to Sunday: A Historical Investigation of the Rise of Sunday Observance in Early Christianity*. (Samuele Bacchiocchi, *From Sabbath to Sunday: A Historical Investigation of the Rise of Sunday Observance in Early Christianity* [Rome: The Pontifical Gregorian University Press, 1977].) Dr. Bacchiocchi is one of my heroes. He kept me on the edge of my seat as I listened to him speak in 1979, and I greatly appreciate his research.

## The Fourth Commandment Is Not
## Restated in the New Testament

It has been said by some in the traditional church that the fourth commandment about the seventh day Shabbat is the only one of the Ten
Commandments not restated in the New Testament. Therefore, the
argument goes, it is no longer a valid commandment for the believer
to follow. Now, it is true that the particular commandment, "Observe
the Sabbath day, to keep it holy" (Deuteronomy 5:12), is not found
in the New Testament. Nevertheless, any casual reader of the New
Testament will see that it teaches more about the seventh day Shabbat
than about any of the other commandments. Dr. Archer agrees:

> In other words, Jesus spent more time discussing the fourth
> commandment than any other commandment in the Decalogue.
> You count up the verses, and you make very sure that you take stock
> of this fact before you take a libertarian attitude about the fourth
> commandment in your own practice. Jesus did care about a proper
> observance of the Sabbath.[3]

Back in the first century among the believing Jews, the Shabbat
was an established day of YHVH. The New Testament did not need to
direct people to observe the Shabbat. They were already remembering
and keeping the day. Rather, the New Testament needed to direct
people how to observe the Shabbat.

Through Yeshua's example and teachings, we see that the Shabbat
was still important in the New Testament: "And he came to Nazareth,
where he had been brought up. And as was his custom, he went to the
synagogue on the Sabbath day, and he stood up to read" (Luke 4:16).
Yeshua went to the synagogue on the Shabbat, as was his custom, not
because it was the custom of the Jews. According to the Torah (Leviticus
23:3), the Shabbat was to be a holy convocation or assembly. Yeshua
met other Jews in the synagogue to keep the commandment himself.

Yeshua also distinctly taught on many occasions about the
proper observance of the seventh day Shabbat. The rabbinic Oral Law
at the time of Yeshua had placed burdensome restrictions upon the
activities of the people on the Shabbat day. Yeshua corrected several

misunderstandings about the Shabbat. For instance, he clarified that acute human need takes precedence over the commandment not to work on the Shabbat. The Shabbat was made for man, and not man for the Shabbat (Mark 2:27).[4¶]

Yeshua also taught that the Shabbat is a day of redemption. Linking the Shabbat to redemption is first seen in the Torah. The reason given to observe the Shabbat in the Exodus passage cited previously is because God rested from His work on the seventh day (Exodus 20:11). In the repetition of the Ten Commandments in Deuteronomy, however, a second reason is given for us to observe the Shabbat. In the Deuteronomy passage, we are asked to remember the Exodus from Egypt and our redemption there during the Shabbat:[5]

> You shall remember that you were a slave in the land of Egypt, and the LORD [YHVH] your God brought you out from there with a mighty hand and an outstretched arm. Therefore the LORD [YHVH] your God commanded you to keep the Sabbath day (Deuteronomy 5:15).

Yeshua reinforced this concept by showing that redemptive acts such as healing and the reversal of the effects of sin in the world are appropriate on the Shabbat. He brought out this teaching by his interaction on the Shabbat with:

- The man with the withered right hand (Matthew 12:9–13, Mark 3:1–6, Luke 6:6–11).
- The woman bent double (Luke 13:10–17).
- The man with dropsy (Luke 14:1–6).[**]

---

¶ For instance, the overriding intent to rest on the Shabbat is not violated by the casual picking of grain to satisfy acute hunger (Matthew 12:1–8, Mark 2:23–28, Luke 6:1–5). In this context he may also have been saying that man himself is lord of the Shabbat (Matthew 12:8, Mark 2:28, Luke 6:5). (David H. Stern, *Jewish New Testament commentary* [Clarksville, MD: Jewish New Testament Publications., 1992], p. 89.) In addition, Yeshua seemed to imply that man with his acute needs is even greater than the Temple (Matthew 12:5–6). (R. Steven Notley, "The Sabbath Was Made for Man," Jerusalem Perspective: Exploring the Jewish Background to the Life and Words of Jesus, January 1, 2004, www.jerusalemperspective.com/4616/.)

** See also the illustrations in the book of John: the ill man by the pool of

Yeshua was teaching in one of the synagogues on Shabbat. A woman came up who had a spirit which had crippled her for eighteen years; she was bent double and unable to stand erect at all. On seeing her, Yeshua called her and said to her, "Lady, you have been set free from your weakness!" He put his hands on her, and at once she stood upright and began to glorify God. But the president of the synagogue, indignant that Yeshua had healed on Shabbat, spoke up and said to the congregation, "There are six days in the week for working; so come during those days to be healed, not on Shabbat!" However, the Lord answered him, "You hypocrites! Each one of you on Shabbat—don't you unloose your ox or your donkey from the stall and lead him off to drink? This woman is a daughter of Avraham, and the Adversary kept her tied up for eighteen years! Shouldn't she be freed from this bondage on Shabbat?" (Luke 13:10–16, *Complete Jewish Bible*).

If a bound animal can be released to drink water on the Shabbat, how much more should a human be unbound from Satan on the Shabbat? The Torah and Yeshua were elevating the Shabbat and characterizing it as a day of redemption.[6] Only after a man is redeemed through Yeshua's atonement can he enter God's rest.

The continued value of the Shabbat in the New Testament is also revealed by Sha'ul's recorded observance of the Shabbat (Acts 13:13–15, Acts 13:42–44, Acts 16:13–15, Acts 17:1–4, Acts 18:1–4). Acts 17:1–2 states that Sha'ul went into the synagogue on the Shabbat according to his custom.

Dr. Archer admits that Sha'ul and the other early followers of Yeshua worshiped on the Shabbat, but he feels they did it in order to evangelize the Jews, not because of their own adherence to the Shabbat commandment:

> We observe that in the record of the book of Acts, and, of course, the subsequent books that are post-resurrection, the apostles made a practice of attending worship on the seventh day Sabbath. Now, of course, this meant that they would have contact with their countrymen, and if you don't have contact with your countrymen, you will have scant opportunity to lead them to the Lord.[7]

Bethesda (John 5:1–18, John 7:21–24) and the blind man (John 9:13–16).

Since we know that Sha'ul also walked orderly, keeping the Law (Acts 21:21–26, Acts 25:7–8), however, it is absurd to think that Sha'ul only worshiped on the Shabbat so that he could have contact with other Jews.

It is clear from this short survey that the New Testament does not minimize the fourth commandment but shows that it continues to carry significant weight.

## Evidence in the New Testament for a New Day of Worship?

The second argument against the seventh day Shabbat focuses on the custom of the early believers. It is said that the New Testament, along with extrabiblical writings, seems to suggest that after Yeshua's death the early believers immediately chose the first day of the week, Sunday, as the new holy day for "Christian" gathering, worship, and rest, and rejected the seventh day. There are five New Testament passages used to support this claim—John 20:19–20, John 20:26–27, Acts 20:7–11, 1 Corinthians 16:1–4, and Revelation 1:9–11.

### John 20:19–20

On the evening of that day, the first day of the week, the doors being locked where the disciples were for fear of the Jews, Jesus [Yeshua] came and stood among them and said to them, "Peace be with you." When he had said this, he showed them his hands and his side. Then the disciples were glad when they saw the Lord.

In this passage, the disciples were seen huddled together out of fear of "the Jews," on the same day that Yeshua was raised from the dead, which happened to be the first day of the week. This gathering hardly constituted the establishment of a new day for the Shabbat or a new day of required worship.[8]

### John 20:26–27

Eight days later [again the first day of the week], his disciples were inside again, and Thomas [Toma] was with them. Although the doors were locked, Jesus [Yeshua] came and stood among them and said, "Peace be with you." Then he said to Thomas [Toma], "Put your finger here, and see my hands; and put out your hand, and place it in my side. Do not disbelieve, but believe."

It appears that the disciples were living together in Jerusalem prior to Shavuot (Pentecost), according to Acts 1:13–14, and, therefore, they saw each other daily. This particular first day of the week was mentioned not because the disciples came together for a special meeting, but because Yeshua appeared on this day. The text suggests that the main reason he appeared on this particular day was that Toma (Thomas), who had been absent previously, was now present.[9]

**Acts 20:7–11**

On the first day of the week, when we were gathered together to break bread, Paul [Sha'ul] talked with them, intending to depart on the next day, and he prolonged his speech until midnight. There were many lamps in the upper room where we were gathered. And a young man named Eutychus, sitting at the window, sank into a deep sleep as Paul [Sha'ul] talked still longer. And being overcome by sleep, he fell down from the third story and was taken up dead. But Paul [Sha'ul] went down and bent over him, and taking him in his arms, said, "Do not be alarmed, for his life is in him." And when Paul [Sha'ul] had gone up and had broken bread and eaten, he conversed with them a long while, until daybreak, and so departed.

Here, Sha'ul met with the believers in Troas, evidently at night on the first day of the week, since Eutychus fell out of the window after midnight. Luke is most likely using a Jewish reckoning to define a day from evening to evening rather than the Roman reckoning from midnight to midnight. Therefore, this meeting was occurring after the Shabbat was over that Saturday night, the first day of the week.[10]

Some commentators feel that Roman time reckoning was most likely being used since Sha'ul intended to leave "the next day." This opinion would mean that this first day of the week at night would be the last hours of Sunday. However, according to Bacchiocchi, the Greek here for "next day" can also mean "next morning" without reference to a new day. Sha'ul's leaving on the next morning continued to be the first day of the week.[11] Sha'ul most likely would not have traveled by land on the Shabbat, and, therefore, it is not surprising to see the documentation that he probably left the morning after the Shabbat.[12]

Those who would say that the believers here participated in the new tradition of communion on the first day of the week, on Sunday night, have a problem in that the group did not break bread until after midnight. Using the Roman time reckoning, the breaking of bread would have occurred on Monday morning, the second day of the week.[13] The reference to the breaking of bread here most likely meant that they merely were eating together anyway, and not participating in communion.[14] This passage falls short of establishing a new day for Christian gatherings and worship.

### 1 Corinthians 16:1–4

Now concerning the collection for the saints: as I directed the churches of Galatia, so you also are to do. On the first day of every week, each of you is to put something aside and store it up, as he may prosper, so that there will be no collecting when I come. And when I arrive, I will send those whom you accredit by letter to carry your gift to Jerusalem. If it seems advisable that I should go also, they will accompany me.

Here, we see that Sha'ul was instructing believing communities in Asia Minor to set aside money for the saints in Jerusalem each week on the first day of the week. Collecting money on the seventh day Shabbat would have been a violation of the Shabbat, and, therefore, we see Sha'ul being consistent with the Scriptures by not using that day. Maybe a collection at the beginning of the week ensured that money would still be available before the monetary demands of the upcoming week.[15] Using the first day of the week to collect money seems to be as good a time as any. The instruction to take a monetary collection on the first day of the week also does not justify the church's changing of the Saturday Shabbat to Sunday.

### Revelation 1:9–11

I, John [Yochanan], your brother and partner in the tribulation and the kingdom and the patient endurance that are in Jesus [Yeshua], was on the island called Patmos on account of the word of God and the testimony of Jesus [Yeshua]. I was in the Spirit on the Lord's day, and I heard behind me a loud voice like a trumpet saying, "Write what you see in a book and send it to the seven churches, to Ephesus and to Smyrna and to Pergamum and to Thyatira and to Sardis and to Philadelphia and to Laodicea."

Yochanon said that he was in the spirit on "the Lord's day." Most commentators would say that he was referring to Sunday by this expression. However, if this phrase were referring to a particular day of the week, why would Saturday not be the Lord's day? As argued by Bacchiocchi, Yochanon was using the expression "the Lord's day" to mean "the day of the Lord," which would be the future day of God's final judgment. This interpretation is more consistent with the context of the book of Revelation.[16]

These five passages are the biblical evidence given that the well-established seventh day Shabbat, the fourth of the Ten Commandments, has been changed to the first day of the week. These are all there are! None of these passages justifies the change of YHVH's seventh day Shabbat to the first day of the week, nor do these passages suggest a new day of worship for the believer. The evidence is just not there.

## An Early Change for the Wrong Reasons

Could some of the earliest extrabiblical Christian writings that document the early believers worshipping on Sunday be the overwhelming evidence needed to prove that the new day of "Christian" worship is now Sunday? Dr. Archer states:

> So the statement is made by Justin Martyr, who was a second-century church leader, "On the day called Sunday, all who live in the city or the country gather together in one place, and the memoirs of the apostles or the writings of the prophets are read. Sunday is the day on which we all hold our common assembly because it is the first day on which God made the world and, Jesus our Savior, on the first day, rose from the dead. So he appeared to his apostles and disciples and taught these things which we have submitted to you for your consideration" [The First Apology of Justin, chapter 67]. Justin Martyr was writing to the Roman emperor at the time, and the apology, of course, meant

that he was writing in defense of the Christian faith and showing that they were not unpatriotic or disobedient subjects of the Roman Empire.[17]

I might add that he was also trying to show the emperor that the Christians were not Jews. How convenient for Justin to make up his own nonbiblical explanations for Sunday observance. It is no longer the day God rested that is important (according to the Scriptures), but "the first day on which God made the world."

Justin wrote other things also. In his *Dialogue with Trypho* the Jew, he states:

> For we too would observe the fleshly circumcision, and the Sabbaths, and in short all the feasts, if we did not know for what reason they were enjoined you—namely, on account of your transgressions and the hardness of your hearts (*Dialogue with Trypho*, 18).[18]

> For the circumcision according to the flesh, which is from Abraham, was given for a sign; that you may be separated from other nations, and from us; and that you alone may suffer that which you now justly suffer; and that your land may be desolate, and your cities burned with fire; and that strangers may eat your fruit in your presence, and not one of you may go up to Jerusalem. For you are not recognized among the rest of men by any other mark than your fleshly circumcision (*Dialogue with Trypho*, 16).[19]

> Moreover, that God enjoined you to keep the Sabbath, and impose on you other precepts for a sign, as I have already said, on account of your unrighteousness, and that of your fathers (*Dialogue with Trypho*, 21).[20]

I do not think that Justin or any of the other "church fathers" who had negative feelings toward the Jews were able to give us any reliable information about God's plan for the Shabbat.[21]

The New Testament and the extrabiblical record do not support the claim that God somehow directed the earliest Jewish believers to choose Sunday as a new Christian holy day immediately after Yeshua's death.

# Does the New Testament Abrogate the Seventh Day Shabbat?

The third argument put forth against the seventh day Shabbat is that the New Testament writings abrogate the seventh day Shabbat along with the rest of the Torah instructions. Three passages written by Sha'ul are cited in this argument—Romans 14:5–6, Galatians 4:7–11, and Colossians 2:13–17. As we study these passages in their full context, we need to ask whether Sha'ul was condemning the Torah-appointed days or whether he was condemning the way the people he was writing to were observing some days. The same question can be asked of Isaiah in Isaiah 1:13–14. Did he condemn YHVH's Torah-appointed days and sacrifices, or was he speaking against the insincere way these days were being observed?

These Pauline passages that we will be looking at are difficult to understand, because we no longer know the exact problems that Sha'ul was confronting. We cannot be too dogmatic about our conclusions. We do have enough hints, though, in each passage to determine that Sha'ul, like Isaiah, could not have been speaking against the days of YHVH as outlined in the Torah.

### Romans 14:5–6

One person esteems one day as better than another, while another esteems all days alike. Each one should be fully convinced in his own mind. The one who observes the day, observes it in honor of the Lord. The one who eats, eats in honor of the Lord, since he gives thanks to God, while the one who abstains, abstains in honor of the Lord and gives thanks to God.

Most commentators are convinced that this passage abolished the Torah-appointed days and now we can choose any days we like in which to worship God. When we look for hints in the full context of Romans 14, however, we can see that Sha'ul was not talking about the Torah-appointed times:

One person believes he may eat anything, while the weak person eats only vegetables (Romans 14:2).

It is good not to eat meat or drink wine or do anything that causes your brother to stumble (Romans 14:21).

The food restrictions the weaker brothers were trying to impose on everyone included eating only vegetables, not eating meat, and not drinking wine. This conflict was not over Torah commandments, which Sha'ul never writes were repealed, but over various ascetic practices that must have been prevalent at the time of this writing. The same is true of the "days" mentioned in this passage. Sha'ul was saying if someone feels it is necessary for him to be a vegetarian for God or to observe a particular day for God, do not condemn him. God does not command anyone to be a vegetarian or to observe days other than those in the Torah. It is not harmful, however, for a weak brother to be a vegetarian or to observe other days to YHVH.[22]

**Galatians 4:7–11**

So you are no longer a slave, but a son, and if a son, then an heir through God. Formerly, when you did not know God, you were enslaved to those that by nature are not gods. But now that you have come to know God, or rather to be known by God, how can you turn back again to the weak and worthless elementary principles of the world, whose slaves you want to be once more? You observe days and months and seasons and years! I am afraid I may have labored over you in vain.

In verse 9, Sha'ul was characterizing the Galatians' problem as turning back again to weak and worthless elemental things. Sha'ul, here, could not possibly have been characterizing God's appointed times as weak and worthless elementary principles of the world, since for Sha'ul "the law is holy, and the commandment is holy and righteous and good" (Romans 7:12). Although we do not know what the Galatians were doing here exactly, the observance of these days was causing them to be enslaved once more to weak and worthless elementary principles of the world. Daniel Juster suggests that the Galatians might have been involved in astrology.[23] In its full context, the passage does not annul YHVH's appointed days.

**Colossians 2:13–17**

And you, who were dead in your trespasses and the uncircumcision of your flesh, God made alive together with him, having forgiven us all our trespasses, by canceling the record of debt that stood against us with its legal demands. This he set aside, nailing it to the cross. He disarmed the rulers and authorities and put them to open shame, by triumphing over them in him. Therefore let no one pass judgment on you in questions of food and drink, or with regard to a festival or a new moon or a Sabbath. These are a shadow of the things to come, but the substance belongs to Christ [Messiah].

This passage certainly appears to have abolished the kosher laws, as well as the Torah-appointed days. Let us clear up some of the misunderstandings about this passage, however.

Verse 14 says that the record of debt consisting of legal demands against us was nailed to the cross. Many would say that it was the "law" or Torah that was nailed to the cross. Nevertheless, this is clearly referring to a written record of our sins, which have been nailed to the cross, not the Torah.[24]

Verse 16 says that no one is to act as your judge regarding "food or drink." The Greek words here, however, mean the act of eating and drinking, and, therefore, could refer to fasting or not fasting, and not the Torah commandments related to food.[25] Even if this verse was saying "food or drink," the Torah does not prohibit any drinking except in relationship to the *Nazirite* vow (Numbers 6:1–4) or to the Temple priest on duty (Leviticus 10:8-9).[26] Therefore, it is unlikely that this phrase was referring to the kosher food laws.

Before we examine the specific days mentioned in verse 16, let us first look at the surrounding context of Colossians 2:8: "See to it that no one takes you captive by philosophy and empty deceit, according to human tradition, according to the elemental spirits of the world, and not according to Christ [Messiah]." The corruption of the faith was over "philosophy and empty deceit, according to human tradition, according to the elemental spirits of the world." Sha'ul was not criticizing here God's instructions found in the Torah, although he may have been partially criticizing the way that individual men were using the Torah instructions corruptly. It seems likely that there had also been the fusion of pagan philosophy into the Messianic faith:[27]

Let no one disqualify you, insisting on asceticism and worship of angels, going on in detail about visions, puffed up without reason by his sensuous mind (Colossians 2:18).

If with Christ [Messiah] you died to the elemental spirits of the world, why, as if you were still alive in the world, do you submit to regulations—"Do not handle, Do not taste, Do not touch" (referring to things that all perish as they are used)—according to human precepts and teachings? These have indeed an appearance of wisdom in promoting self-made religion and asceticism and severity to the body, but they are of no value in stopping the indulgence of the flesh (Colossians 2:20–23).

Again, Sha'ul was not writing in opposition to the Torah, but against the self-made instructions of men. As in the Galatians chapter 4 passage examined previously, it is unclear exactly what Sha'ul was combatting here.[28††]

When we come back to verse 16 and examine the Torah-appointed days mentioned by Sha'ul, we must understand that he was not abrogating these days or condemning their observance. In fact, he says in verse 17 that they are a shadow of what is to come. They have significance for us as long as we remember to what the shadows are pointing (see appendix 1).[29] Sha'ul was telling the Colossians here to follow the ways of God rather than the commandments and religions of men. He was pointing out that there had been a perversion associated with God's Torah-appointed times, and that the Colossians should not allow false teachers to pressure them into following the perverted teachings. It may be that some men were demanding a particular form of observance in order to be "saved." Sha'ul was not nullifying or condemning God's Torah-appointed days.[30]

---

†† What may complicate Colossians chapter 2 more is that Colossians 2:8–15 may be a hymnic passage—a section not originally composed by Sha'ul. (Dean L. Overman, *A Case for the Divinity of Jesus: Examining the Earliest Evidence* [New York: Rowman & Littlefield Publishers, Inc., 2010], p. 244.) I will discuss more about hymnic passages in chapter 12.

## Could God Allow Christians to Make Such a Big Mistake?

After going through the weak evidence, Dr. Archer comes to the bottom line for himself and most traditional Christians. He will fight for Sunday as the new day for the "Christian Sabbath" regardless of the evidence because this has been the tradition of the church for 2,000 years, and the church could not have made a mistake since God's Holy Spirit has guided it:

> And so, what we have here is a shift of the sanction of the fourth commandment from the Old Testament seventh day to the New Testament first day. It is quite inconceivable that this shift could have been made against the will of God as if somehow the Holy Spirit had no control over the decisions of the leadership of the New Testament church. And so, we need to take very careful heed to this early testimony on the part of Justin Martyr.[31]

This assertion coming from a Protestant believer who stands behind the Protestant Reformation is astonishing.

## Sunday Sabbath: A Form of Replacement Theology

Dr. Archer's final point is most revealing. He takes a passage from the Scriptures that is plainly speaking about the seventh-day Shabbat and transforms it into a passage that is now speaking about the "Christian Sabbath." This makeover is a subtle form of replacement theology where God's blessings to Israel are taken away and given to the church:

> But we are to regard the Sabbath as a delight. There's a beautiful passage in Jeremiah 17 that I would like you to turn to. I know that it has to do with the seventh day Sabbath, but there is a carryover of principle here. The seventeenth chapter of Jeremiah beginning at verse 19.[32]

He is taking the promises and blessings related to the "Jewish Sabbath" and placing them upon the "Christian Sabbath."

The evidence is clear that the seventh day Shabbat has not been changed to another day or been abrogated.

## A Stumbling Block for Jews

Now, it is not wrong to worship on Sunday. Sha'ul is clear in Romans 14 that if a man wishes to observe a day to YHVH, he is free to do so, whether the day is Sunday, Tuesday, or Friday. One is not free, however, to cancel out God's instructions relating to the seventh day Shabbat, neglecting the commandment of God and holding to the tradition of men (Mark 7:8). One is not free to change the Shabbat to any day he pleases. Unfortunately, Christian Sunday observance, with the corresponding rejection of the seventh day Shabbat, has done harm. The replacement of the "Jewish" or biblical Holy Days by "Christian" holidays, not found anywhere in the Scriptures, has been one of the many stumbling blocks that have prevented the Jewish people from seeing the Messianic faith as their own.

## The Transcendent Nature of Shabbat

How serious is God about the seventh day Shabbat? He is dead serious. The person who worked on the Shabbat in ancient Israel was to be put to death (Exodus 35:1–2, Numbers 15:32–36). God must consider the sin of profaning the Shabbat as reprehensible as the sins of murder and adultery since the punishment for violators of all three was the same. Profaning the Shabbat was also one of the reasons for Israel's dispersal among the nations (Ezekiel 20:23–24). YHVH seems serious about His Shabbat.

Why does God raise the Shabbat to such heights? By keeping the Shabbat, we are in a sense maintaining the whole covenant between God and his people. In Isaiah chapter 56, we have parallel poetic lines equating the keeping of the Shabbat with holding fast to God's covenant. The eunuchs and foreigners in Isaiah 56:4 and 56: 6 who join themselves to YHVH and choose what pleases Him will be keeping the Shabbat/holding fast to the covenant:

> And the foreigners who join themselves to the LORD [YHVH], to minister to him, to love the name of the LORD [YHVH], and to be his servants, everyone who keeps the Sabbath and does not profane it, and holds fast my covenant (Isaiah 56:6).

If we want to maintain this divine agreement, we should start by keeping the Shabbat.

Some would say that the Shabbat is just an ancient shadow of something already fulfilled. Therefore, we do not have to deal with an outward observance of it anymore. We see in Isaiah 56:6, however, that Gentile followers of God will be observing the Shabbat in a future age. In addition, Yeshua suggested that the Shabbat would be in existence well into the future, after his death; for he asked us to pray that our flight from a future tribulation would not occur on a Shabbat day:

> So when you see the abomination of desolation spoken of by the prophet Daniel, standing in the holy place (let the reader understand), then let those who are in Judea flee to the mountains. Let the one who is on the housetop not go down to take what is in his house, and let the one who is in the field not turn back to take his cloak. And alas for women who are pregnant and for those who are nursing infants in those days! Pray that your flight may not be in winter or on a Sabbath. For then there will be great tribulation, such as has not been from the beginning of the world until now, no, and never will be (Matthew 24:15–21).

It is curious why he listed the Shabbat here among the other impediments to a swift flight such as being pregnant, nursing a child, or winter. Whatever the reason, though, he suggested that the Shabbat would remain in effect into the future.[33]

Are there any benefits to keeping the Shabbat? The Shabbat foreshadows our future rest in the messianic age (Hebrews 4). The Shabbat helps us to recall God's redemptive acts on our behalf. Moreover, by obeying God and keeping the Shabbat, we will ride on the heights of the earth:

> If you turn back your foot from the Sabbath, from doing your pleasure on my holy day, and call the Sabbath a delight and the holy day of the LORD [YHVH] honorable; if you honor it, not going your own ways, or seeking your own pleasure, or talking idly; then you shall take delight in the LORD [YHVH], and I will make you ride on the heights of the earth; I will feed you with the heritage of Jacob your father, for the mouth of the LORD [YHVH] has spoken (Isaiah 58:13–14).

I cannot entirely grasp what it means to ride on the heights of the earth, but it sounds great! (See also Deuteronomy 32:13.) Without a doubt, God will bless us when we follow His instructions, as He promised. The Shabbat was made for man.

In the early days of the church, the seventh day Shabbat was removed from the church's memory and exchanged for another tradition. The overwhelming evidence does not justify such a change. The fourth commandment should be chiseled back onto the tablets of stone.

As we will see in the next chapter, the kosher food laws experienced a similar demise.

# (Endnotes)

1   John Sailhamer, *Genesis Unbound: A Provocative New Look at the Creation Account* (Sisters, OR: Multnomah Books, 1996).

2   *From Sabbath to Lord's Day: A Biblical, Historical, and Theological Investigation*, ed. by D. A. Carson (Grand Rapids, MI: Zondervan Publishing House, 1982).

3   Gleason L. Archer, "Is the Sabbath Saturday or Sunday According to the Bible?" taped message in 1991 at a John Ankerberg apologetics conference.

4   Samuele Bacchiocchi, *From Sabbath to Sunday: A Historical Investigation of the Rise of Sunday Observance in Early Christianity* (Rome: The Pontifical Gregorian University Press, 1977), pp. 48–51.

5   Ibid., pp. 21–24.

6   Ibid., pp. 29–48.

7   Gleason L. Archer, "Is the Sabbath Saturday or Sunday According to the Bible?" taped message in 1991 at a John Ankerberg apologetics conference.

8   Samuele Bacchiocchi, *From Sabbath to Sunday: A Historical Investigation of the Rise of Sunday Observance in Early Christianity*, pp. 85–86.

9   Ibid., p. 87.

10  David H. Stern, *Jewish New Testament Commentary* (Clarksville, MD: Jewish New Testament Publications, 1992), pp. 297–298.

11  Samuele Bacchiocchi, *From Sabbath to Sunday: A Historical Investigation of the Rise of Sunday Observance in Early Christianity*, pp. 103–104.

12  Ibid., p. 106.

13  Ibid., p. 104.

14  Ibid., pp. 107–110.

15  Ibid., pp. 100–101.

16  Ibid., pp. 111–131.

17  Gleason L. Archer, "Is the Sabbath Saturday or Sunday According to the Bible?" taped message in 1991 at a John Ankerberg apologetics conference.

18  "The Apostolic Fathers, Justin Martyr, Irenaeus," Vol. I in *Ante-Nicene Fathers* ed. by Alexander Roberts and James Donaldson, revised and arranged by A. Cleveland Coxe, 10 Vols. (Peabody, MA: Hendrickson Publishers, 1994), p. 203.

19  Ibid., p. 202.

20   Ibid., p. 204.

21   Samuele Bacchiocchi, *From Sabbath to Sunday: A Historical Investigation of the Rise of Sunday Observance in Early Christianity*, pp. 223–233.

22   David H. Stern, *Jewish New Testament Commentary* (Clarksville, MD: Jewish New Testament Publications, 1992), pp. 431–434.

23   Daniel Juster, *Jewish Roots: A Foundation of Biblical Theology*, second ed. (Gaithersburg, MD: DAVAR Publishing Co., 1986).

24   Ariel and D'vorah Berkowitz, *Take Hold: Embracing Our Divine Inheritance with Israel* (Littleton, CO: First Fruits of Zion, 1998), pp.227–228.

25   David H. Stern, *Jewish New Testament Commentary*, p. 610.

26   Ibid., p 433.

27   Daniel Juster, *Jewish Roots: A Foundation of Biblical Theology*, pp. 130–131.

28   Ibid., p. 130.

29   David H. Stern, *Jewish New Testament Commentary*, p. 611.

30   Ibid., pp. 611–612.

31   Gleason L. Archer, "Is the Sabbath Saturday or Sunday According to the Bible?" taped message in 1991 at a John Ankerberg apologetics conference.

32   Ibid.

33   Samuele Bacchiocchi, *From Sabbath to Sunday: A Historical Investigation of the Rise of Sunday Observance in Early Christianity*, p. 71.

# Chapter 6: Have the Kosher Laws Been Abrogated?

## What Is Food?

In the Torah, in the book of Leviticus, chapter 11, one finds instructions about clean and unclean animals. This chapter told the people of Israel what they could and could not eat. These guidelines give a person much food for thought. If God defined the nature of food for the ancient Israelites, why do God's people today in the traditional church eat whatever they please?

The answer to this question, as I have discussed previously, lies in the fact that most believers in the traditional church believe that the Torah has been abrogated. The Torah instructions are not part of the mindset of those in the traditional church. Unfortunately, it appears that many in the church, who think they are standing firm, are frequently falling because of this. Even though most believers observe large portions of the Torah,* they do so usually because the "New Testament" has restated some of these "Old Testament" instructions. Most believers would say that the New Testament specifically annuls

---

* Andrew Roth has actually tried to make the calculations. Of the 613 commandments the rabbis have catalogued from the Torah (many of these related to the Temple and priesthood, which cannot be performed today) he states that the majority of Christians are keeping about 203. (*Aramaic English New Testament*, compiled, ed., and trans. by Andrew Gabriel Roth [Sedro-Woolley, WA: Netzari Press LLC, 2008], pp. 845–864.)

the kosher food laws found in the Torah. If one could show that the New Testament has not invalidated the kosher food instructions found in Leviticus chapter 11, then one could smash one more barrier separating God's people from His instructions found in the Torah.

## Respecting Context

The traditional church defends its nonkosher food stance with eight New Testament passages—Mark 7:18–19, Acts 10:13–15, Galatians 2:11–12, Romans 14:2, 1 Timothy 4:4–5, 1 Corinthians 10:27, 1 Corinthians 8:8, and Colossians 2:16–17. Even though in isolation each of these passages seems very convincing, all have been wrenched free from their context. When restored to their full context, none of these passages has anything negative to say about the kosher food laws.

Those not honoring the context of their proof texts have established many false biblical "truths." A humorous story is told about a man who was trying to get direction from God.[1] He opened his King James Bible and with his eyes closed, landed his pointed finger on Matthew 27:5, "He went and hanged himself." Confused by this message, he tried again and came down upon Matthew 24:33, "So likewise ye." Not anxious to carry out these instructions, he tried one more time and picked John 13:27, "That thou doest, do quickly." When the context of a scriptural verse or phrase is lost, almost anything can be justified.[†]

## Unraveling the Anti-Kosher Proof Texts

Let us begin to study these New Testament food passages one by one.

### Mark 7:18–19

And he said to them, "Then are you also without understanding? Do

---

† A man once told me that he drank cups of his urine every day to stay healthy. He explained to me that this practice came straight out of the Bible: "Drink water from your own cistern, flowing water from your own well" (Proverbs 5:15). Clearly, though, the context in this Proverb is to be faithful to your wife, not to drink your own urine.

you not see that whatever goes into a person from outside cannot defile him, since it enters not his heart but his stomach, and is expelled?" (Thus he declared all foods clean.)‡

These short verses are taken from the larger passage Mark 7:1–23. Here, Yeshua was mainly criticizing the Pharisees for following the traditions of men rather than the commandments of God:

> And he said to them, "Well did Isaiah prophesy of you hypocrites, as it is written, 'This people honors me with their lips, but their heart is far from me; in vain do they worship me, teaching as doctrines the commandments of men.' You leave the commandment of God and hold to the tradition of men." And he said to them, "You have a fine way of rejecting the commandment of God in order to establish your tradition!" (Mark 7:6–9).

Since Yeshua was chastising the Pharisees for not following the Torah, he could not have possibly then turned around and canceled out all of the kosher food commandments given by God in the Torah.

The principal controversy in this passage was not over the God-given kosher food commandments, but over the man-made tradition of hand washing before eating: "And the Pharisees and the scribes asked him, 'Why do your disciples not walk according to the tradition of the elders, but eat with defiled hands?'" (Mark 7:5). In fact, those who understand this passage as saying that one can now eat whatever he desires have removed the definition of what food is.

Some believers say that food is now defined by the culture in which one is living. Can we now eat bats and rats, however? Imagine being a missionary living in a cannibal village. After a justified war, the village men bring home the brains of the dead enemy for supper.

---

‡ Note that the text of the *New King James Version*, based on the *Received Text*, gives a completely different meaning to the passage, "So He said to them, 'Are you thus without understanding also? Do you not perceive that whatever enters a man from outside cannot defile him, because it does not enter his heart but his stomach, and is eliminated, *thus* purifying all foods?'" (Mark 7:18–19, New King James Version).

May you eat this?

There is no evidence that this passage has removed the Torah definition of food. Whenever Yeshua was talking about food, he could only be talking about food as the Torah specifies it. Therefore, in Mark 7:18–19, Yeshua was saying that food delineated already by the Torah is not made unclean when a person does not wash his hands.[28]§

**Acts 10:13–15**

> And there came a voice to him: "Rise, Peter [Kefa]; kill and eat." But Peter [Kefa] said, "By no means, Lord; for I have never eaten anything that is common or unclean." And the voice came to him again a second time, "What God has made clean, do not call common."

This second group of verses is found within the larger passage of Acts 10:1–48. This passage does not have food as its central theme, but Gentiles. In this passage, Kefa (Peter) had a strange dream:

> And he became hungry and wanted something to eat, but while they were preparing it, he fell into a trance and saw the heavens opened and something like a great sheet descending, being let down by its four corners upon the earth. In it were all kinds of animals and reptiles and birds of the air. And there came a voice to him: "Rise, Peter [Kefa]; kill and eat." But Peter [Kefa] said, "By no means, Lord; for I have never eaten anything that is common or unclean." And the voice came to him again a second time, "What God has made clean, do not call common." This happened three times, and the thing was taken up at once to heaven (Acts 10:10–16).

First, note that Kefa did not actually eat from the animals in the vision. The second point to observe is that Kefa at first did not understand the meaning of the dream:

> Now while Peter [Kefa] was inwardly perplexed as to what the vision that he had seen might mean, behold, the men who were sent by Cornelius,

---

§   Geza Vermes points out that if Yeshua was really teaching that all foods are clean, then one of his right-hand men, Kefa (Peter), never learned the lesson. Kefa declares in Acts 10:13–15 that he never ate "common or unclean" animals in his life. (Geza Vermes, *Christian Beginnings: From Nazareth to Nicaea* [New Haven, CT: Yale University Press, 2013], pp. 52–53.)

having made inquiry for Simon's house, stood at the gate (Acts 10:17).

And while Peter [Kefa] was pondering the vision, the Spirit said to him, "Behold, three men are looking for you" (Acts 10:19).

It seems that if God were telling Kefa that he is now free to eat unclean animals, he would have understood this without much difficulty. Notice that when Kefa comprehended the vision, he did not say, "God has shown me that I should not call any person *or any animal* common or unclean." It is clear that Kefa understood the vision to be about men only, and not about food:[3]

> And he said to them, "You yourselves know how unlawful it is for a Jew to associate with or to visit anyone of another nation, but God has shown me that I should not call any person common or unclean" (Acts 10:28).

> So Peter [Kefa] opened his mouth and said: "Truly I understand that God shows no partiality, but in every nation anyone who fears him and does what is right is acceptable to him" (Acts 10:34–35).

Why, then, did God give Kefa this vision about unclean animals?

Periodically in Scripture, as Gary Smalley and John Trent would say in *The Language of Love*, God uses "emotional word pictures" to convict someone of a particular error. The classic example of a provocative, emotional word picture in the Scriptures is the word picture presented by the prophet Nathan to King David after he committed the sin with Bathsheba. Nathan pulled David into a story about a rich man, a poor man, and the poor man's lamb, and convicted David of his horrible sin (2 Samuel 12:1–10).[4] Likewise, since Kefa was hungry and had kept the kosher food commandments all of his life, he, too, was emotionally drawn into the message that God was giving to him about Gentiles.

### Galatians 2:11–12

> But when Cephas [Kefa] came to Antioch, I opposed him to his face, because he stood condemned. For before certain men came from James [Ya'akov], he was eating with the Gentiles; but when they came he drew back and separated himself, fearing the circumcision party.

In Galatians 2:11–16, most commentators say that Sha'ul's

criticism of Kefa was over his refusal to eat nonkosher food when he was with the Gentiles. Nevertheless, I do not believe that food is the issue here. The circumcision party, those who were saying that the Gentiles must be circumcised in order for them to be saved, intimidated Kefa. We already know from the passage we just studied, Acts 10:28, that it was unlawful, according to the tradition, for a man who is a Jew to intermingle with a foreigner: "And he said to them, 'You yourselves know how unlawful it is for a Jew to associate with or to visit anyone of another nation, but God has shown me that I should not call any person common or unclean'" (Acts 10:28). The circumcision party must have upheld this tradition in this particular instance. Since these Gentiles were not circumcised, the circumcision party probably was hard on Kefa for socializing with them. Keep in mind that people often associated with each other during meals.

I believe the conflict in this passage was over the association and not over the food that was being eaten. It is inconsistent with the rest of the Scriptures to suggest that Kefa or Sha'ul ate nonkosher foods. If one says that Sha'ul ate nonkosher foods one would have to call him a liar, for in at least two passages Sha'ul affirmed that he followed the Torah— Acts 21:21–26, which we have viewed previously, and Acts 25:7–8:

> When he had arrived, the Jews who had come down from Jerusalem stood around him, bringing many and serious charges against him that they could not prove. Paul [Sha'ul] argued in his defense, "Neither against the law of the Jews, nor against the temple, nor against Caesar have I committed any offense."

Sha'ul was neither a liar nor a hypocrite. He could have criticized Kefa for not wanting to associate with Gentiles, but not for keeping kosher.

### Romans 14:2

> One person believes he may eat anything, while the weak person eats only vegetables.

Some have used this Romans passage to suggest that those who continue to follow the Torah instructions are the weaker brothers in the faith. After reviewing the full context of Romans 14:1–23, however, it is clear the weaker brothers in faith were putting particular non-Torah restrictions on their oral intake. Sha'ul argued that these petty non-Torah restrictions were not worth fighting over. He did not nullify the kosher food laws. I have already discussed this passage in chapter 5 in my defense of Shabbat.[5]

**1 Timothy 4:4–5**

For every creature of God *is* good, and nothing is to be refused if it is received with thanksgiving; for it is sanctified by the word of God and prayer (1 Timothy 4:4–5, New King James Version).

After reading this verse in 1 Timothy, we come away with the idea that every creature God created is good for eating. At first this verse seems devastating to those who would maintain that the kosher food laws have not been abolished, but if we investigate the full context of this verse, it also does not do away with the kosher food laws:

Now the Spirit expressly says that in latter times some will depart from the faith, giving heed to deceiving spirits and doctrines of demons, speaking lies in hypocrisy, having their own conscience seared with a hot iron, forbidding to marry, *and commanding* to abstain from foods which God created to be received with thanksgiving by those who believe and know the truth. For every creature of God *is* good, and nothing is to be refused if it is received with thanksgiving; for it is sanctified by the word of God and prayer (1 Timothy 4:1–5, New King James Version).

Verse 1 states that some will fall away from the faith because they will be paying attention to "deceiving spirits" and "doctrines of demons." Could Sha'ul possibly be referring to the Torah instruction in this way? In verse 3, Sha'ul defined the philosophy of these men more clearly. They were men who abstained from marriage. They certainly did not find this teaching in the Torah. They also abstained from certain foods that God had created. As we saw already in Romans 14, some men were apparently advocating abstention from meat altogether, as well as from wine (Romans 14:2, 14:21). The Torah commandments restricted neither of these for the average person. How do we know what creatures are fit for eating? Verse 5 tells us that it is those creatures that are sanctified by means of the word of

God and prayer. The Scriptures, mainly the Torah, still define what creatures are to be eaten. The Torah still delineates what food is. Does verse 5, however, suggest that we can make a pig kosher by praying over it? The typical Christian grace before meals would suggest that this could be done: "Bless this food for our bodies." The Jewish prayer before the meal, however, is blessing and thanking God for what He has given to us, not blessing the food.¶

The kosher food laws have already defined what foods are appropriate to eat. This passage in 1 Timothy was not proclaiming that we can now eat any creature that we want. It was warning against men who were advocating certain ascetic practices that are not the teachings of God, such as abstaining from marriage, meats, and wine.[6]

### 1 Corinthians 10:27

If one of the unbelievers invites you to dinner and you are disposed to go, eat whatever is set before you without raising any question on the ground of conscience.

Another misunderstood passage is 1 Corinthians 10:27. I know of some Gentile believers who purposely served pork to their Messianic Jewish friends because of this verse. The full context of this passage from 1 Corinthians 10:14–33, however, is clearly speaking about food sacrificed to idols, not unclean animals:

Therefore, my beloved, flee from idolatry (1 Corinthians 10:14).

What do I imply then? That food offered to idols is anything, or that an idol is anything? No, I imply that what pagans sacrifice they offer to demons and not to God. I do not want you to be participants with demons. You cannot drink the cup of the Lord and the cup of demons. You cannot partake of the table of the Lord and the table of demons (1 Corinthians 10:19–21).

Eat whatever is sold in the meat market without raising any question

---

¶   The Jewish blessing before eating bread is, "Blessed are You, YHVH our God, King of the universe, who brings forth bread from the earth." This is most likely the blessing given by Yeshua when he fed the multitude with bread and fish (Mark 8:6).

on the ground of conscience. For "the earth is the Lord's, and the fullness thereof." If one of the unbelievers invites you to dinner and you are disposed to go, eat whatever is set before you without raising any question on the ground of conscience. But if someone says to you, "This has been offered in sacrifice," then do not eat it, for the sake of the one who informed you, and for the sake of conscience (1 Corinthians 10:25–28).

Sha'ul was informing the believers here that if the meat of a clean animal was placed before them, they should not question whether it had been sacrificed to idols or not. He was not saying if a hot dog is placed before you, do not question whether the brand is Oscar Mayer or Aaron Kosher. In this passage, Sha'ul was not giving us the freedom to violate the Torah instructions so as not to offend a brother or a nonbeliever. For instance, if I go to someone's house for supper, and they say that we are going to have a séance for the evening entertainment or a wife-swapping experience, I would be forced to offend that person and say: "I am sorry, brother, but I cannot violate the Torah." Why should my response be any different if unclean animals are set before me?

### 1 Corinthians 8:8

Food will not commend us to God. We are no worse off if we do not eat, and no better off if we do.

The context of this verse is all of 1 Corinthians chapter 8. This chapter, like the 1 Corinthians 10 passage, has meat sacrificed to idols as its subject, and nothing more:

Now concerning food offered to idols: we know that "all of us possess knowledge." This "knowledge" puffs up, but love builds up (1 Corinthians 8:1).

Therefore, as to the eating of food offered to idols, we know that "an idol has no real existence," and that "there is no God but one" (1 Corinthians 8:4).

For if anyone sees you who have knowledge eating in an idol's temple, will he not be encouraged, if his conscience is weak, to eat food offered to idols? (1 Corinthians 8:10).

Sha'ul was saying in this passage not to offend a weaker brother over the matter of meat sacrificed to idols. He was not giving us permission to ingest unclean animals.

### Colossians 2:16–17

Therefore let no one pass judgment on you in questions of food and drink, or with regard to a festival or a new moon or a Sabbath. These are a shadow of the things to come, but the substance belongs to Christ [Messiah].

I have already reviewed this passage in the previous chapter dealing with the seventh day Shabbat. Sha'ul was also not repealing or condemning the kosher food laws here.[7]

I have attempted to restore the context of these eight New Testament passages. The New Testament does not annul the kosher food laws found in the Torah. This knowledge should give us confidence that the Torah instructions have not been abrogated. We can still wrestle with them:

"For I am the LORD [YHVH] who brought you up out of the land of Egypt to be your God. You shall therefore be holy, for I am holy." This is the law about beast and bird and every living creature that moves through the waters and every creature that swarms on the ground, to make a distinction between the unclean and the clean and between the living creature that may be eaten and the living creature that may not be eaten (Leviticus 11:45–47).

An old Messianic Jewish bumper sticker once proclaimed, "Yeshua made me kosher." Now, we have the responsibility to keep kosher.

God expected people of faith to live in community. The next three chapters will describe features of His holy community

## (Endnotes)

1   Thanks to Farrokh Patell for this story.

2   David H. Stern, *Jewish New Testament Commentary* (Clarksville, MD: Jewish New Testament Publications, 1992), pp. 92–94. Ariel and D'vorah Berkowitz, *Take Hold: Embracing Our Divine Inheritance with Israel* (Littleton, CO: First Fruits of Zion, 1998), pp. 199–201.

3   David H. Stern, *Jewish New Testament Commentary*, pp. 257–259. Ariel and D'vorah Berkowitz, *Take Hold: Embracing Our Divine Inheritance with Israel*, pp. 201–203.

4   Gary Smalley and John Trent, *The Language of Love: A Powerful Way to Maximize Insight, Intimacy and Understanding* (New York: Pocket Books, 1991), pp. 58–65.

5   David H. Stern, *Jewish New Testament Commentary*, pp. 431–436.

6   Ibid., pp. 643–645.

7   Ibid., pp. 611–612.

# Chapter 7: God's Holy Community*

## Who Makes up God's Holy Community?

All of us can appreciate the beauty in a bouquet of flowers. Our experience tells us, however, that after a few days, the bouquet's beauty begins to fade, and no new flowers grow from the cut plants. I once took a plant physiology course in college. Unfortunately, I cannot remember many facts, but I do remember one profound truth. Most flowering plants have and need roots. Roots stabilize a plant and allow it to have better access to life-sustaining water and nutrients. Cut plants in a bouquet no longer have their roots, allowing corruption to eventually overtake them.

The traditional Gentile Christian church has established itself as God's holy community today. However, the traditional Gentile Christian church has separated itself from its Jewish roots. Like an old, wilted bouquet of flowers, this community is becoming dried and withered, and I fear it may be beyond the point of recovery unless some drastic steps are taken to plug it back into its root system. What should God's holy community look like today? What should have been the relationship between Gentile believers and the Jewish people?

There are different ideas today concerning the makeup of God's holy community. Traditional Jews would say that only Jews make up

---

* "Holy community" is the terminology used by Ariel and D'vorah Berkowitz. (Ariel and D'vorah Berkowitz, *Take Hold: Embracing Our Divine Inheritance with Israel* [Littleton, CO: First Fruits of Zion, 1998], p. 140.)

God's holy community.[1] Various Christian groups would have other ideas. Some would say that Israel was once God's people, but when they sinned and rejected Yeshua, God rejected them. They would maintain that Gentile believers now have become God's holy community, thus replacing Israel. The blessings in the Bible to Israel now fall on the church, but the curses remain for the Jews. This idea is commonly known as replacement theology.[2] Another Christian view is that God has two distinct holy communities—Israel and the church. They would say that each has a different function in different periods of history. This model is called dispensational theology. Some would even say that Israel is the earthly people of God and the church the heavenly people.[3] There are many variations on these themes, and reading about them is dizzying.[4] Can we get closer to the simple truth by reexamining the Scriptures?

## Israel Is God's Foundational Holy Community

From the beginning of the book of Genesis, we see God separating out a distinct people or "seed" for Himself. His plan is to use this seed to restore His original blessings to humanity.[5] It is important to realize that He does not choose an established nation. This seed runs from Adam, to Seth, to Noah, to Shem, to Peleg, and eventually through the patriarchs Abraham, Isaac, and Jacob:

> Now the LORD [YHVH] said to Abram, "Go from your country and your kindred and your father's house to the land that I will show you. And I will make of you a great nation, and I will bless you and make your name great, so that you will be a blessing. I will bless those who bless you, and him who dishonors you I will curse, and in you all the families of the earth shall be blessed (Genesis 12:1–3).

Ultimately, the Messiah comes from this line.

I have some good news and bad news for Gentiles, those not from the above line. The bad news is that the Gentiles for many years were separated from Messiah, "alienated from the commonwealth of Israel and strangers to the covenants of promise, having no hope and without God in the world" (Ephesians 2:12). That is awfully bad news.

In fact, all the covenants made to mankind after the covenant God made with Noah were made only to the people of Israel, including the new covenant reported by Jeremiah:[6] "Behold, the days are coming, declares the LORD [YHVH], when I will make a new covenant with the house of Israel and the house of Judah" (Jeremiah 31:31). Being outside of the covenant people, the house of Israel and the house of Judah, was not a good thing.

The good news, however, is that God, in His mercy, made a way for the Gentiles also to come near to Himself: "But now, you who were once far off have been brought near through the shedding of the Messiah's blood" (Ephesians 2:13, *Complete Jewish Bible*). The Messiah's death did more than just bring the Gentiles closer to God. It also gave them a way to become a part of God's people:

> For he himself is our shalom—he has made us both one and has broken down the *m'chitzah* which divided us by destroying in his own body the enmity occasioned by the Torah, with its commands set forth in the form of ordinances. He did this in order to create in union with himself from the two groups a single new humanity and thus make shalom, and in order to reconcile to God both in a single body by being executed on a stake as a criminal and thus in himself killing that enmity. Also, when he came, he announced as Good News shalom to you far off and shalom to those nearby, news that through him we both have access in one Spirit to the Father. So then, you are no longer foreigners and strangers. On the contrary, you are fellow-citizens with God's people and members of God's family (Ephesians 2:14–19, *Complete Jewish Bible*).

It is implied that through the Messiah, Gentiles can now be brought in, to become fellow citizens with Israel. As David Stern translates, they can enjoy the "national life of Israel" and no longer be "foreigners to the covenants."[7] In the next chapter, Sha'ul calls this the hidden mystery of the Messiah, "that in union with the Messiah and through the Good News the Gentiles were to be joint heirs, a joint body and joint sharers with the Jews in what God has promised" (Ephesians 3:6, *Complete Jewish Bible*).

In Galatians 3, Sha'ul relates the same information: "Also, if you belong to the Messiah, you are seed of Avraham and heirs according to the promise" (Galatians 3:29, *Complete Jewish Bible*). Gentiles, when they believe, are joined to the nation of Israel. They do not become some new independent entity called "The New Testament Church," and they do not establish a new religion. Yeshua, Kefa (Peter), and Sha'ul did not leave the biblical religion of Israel and become "Christians." God's original plan that it will be through the "seed of Abraham" that the families of the earth are to be blessed is still going forward. The mystery that was not understood at first was that through Yeshua, Gentiles could also join the existing nation of Israel.[8]

## Olive Tree Theology

Now, some believers might be saying, "Wait a minute! How could believing Gentiles ever have a relationship with nonbelieving Jews? Believers and nonbelievers could never be yoked together" (2 Corinthians 6:14–15). Many think that any relationship between believing Gentiles and the nation of Israel can only exist through the small remnant of Jewish believers.

Sha'ul gives us a model in Romans 11 that helps us to understand this relationship better. In *Messianic Jewish Manifesto*, David Stern calls this "olive tree theology":[9]

> If the dough offered as first fruits is holy, so is the whole lump, and if the root is holy, so are the branches. But if some of the branches were broken off, and you [Gentiles], although a wild olive shoot, were grafted in among the others and now share in the nourishing root of the olive tree, do not be arrogant toward the branches. If you are, remember it is not you who support the root, but the root that supports you. Then you will say, "Branches were broken off so that I might be grafted in." That is true. They were broken off because of their unbelief, but you stand fast through faith. So do not become proud, but fear. For if God did not spare the natural branches, neither will he spare you. Note then the kindness and the severity of God: severity toward those who have fallen, but God's kindness to you, provided you continue in his kindness. Otherwise you too will be cut off. And even they, if they do not continue in their unbelief, will be grafted in, for God has the power to graft them in again. For if you were cut from what is by nature a wild

olive tree, and grafted, contrary to nature, into a cultivated olive tree, how much more will these, the natural branches, be grafted back into their own olive tree (Romans 11:16–24).

In this model, there is only one cultivated olive tree. There is only one "called out"[10] people of God. Most commentators agree that this tree is growing from the roots of the patriarchs, Abraham, Isaac, and Jacob, for Abraham is called the father of us all in Romans chapter 4.[11] Therefore, Abraham and the other patriarchs are the roots and the first fruits of our faith. Since this tree is growing from the roots of the patriarchs, it represents the one and only Israel.[12]

At this point, it is critical to recognize that there are two levels to this model. The model represents Israel as a *nation* on one level and *individuals* of all the nations on another level.[13]

As the olive tree model symbolizes Israel as a nation, recognize that it is common for God to deal with people on a national level rather than on an individual level. For instance, the sacrifice for Yom Kippur was a sacrifice for the nation of Israel as a whole, not specifically for individuals (Leviticus 16:34). In addition, we see God dealing with other nations as a whole, such as Assyria and Egypt (Isaiah 19:23–25).[14†]

It is important to remember, when looking at this model, that God made unconditional, covenantal promises to Abraham concerning his descendants, the nation of Israel (Genesis 15, Genesis 17:1–14, Genesis 22:15–18). This same covenant was reaffirmed to Isaac (Genesis 26:1–5) and Jacob (Genesis 28:10–17, Genesis 35:9–13). The covenant is an everlasting covenant. The covenant is extended to the nation as a whole. The nation of Israel could do nothing to lose the covenant promises, "For the gifts and the calling of God are irrevocable" (Romans 11:29).[15] When Israel sinned, she suffered. The

---

† Various authors claim that this prophecy concerning Assyria and Egypt in Isaiah is speaking about the Arab peoples currently living in the previous Assyrian and Egyptian land boundaries. However, the descendants of the historical Egyptians (the Copts) and Assyrians live today. Both communities are Christian and followers of YHVH. I suspect this prophecy is concerning them.

nation of Israel was scattered among the nations and was persecuted at every turn in the road, as was predicted in Deuteronomy 28:15–68. Nevertheless, the covenant to the nation of Israel remains in force, even to this day.

The holy community or nation represented in this olive tree model is composed of three different types of branches. Some branches are the natural branches still attached to the tree, which represent the believing Jews. Another group of branches is the cut-off natural branches, which represent the nonbelieving Jews. According to David Stern, this second group of branches has been removed from the "living sap of the tree." Nevertheless, God is still preserving this group of branches in their detached state. They are not left to dry out and decay, losing all potential to be used again, for they remain in a condition where they can be grafted back into their own tree. They are still part of the tree—part of the nation of Israel. The third group of branches is the grafted-in wild branches, which represents the believing Gentiles.[16]

In this nation-level model, when Gentiles believe, they are grafted into the nation of Israel. They join that existing, ancient, "called out" covenant people of God, whether most in Israel believe or not.[17]

The second level of this olive tree model concerns individuals, specifically believers and nonbelievers. The attached individual branches are the only ones who will obtain salvation, through Yeshua's death. The separated branches, as individuals, will not be saved if they continue to reject the atonement of Yeshua. This certainty will follow even if they are physical descendants of Abraham.[18]

## The Commonwealth Concept

From Ephesians chapter 2, Daniel Juster and David Stern have developed an analogy that also helps to clarify this issue, using the concept of a commonwealth.[19] Juster calls this the "commonwealth concept."[20] They represent the nation of Israel by Great Britain. The Gentiles, who are brought near to God through Yeshua, represent members of the British Commonwealth of Nations. Imagine that Great Britain did not recognize the reigning English monarch, even though she was the rightful queen, but that all of the other Commonwealth nations did continue to acknowledge the English queen. This illustration would be analogous to Israel not recognizing Yeshua as the promised Jewish Messiah while many Gentiles do acknowledge him. In this circumstance, it would be wrong to say that Great Britain was no longer a member of the Commonwealth when in fact it would still be the central member among equals. The other Commonwealth countries also would remain bound to Great Britain, even at this time when Great Britain did not recognize their queen. The job of the other Commonwealth countries at this point would be to convince individual Englishmen, and their government in Great Britain, to honor the queen.

The nation of Israel is still God's chosen people, whether most of the nation believes at this time or not. Most Jewish believers have never had a problem considering themselves as a part of the nation of Israel, even though most of the nation does not believe at this time. In the same way, Gentile believers should consider themselves bound to the current nation of Israel, even though most of the nation today do not believe.

Sha'ul says in Romans 11:

> Lest you be wise in your own sight, I do not want you to be unaware of this mystery, brothers: a partial hardening has come upon Israel, until the fullness of the Gentiles has come in. And in this way all Israel will be saved, as it is written, "The Deliverer will come from Zion, he will banish ungodliness from Jacob"; "and this will be my covenant with them when I take away their sins" (Romans 11:25–27).

This prophecy confirms that Israel as a nation will one day believe—a promise on which we can rely. We are allowed to identify Israel as the perpetual backbone of the olive tree, even in these days when she does not believe.

## Do Gentile Believers Become Jews?

If Gentiles become bound to the nation of Israel, do the Gentile believers then become Jews? The Gentile believer, grafted in, has the same rights as a Jewish citizen and is a full member of God's household, but this person does not become a true physical descendant of Abraham.[21] The New Testament discouraged Gentiles from trying to become Jews:

> Only let each person lead the life that the Lord has assigned to him, and to which God has called him. This is my rule in all the churches. Was anyone at the time of his call already circumcised? Let him not seek to remove the marks of circumcision. Was anyone at the time of his call uncircumcised? Let him not seek circumcision. For neither circumcision counts for anything nor uncircumcision, but keeping the commandments of God. Each one should remain in the condition in which he was called (1 Corinthians 7:17–20).

Physical circumcision is clearly a rite not required for Gentiles in order to be saved. We see this also discussed in Acts chapter 15. Moreover, in the olive tree model in Romans 11, the Gentile believers are still recognized as "wild branches." They are not transformed into natural branches.[22]

Some believers would say that the Jewish distinction was done away with for those in Yeshua, since Sha'ul writes in Galatians 3:26–28:

> For in union with the Messiah, you are all children of God through this trusting faithfulness; because as many of you as were immersed into the Messiah have clothed yourselves with the Messiah, in whom there is neither Jew nor Gentile, neither slave nor freeman, neither male nor female; for in union with the Messiah Yeshua, you are all one. Also, if you belong to the Messiah, you are seed of Avraham and heirs according to the promise (Galatians 3:26–29, *Complete Jewish Bible*).

However, just as there are still distinctions between males and females, and just as there remained, at the time of Sha'ul's writing, differences between slaves and freemen, there are still distinctions between Jews and Gentiles.[23] Even though we are all full members of God's household, and all of us, Jew or Gentile, are equal before God, all of us have different responsibilities.

One of the best examples of one subset in a nation having different responsibilities from other equal members of that same nation can be seen among the priests and common people in ancient Israel. Only the Levites were allowed to serve in the Temple, but in the eyes of God they were not more superior than members of any other tribe. Jews and Gentiles, though equal before God, seem to have been given different acts of service before God (more about this in chapter 9).

To summarize, the wild olive branches, grafted into the cultivated olive tree, create an expanded "seed" of Abraham. These previously separated groups existing without enmity are brought together through the Messiah as one new humanity or new man. Realize, however, that the new man is the same old cultivated olive tree now expanded surprisingly with wild branches. The Gentile believers are blessed as they follow the Messiah Yeshua, Abraham's greatest descendant. They also are blessed when they come alongside the original "called out" people of God—Israel—and are grafted in. God clearly promises that all the families of the earth will be blessed in Abraham. From God's promise to Abraham that "I will bless those who bless you," I believe that Gentiles and even individual Jews, who bless the nation of Israel, are blessed.

Therefore, the real olive tree is not the lone nation of Israel composed only of Jews. The real olive tree is not the lone New Testament church devoid of Jews. Moreover, the real olive tree is not two distinct trees, Israel and the New Testament church, going their separate ways into the future. The true olive tree, God's holy community, is a tree growing from the roots of the patriarchs, composed of three different types of branches, where Jew and Gentile are a new humanity, a new commonwealth, a new family:

> Let not the foreigner who has joined himself to the LORD [YHVH] say, "The LORD [YHVH] will surely separate me from his people"; and let not the eunuch say, "Behold, I am a dry tree." For thus says the LORD [YHVH]: "To the eunuchs who keep my Sabbaths, who choose the things that please me and hold fast my covenant, I will give in my house and within my walls a monument and a name better than sons and daughters; I will give them an everlasting name that shall not be cut off. And the foreigners who join themselves to the LORD [YHVH], to minister to him, to love the name of the LORD [YHVH], and to be his

servants, everyone who keeps the Sabbath and does not profane it, and holds fast my covenant—these I will bring to my holy mountain, and make them joyful in my house of prayer; their burnt offerings and their sacrifices will be accepted on my altar; for my house shall be called a house of prayer for all peoples." The Lord GOD [YHVH], who gathers the outcasts of Israel, declares, "I will gather yet others to him besides those already gathered" (Isaiah 56:3–8).

Even if Gentiles can belong to God's holy community, do they have the responsibility to uphold the Torah instructions, or are these instructions only for the Jews?

# (Endnotes)

1 David H. Stern, *Jewish New Testament Commentary* (Clarksville, MD: Jewish New Testament Publications, 1992), p. 415.

2 Ibid., p. 415.

3 Ibid., p. 416.

4 Arnold G Fruchtenbaum, *Israelology: The Missing Link in Systematic Theology* (Tustin, CA: Ariel Ministries Press, 1993).

5 John H. Sailhamer, *Genesis*, Vol. 2 of *The Expositor's Bible Commentary*, ed. by Frank E. Gaebelein, 12 vols. (Grand Rapids, MI: Zondervan Publishing House, 1990), pp. 70–71.

6 Ariel and D'vorah Berkowitz, *Take Hold: Embracing Our Divine Inheritance with Israel* (Littleton, CO: First Fruits of Zion, 1998), p. 37.

7 David H. Stern, *Jewish New Testament Commentary*, pp. 582–583.

8 Ariel and D'vorah Berkowitz, *Take Hold: Embracing Our Divine Inheritance with Israel*, pp. 109–127. Daniel Juster, *Growing to Maturity (A Messianic Jewish Guide)* (Gaithersburg, MD: UMJC, 1982), pp. 252–255. David H. Stern, *Jewish New Testament Commentary*, pp. 581–588.

9 David H. Stern, *Messianic Jewish Manifesto* (Jerusalem: Jewish New Testament Publications, 1988), p. 47.

10 Ariel and D'vorah Berkowitz, *Take Hold: Embracing Our Divine Inheritance with Israel*, pp. 138–140.

11 David H. Stern, *Messianic Jewish Manifesto*, p. 49.

12 Ibid., p. 49.

13 Ibid., p. 56.

14 Ibid., p. 56.

15 Daniel Juster, *Jewish Roots: A Foundation of Biblical Theology* (Rockville, MD: DAVAR Publishing Co., 1986), pp. 37–39.

16 David H. Stern, *Messianic Jewish Manifesto*, pp. 55–56.

17 Ariel and D'vorah Berkowitz, *Take Hold: Embracing Our Divine Inheritance with Israel*, pp. 103–107.

18 David H. Stern, *Messianic Jewish Manifesto*, p. 56.

19 Daniel Juster, *Growing to Maturity (A Messianic Jewish Guide)*, pp. 253–255. David H. Stern, *Messianic Jewish Manifesto*, p. 57.

20  Daniel Juster, *Growing to Maturity (A Messianic Jewish Guide)*, pp. 254.

21  Ariel and D'vorah Berkowitz, *Take Hold: Embracing Our Divine Inheritance with Israel*, p. 107.

22  Ibid., p. 107.

23  Daniel Juster, *Jewish Roots: A Foundation of Biblical Theology*, pp. 38–39.

# Chapter 8: Gentiles and the Torah*

## Is Torah Observance Limited to Israel?

In the days of Moses, Israel was to separate itself from the surrounding pagan, idol-worshipping nations, to protect itself from foreign influence. In the book of Numbers, the pagan prophet Balaam describes this separation: "For from the top of the crags I see him, from the hills I behold him; behold, a people dwelling alone, and not counting itself among the nations!" (Numbers 23:9). When Israel did not maintain this separation, it fell away from God. For instance, when the people of Israel began to mingle with the daughters of Moab, they became attracted to the Baal of Peor, a foreign god (Numbers 25:1–3).

As discussed in chapter 3, the separation of Israel from the other nations came from Israel's willingness to follow God's instructions in the Torah. Undoubtedly, Torah observance enriched the nation of Israel through the centuries. Many Jews would argue that the Torah instructions should remain the privileged possession of Israel. Gentile Christians customarily reject the Torah instructions. What relationship should Gentile believers have to the Torah?

In the last chapter, I tried to show that a bond exists today between the nation of Israel and Gentile believers. Even though Gentile believers do not become physical descendants of Abraham when they

---

\* By the word "Torah," I am mainly focusing on the instructions, commandments, statutes, and judgments given to us by God in the Five Books of Moses.

believe, they still have been grafted into the olive tree of Israel and have become members of the Commonwealth of Israel. Today, however, the Jewish people remain wary of Gentiles believers. Unfortunately, much of this distrust stems from "Christian" anti-Semitism. The Jewish people tend to keep Gentile believers at a distance and do not typically encourage Torah observance for this group. Jewish believers also sometimes discourage Torah observance for Gentile believers, and some even bar Gentile believers from worshipping in Messianic synagogues.

God-fearing Jews should still separate themselves from the pagan elements in our society. Since true Gentile believers are no longer pagans, however, I would suggest that it is inappropriate for Jews today to apply this ancient principle of separation toward them. Jews should not shun Gentile believers who are trying to attach themselves to the God of Israel and the people of Israel. More specifically, Jews should encourage true Gentile believers to follow the Torah, allowing the Torah to separate Gentile believers also from the pagan elements in our society.

## Gentiles in the Past Joined Themselves to Israel and the Torah

At the time of Moses, when the people of Israel were to separate themselves from the surrounding pagan nations through observance of the Torah, some Gentiles did have a relationship with Israel. In Hebrew, there are four different words to designate Gentiles in the Torah. Each word seems to offer a different level of relationship with Israel: 1) the *ger* who had the closest relation, 2) the *toshav* with a little less, 3) the *nechar*, a foreigner without a relationship, and 4) the *zur* who was often Israel's enemy.[1] Usually, in different English translations, all of these Hebrew words are translated into the same English word. Depending on the English translation, they are all either "strangers," "foreigners," "sojourners," or "aliens."

The *ger* was a Gentile who would join himself to the nation of Israel and the God of Israel and keep most of the precepts of the Torah. Torah observance was not only allowed, but also required for this group of people:

> If a stranger [*ger*] shall sojourn with you and would keep the Passover to the LORD [YHVH], let all his males be circumcised. Then he may come near and keep it; he shall be as a native of the land. But no uncircumcised person shall eat of it. There shall be one law for the native and for the stranger [*ger*] who sojourns among you (Exodus 12:48–49).

> And if a stranger [*ger*] is sojourning with you, or anyone is living permanently among you, and he wishes to offer a food offering, with a pleasing aroma to the LORD [YHVH], he shall do as you do. For the assembly, there shall be one statute for you and for the stranger [*ger*] who sojourns with you, a statute forever throughout your generations. You and the sojourner [*ger*] shall be alike before the LORD [YHVH]. One law and one rule shall be for you and for the stranger [*ger*] who sojourns with you (Numbers 15:14–16).

> You shall have the same rule for the sojourner [*ger*] and for the native, for I am the LORD [YHVH] your God (Leviticus 24:22).

In almost every way, this ancient group of foreigners was treated as the native-born in Israel when it came to following the Torah.

## Future Gentiles Will Join Themselves to Israel and the Torah

In a future day also, Isaiah 56:3–8 tells us, covenant-keeping Gentiles will similarly bind themselves to YHVH and His people.† They will not be separated from the Torah.[2] We looked at this passage at the end of the last chapter:

> Let not the foreigner who has joined himself to the LORD [YHVH] say, "The LORD [YHVH] will surely separate me from his people";

---

† Some Jewish believers argue that these prophecies tying Gentiles to the Torah speak of a future time and do not apply to Gentiles in the present. Therefore, they would say, Gentiles today should not be Torah observant. These same individuals, however, see Israel's return to the land of Israel today as a fulfillment of prophecy, even though many details of those prophecies have not yet come to fruition.

and let not the eunuch say, "Behold, I am a dry tree." For thus says the LORD [YHVH]: "To the eunuchs who keep my Sabbaths, who choose the things that please me and hold fast my covenant, I will give in my house and within my walls a monument and a name better than sons and daughters; I will give them an everlasting name that shall not be cut off. And the foreigners who join themselves to the LORD [YHVH], to minister to him, to love the name of the LORD [YHVH], and to be his servants, everyone who keeps the Sabbath and does not profane it, and holds fast my covenant—these I will bring to my holy mountain, and make them joyful in my house of prayer; their burnt offerings and their sacrifices will be accepted on my altar; for my house shall be called a house of prayer for all peoples." The Lord GOD [YHVH], who gathers the outcasts of Israel, declares, "I will gather yet others to him besides those already gathered" (Isaiah 56:3–8).

What is curious here is that the Hebrew word for "foreigner" in this Isaiah passage is *ben ha-nechar* ("son of the *nechar*"), which usually designates someone without a close relationship with Israel or YHVH. Therefore, in a future day, even Gentiles who never had a relationship with Israel or with YHVH will be zealously seeking one.

Ariel and D'vorah Berkowitz wrote a book entitled *Take Hold*, in reference to another future prophecy out of Zechariah in which Gentiles will be grabbing onto Jews by their *tzitziyot* (fringes) because they will want to follow the God of Israel and the Torah:

"Thus says the LORD [YHVH] of hosts: Peoples shall yet come, even the inhabitants of many cities. The inhabitants of one city shall go to another, saying, 'Let us go at once to entreat the favor of the LORD [YHVH] and to seek the LORD [YHVH] of hosts; I myself am going.' Many peoples and strong nations shall come to seek the LORD [YHVH] of hosts in Jerusalem and to entreat the favor of the LORD [YHVH]. Thus says the LORD [YHVH] of hosts: In those days ten men from the nations of every tongue shall take hold of the robe [*kanaf*—corner] of a Jew, saying, 'Let us go with you, for we have heard that God is with you'" (Zechariah 8:20–23).

By grabbing the *tzitziyot* or corners, they will be holding the remembrance of the Torah (Numbers 15:37–40).[3]

## Present Day Gentiles Should Be Able to Join Themselves to Israel and the Torah

The bottom line is if there was no separation of the true Gentile believer from the Torah in the past, and if there will be no separation of the true Gentile believer from the Torah in the future, surely there should be no separation of the true Gentile believer from the Torah in the present.[4] The Torah was to protect Israel from the influence of pagans. It was not to barricade other followers of God from Israel.

Another purpose for Israel's separation through Torah observance was to allow the people of Israel to be an example to the surrounding nations who needed to see how a nation, separated (or holy) to YHVH, should live:

> See, I have taught you statutes and rules, as the LORD [YHVH] my God commanded me, that you should do them in the land that you are entering to take possession of it. Keep them and do them, for that will be your wisdom and your understanding in the sight of the peoples, who, when they hear all these statutes, will say, 'Surely this great nation is a wise and understanding people.' For what great nation is there that has a god so near to it as the LORD [YHVH] our God is to us, whenever we call upon him? And what great nation is there, that has statutes and rules so righteous as all this law that I set before you today? (Deuteronomy 4:5–8).

Jewish believers Ariel and D'vorah Berkowitz argue that since the righteous statutes and rules in the Torah were to attract the Gentile nations to the God of Israel, it makes no sense to bar devoted Gentile believers from following this great Torah themselves.[5] God's perfect instructions for how men and women should live life to the fullest should be the same for all believers in YHVH.

It is the Mosaic covenant that prescribed Torah observance. Some argue that since God made this covenant with the people of Israel only, Torah observance should only be for Israel. This reasoning is flawed, however, since the new covenant described in Jeremiah 31 was also made to Israel and Judah alone (Jeremiah 31:31–34).[6] Can one say that the new covenant, based on the death of Yeshua for the sins of all humanity, has nothing to do with Gentiles? It is obvious that Gentiles can plug into this new covenant by accepting Yeshua's death and by becoming part of the Commonwealth of Israel. Also, since the result of the new covenant will be the writing of the Torah on the heart, this part also must apply to Gentiles, who accept Yeshua's atoning death. The clear teaching of the Scriptures is:

> Turn to me and be saved, all the ends of the earth! For I am God, and there is no other. By myself I have sworn; from my mouth has gone out in righteousness a word that shall not return: "To me every knee shall bow, every tongue shall swear allegiance" (Isaiah 45:22–23).

The goal is for all of humankind to come back to YHVH.

## Does Acts Chapter 15 Free Gentile Believers from Torah Observance?

Some Jewish believers think Acts chapter 15 teaches that Gentile believers today should not try to adopt the Torah instructions. They feel that the Torah is only for the Jews—allowing Jews to maintain their identity as Jews through this unique responsibility. There is the fear that Jewish believers will lose their distinctiveness if overwhelmed by Torah-keeping Gentiles. Unfortunately, there is also the idea found among some Messianic Jewish congregations that they need to keep up a certain "Jewish" appearance for the traditional Jewish community. What will the nonbelieving Jewish community think if they see many Gentiles behaving like Jews in these Messianic congregations? (My take on this can be found in chapter 9.)

Since Acts chapter 15 is the proof text used by those who would deny Gentile believers the right to Torah observance, we need to look at that text in context. Frankly, if the Jewish believers in Jerusalem were actually saying that Gentile believers have no responsibility to follow the Torah, then they were wrong. However, in fact, the clear message of Acts chapter 15 is introduced at the beginning of the passage: "But some men came down from Judea and were teaching the brothers, 'Unless you are circumcised according to the custom of Moses, you cannot be saved'" (Acts 15:1).

The false teaching circulating among the first believers at the time was that a person could only be saved by performing righteous acts such as circumcision or the Law of Moses. However, there is nothing that one can do to be saved except to acknowledge the atonement of Yeshua. Kefa (Peter) understood that neither they nor their fathers were able to gain their salvation by using the Mosaic Law or circumcision in a legalistic way—a yoke on their necks:

> Why are you putting God to the test by placing a yoke on the neck of the [Gentile] disciples that neither our fathers nor we have been able to bear? But we believe that we will be saved through the grace of the Lord Jesus [Yeshua], just as they will (Acts 15:10–11).

Nevertheless, Kefa was not casting off the Torah instructions for himself or the other Jews. He recognized that obedience to God was essential, but that man's best efforts at obedience cannot win his salvation.

The Jerusalem assembly in Acts does not appear to instruct Gentile believers to forsake the Torah either, but they are set free from the troubling obligation of circumcision. The leader Ya'acov (James) proclaims:

> Therefore my judgment is that we should not trouble those of the Gentiles who turn to God, but should write to them to abstain from the things polluted by idols, and from sexual immorality, and from what has been strangled, and from blood. For from ancient generations Moses has had in every city those who proclaim him, for he is read every Sabbath in the synagogues (Acts 15:19–21).

In verse 20, he gives some basic, entry-level Torah instructions for those Gentiles coming out of paganism. In time, he seems to be telling the Jerusalem community, the Gentiles will keep adding to their Torah instructions as they listen to Moses read in the synagogues every Shabbat.[7]

Sha'ul also discourages Gentiles from trying to become Jewish by being circumcised, but he does not discourage them from following God's instructions in the Torah:

> Only let each person lead the life that the Lord has assigned to him, and to which God has called him. This is my rule in all the churches.

Was anyone at the time of his call already circumcised? Let him not seek to remove the marks of circumcision. Was anyone at the time of his call uncircumcised? Let him not seek circumcision. For neither circumcision counts for anything nor uncircumcision, but keeping the commandments of God (1Corinthians 7:17–19).

Jews do not need to become Gentiles and Gentiles are not required to become Jews. Each group, however, should keep the commandments of God.

The Tanach empowers Gentile believers to keep the Torah, and the New Testament does not rescind this privilege. Genuine Gentile Torah-keepers will not threaten Jewish identity. Israel will remain an identifiable race of people because of the promises of God. There is no justification for separating Gentile believers from God's holy community or the Torah. More specifically, Jewish believers intent on maintaining a Jewish identity in the world should never advocate restraining Gentiles, who are attempting to come closer to God. They should instead keep their focus solely on expanding the population of believing Jews.

The next chapter will explore the different roles of Jews and Gentile believers in community together.

## (Endnotes)

1    Thanks to Elisei Feurdean for this information. "Stranger," *The New International Dictionary of the Bible*, ed. by J. D. Douglas and Merrill C. Tenney (Grand Rapids, MI: Zondervan Publishing House, 1987), pp. 966–967.

2    Ariel and D'vorah Berkowitz, *Take Hold: Embracing Our Divine Inheritance with Israel* (Littleton, CO: First Fruits of Zion, 1998), pp. 65–67.

3    Ibid., pp. 69–74.

4    Ibid., p. 74.

5    Ibid., pp. 45–47.

6    Ibid., p. 37.

7    Ibid., pp. 94–95.

# Chapter 9: The Symbiotic Relationship between Jews and Gentiles

## Defining Symbiotic Relationships

There are many examples in biology of two dissimilar organisms living together in a mutually beneficial relationship. This relationship is called symbiosis. Those greenish plaques often found growing on trees, lichens, are composed of algae and fungi living together as a single unit. The algae produce food for themselves and the fungi through photosynthesis, while the fungi provide structure and support for the algae, putting them into the sunlight. These two organisms live together in a symbiotic relationship. Each helps the other to prosper.

Another symbiotic relationship, not often obvious on the surface, is the relationship between Jews and Gentiles. Each should be assisting the other to flourish. In chapter 7, I tried to demonstrate that God's holy community is made up of both Jews and Gentiles. Even though each group is a full member of God's household, and each group is equal before God, both have different responsibilities. They have been given separate acts of service before God.

## Israel: A Kingdom of Priests to Bless the Families of the Earth

God commissioned the descendants of Abraham, long ago, to bring the other nations of the earth to Himself. We see this in the promise made to Abram in Genesis 12:3:

> Now the LORD [YHVH] said to Abram, "Go from your country and
> your kindred and your father's house to the land that I will show you.
> And I will make of you a great nation, and I will bless you and make
> your name great, so that you will be a blessing. I will bless those who
> bless you, and him who dishonors you I will curse, and in you all the
> families of the earth shall be blessed" (Genesis 12:1–3).

Camped before Mount Sinai, God confirms this promise in Exodus
19:4–6:

> "You yourselves have seen what I did to the Egyptians, and how I bore
> you on eagles' wings and brought you to myself. Now therefore, if you
> will indeed obey my voice and keep my covenant, you shall be my
> treasured possession among all peoples, for all the earth is mine; and
> you shall be to me a kingdom of priests and a holy nation. These are the
> words that you shall speak to the people of Israel."

Unfortunately, the Jews have not become a kingdom of priests
to the other nations.* They have failed God in their responsibility as
"firstborn sons" (Exodus 4:22)—"translating the values" and knowledge
of the Father to His other children.† Regardless of their shortcomings,

---

\* Becoming a kingdom of priests was a job description for Israel, not some
elevated title to puff them up. They would certainly receive honor for a job
well done, but not just for holding the title. They were to help bring all men,
created by God and in the image of God, near to Him.

† This fascinating concept was developed by Rabbi David Fohrman at
AlephBeta. (Rabbi David Fohrman, "Passover: What Does It Mean to Be Chosen?" Segment 8—*What Does It Mean to Be Chosen?*, AlephBeta, accessed June
14, 2015, www.alephbeta.org/course/lecture/what-does-it-mean-to-be-chosen/
autoplay.) The firstborn has a special role in the Torah. For example, after the
Exodus from Egypt, the firstborn males in Israel were to be set apart to YHVH
(Exodus 13:2), most likely to serve in worship. After the golden calf incident,
this role was taken over by the Levites (Numbers 3:12). (John H. Sailhamer,
*The Pentateuch as Narrative* [Grand Rapids, MI: Zondervan Publishing House,
1992], p. 373.) Curiously, in the book of Genesis, the firstborn typically loses his
or her position of prominence to a younger sibling (Cain-Abel, Ishmael-Isaac,
Esau-Jacob, Reuben-Judah). One might wonder if the firstborn, endowed with
a special ability to perform service to YHVH, is under more spiritual attack to

however, God did not take that job away from them, "For the gifts and the calling of God are irrevocable" (Romans 11:29). They still possess the supernatural ability to bring the knowledge of God to the nations.

Occasionally we come across people who seem to have been endowed with an extraordinary set of skills. These people stand head and shoulders above their peers in these skills. One could consider Mozart in music, Michelangelo in art, or Michael Jordan in basketball. God has endowed the Jews with the supernatural ability to communicate the essence of God to the rest of the world. This endowed skill may be why Sha'ul said the good news should go "to the Jew first and also to the Greek" (Romans 1:16).

## Gentiles Are to Restore Israel Through Jealousy

Curiously, Gentile believers have a similar responsibility before YHVH. They are to bring the Jews, who have fallen away from God, back to God:

> But Jeshurun grew fat, and kicked; you grew fat, stout, and sleek; then he forsook God who made him and scoffed at the Rock of his salvation. They stirred him to jealousy with strange gods; with abominations they provoked him to anger. They sacrificed to demons that were no gods, to gods they had never known, to new gods that had come recently, whom your fathers had never dreaded. You were unmindful of the Rock that bore you, and you forgot the God who gave you birth. "The LORD [YHVH] saw it and spurned them, because of the provocation of his sons and his daughters. And he said, "I will hide my face from them; I will see what their end will be, for they are a perverse generation, children in whom is no faithfulness. They have made me jealous with what is no god; they have provoked me to anger with their idols. So I will make them jealous with those who are no people; I will provoke them to anger with a foolish nation"

---

succeed than are others. This potential adversity certainly does not mean that all firstborns will automatically fail; in fact, some studies suggest that firstborns tend to be more successful. (Amber Esping, "Does Birth Order Affect Intelligence?," Human Intelligence, last modified November 7, 2013, www.intelltheory.com/birthOrder.shtml). Firstborns may need to be more vigilant, however.

(Deuteronomy 32:15–21).[1]

The Gentile believers are to do this by making the Jews jealous. Jealousy is an uncomfortable feeling. It is a feeling that can drive people to action.

## An Unusual Symbiotic Relationship

From Romans 11:11–15, we get a glimpse of the interrelated Jewish and Gentile services before God:

> So I ask, did they stumble in order that they might fall? By no means! Rather through their trespass salvation has come to the Gentiles, so as to make Israel jealous. Now if their trespass means riches for the world, and if their failure means riches for the Gentiles, how much more will their full inclusion mean! Now I am speaking to you Gentiles. Inasmuch then as I am an apostle to the Gentiles, I magnify my ministry in order somehow to make my fellow Jews jealous, and thus save some of them. For if their rejection means the reconciliation of the world, what will their acceptance mean but life from the dead? (Romans 11:11–15).

As Gentile believers serve God, through jealousy, they will motivate the Jews to renew their relationship with God. As the Jews accept the atonement of Yeshua, they will orchestrate a supernatural revival among the Gentile nations, "For if their rejection means the reconciliation of the world, what will their acceptance mean but life from the dead?" (Romans 11:11–15). This dual action will ultimately bring a blessing to the whole world according to the promise made to Abraham, "I will bless those who bless you" (Genesis 12:3).[‡] This circumstance where it is the Jew's job to bring the Gentiles closer to God, and the Gentile believer's job to bring the Jews closer to God, places them in a symbiotic relationship.

---

‡   An irony of history is that the Gentile persecutors of the Jews have cursed themselves by postponing the Gentile spiritual renewal that the Jews are to ignite for them. Maybe this outcome partially explains the promise made to Abraham, "Him who dishonors you I will curse" (Genesis 12:3).

## Jealousy through Gentile Torah Observance

How well has the Gentile church done in provoking the Jews to jealousy over the years? In general, over the past 2,000 years, the church has done more to drive the Jews away from God and from knowledge of their Messiah Yeshua rather than to bring them close.§ Even groups of Evangelical Christians today who love the nation of Israel and the Jewish people and who have given financially to them have not provoked the Jewish people to jealousy.

It may be that Torah observance is the key that will unlock this door. As we discussed earlier, the church has taught that the Torah has been abrogated. Most Jews, even those who are not religious, realize deep down that the Torah is one of the central pieces of Judaism. When Gentile believers, who claim to follow the Jewish Messiah, reject the Torah and discard it, they lose any credibility in the eyes of the Jewish community.[2] I think Gentile believers will only be able to provoke the Jews to jealousy when they begin to embrace the Torah.

As we saw in the last chapter, Deuteronomy 4:5–8 states that the Torah was to attract the surrounding nations to Israel's God. The Gentile nations were to understand how great God was when they saw the wonderful instruction, the wonderful Torah that God had given to his people.[3] Could it also be that the Jews will be attracted by their own Torah when they see Gentile believers taking the Torah for themselves and applying it in light of the good news about Yeshua?

Imagine the impact the Gentile believers would have on the Jewish people today if they actually embraced the Torah, came alongside of the Jewish people, and said as Ruth said to Naomi, "Do not urge me to leave you or to return from following you. For where you go I will go and where you lodge I will lodge. Your people shall be my people, and your God my God" (Ruth1:16). Imagine thousands of Ruths who have made the Torah their Torah, the Jewish people their people, and the God of Israel their God. Imagine Gentile believers

---

§   Undoubtedly, there are cases where individual Gentiles have heroically brought the knowledge of God to some Jews, but these examples are rare.

who are truly branches growing from the roots of the patriarchs Abraham, Isaac, and Jacob. That will produce the real jealousy that Sha'ul speaks about in Romans 11. The resulting heavenly symbiotic relationship might lead to the reconciliation of the world and life from the dead.

The next three chapters will challenge the doctrine of the Trinity and the deity of Yeshua. All of these chapters will constitute a three-fold case against the traditional church's most knotty faith position.

## (Endnotes)

1    Dr. Jeff Feinberg introduced me to Ha'azinu.

2    David H. Stern, *Messianic Jewish Manifesto* (Jerusalem: Jewish New Testament Publications, 1988), p. 125.

3    Ariel and D'Vorah Berkowitz, *Take Hold: Embracing our Divine Inheritance with Israel* (Littleton, CO: First Fruits of Zion, 1998), p 46.

## Chapter 10: Is the Messiah Yeshua God?

### Is the Christian Church Infallible?

As I have tried to point out in previous chapters, the traditional Gentile Christian church has lost or misrepresented the real faith of Israel as outlined in the Tanach. The church has rejected the Jewish people. It has rejected the Torah. It has rejected God's Holy Days and created its own. It has changed the day of the Shabbat. Therefore, can we trust the traditional Gentile Christian church in the knowledge it has conveyed to the world about the nature of God, the ultimate truth? I will warn you in advance that these next few chapters will be the most unsettling for those who consider themselves believers in Yeshua.

The church has consistently taught, through the concept of the Trinity, that Yeshua the Messiah is divine. As set down by James White in *The Forgotten Trinity: Recovering the Heart of Christian Belief,* the doctrine of the Trinity states: "Within the one Being that is God, there exist eternally three coequal and coeternal persons, namely, the Father, the Son, and the Holy Spirit."[1] Yeshua is considered the second person, the Son.

### The Incomprehensible Trinity

There are serious contradictions in the doctrine of the Trinity and, therefore, an explanation of the Trinity, even among scholars, always breaks down with the platitude that God is too complicated for us to comprehend. White writes:

The Trinity is a truth that tests our dedication to the principle that God is smarter than we are. As strange as that may sound, I truly believe that in most instances where a religious group denies the Trinity, the reason can be traced back to the founder's unwillingness to admit the simple reality that God is bigger than we can ever imagine. That is really what Christians have always meant when they use the term "mystery" of the Trinity. The term has never meant that the Trinity is an inherently irrational thing. Instead, it simply means that we realize that God is completely unique in the way He exists, and there are elements of His being that are simply beyond our meager mental capacity to comprehend.[2]

As Anthony Buzzard and Charles Hunting point out in their book *The Doctrine of the Trinity: Christianity's Self-Inflicted Wound,* "mystery" does exist "in religion," "but mystery and contradiction are two different things." We will look at some of these contradictions shortly.[3]*

If scholars have trouble understanding the Trinity, certainly the layman is not better off. When Christians pray to God, it is not uncommon for them to pray to the different "persons" of the Trinity, sometimes in the same prayer, depending on the situation. Around the time of September 11, 2001, on Moody Christian Radio, I heard more prayers than usual being addressed to God the Father than to Jesus, implying that the Father was the one to call on for the heavy lifting. For the most part, though, Jesus has become the principal "person" of the Trinity with whom Christians interact. Most contemporary Christian music is sung in worship to Jesus rather than to God the Father. Jesus has become *the* God of the Christian masses.

---

\*  I never believed in the full doctrine of the Trinity. Many Messianic Jews would make the same confession. I did, however, look at Yeshua as the "arm of the Lord," a part of God reaching into the world. I tended not to think about it much. My faith in Yeshua's deity began to weaken after a few situations forced me to see some of the contradictions. *The Doctrine of the Trinity: Christianity's Self-Inflicted Wound* by Buzzard and Hunting became the final stimulus that forced me to think. They bring great arguments to the table. In my opinion, they make one mistake in attempting to defend the reliability of particular New Testament texts that I feel are indefensible.

## The Questions One Dares Not Ask

Most Christians would say that one *must* believe in Yeshua's divinity in order to be "saved." With the real threat of being labeled as a heretic and being cast out from the believing community, the average Christian does not discuss the problems and inconsistencies of the Trinity.[†] They blindly follow the authority of the church on this issue without stepping back to view the evidence for themselves. It is like the story of *The Emperor's New Clothes*. It was said that those who could not see the emperor's "new clothes" were fools. Since no one in the story wanted to be considered a fool, everyone claimed to see the "new clothes" even in the face of the strong visual evidence that there were no new clothes.[‡]

## Contradictions in the Synoptic Texts

To get a flavor for the problem of declaring Yeshua to be divine, let us begin by looking at some of the obvious contradictions in the first three books of the New Testament: Matthew, Mark, and Luke.

At the beginning of his ministry, Yeshua was tempted by the devil: "Then Jesus [Yeshua] was led up by the Spirit into the wilderness to be tempted by the devil" (Matthew 4:1). James 1:13 tells us that God cannot be tempted by evil. How could it be, then, that Satan could have tempted Yeshua as God?

---

[†]  This reminds me of the promotion of evolutionary theory by Darwinists who consider the theory of evolution to be scientific fact. Using academic censure and United States law, they have suppressed further discussion of a theory that can no longer be supported by the evidence. (Phillip E. Johnson, *Defeating Darwinism by Opening Minds* [Downers Grove, IL: InterVarsity Press, 1997].)

[‡]  Some believers are beginning to question the Trinity and the deity of Yeshua. Once per week Moody Christian Radio has a call-in program called "Open Line." Dr. Michael Rydelnik, head of the Jewish studies program at Moody Bible Institute, hosts the program. Just about every week someone calls in to question Dr. Rydelnik about one of the puzzling contradictions concerning the Trinity. Maybe they think a Jewish believer will be able to unravel the mystery. Dr. Rydelnik is bright, and knows the Bible extremely well, but his traditional answers often do not satisfy.

.ı Yeshua taught his disciples how to pray ("the Lord's
, he told them to pray to "our Father in heaven" (Matthew
ıe did not also include an address to "the Son."

While answering a question in the book of Mark, Yeshua clearly
distinguished himself from God:

> And as he was setting out on his journey, a man ran up and knelt before
> him and asked him, "Good Teacher, what must I do to inherit eternal
> life?" And Jesus [Yeshua] said to him, "Why do you call me good? No
> one is good except God alone." (Mark 10:17–18)

Here, Yeshua recognized the one God, who is good. He did not seem
to include himself as a member of a Trinity.

In Luke, while addressing the city of Jerusalem, Yeshua said,
"And I tell you, you will not see me until you say, 'Blessed is he who
comes in the name of the Lord!'" (Luke 13:35). He did not say, "until
you say, 'Blessed is the Lord, who comes.'" He is coming in the name
of the YHVH, not as YHVH.

When the sons of Zebedee, Ya'akov (James) and Yochanan
(John), with their mother, asked Yeshua for a particular position in
his kingdom, he told them he would be unable to grant their request:
"He said to them, 'You will drink my cup, but to sit at my right hand
and at my left is not mine to grant, but it is for those for whom it has
been prepared by my Father'" (Matthew 20:23). If Yeshua is God,
why is it that only the Father can grant positions in heaven?

In Matthew chapter 24, when Yeshua's disciples asked him what
will be the sign of his coming and the end of the age, he answered,
"But concerning that day and hour no one knows, not even the angels
of heaven, nor the Son, but the Father only" (Matthew 24:36). If
Yeshua is God, how could the Father know something that Yeshua
does not know?

As he was contemplating his approaching death, Yeshua prayed
to the Father:

> Then he said to them, "My soul is very sorrowful, even to death; remain
> here, and watch with me." And going a little farther he fell on his face
> and prayed, saying, "My Father, if it be possible, let this cup pass from
> me; nevertheless, not as I will, but as you will" (Matthew 26:38–39).

How can Yeshua as God pray to God the Father? Does not God the Father already know what God the Son is going to say to himself? Furthermore, how could the will of Yeshua be different from the will of the Father if Yeshua were God also?

During his trial before the high priest and the "council" (Sanhedrin), the following dialogue was recorded in Mark:

> But he remained silent and made no answer. Again the high priest asked him, "Are you the Christ [Messiah], the Son of the Blessed?" And Jesus [Yeshua] said, "I am, and you will see the Son of Man seated at the right hand of Power, and coming with the clouds of heaven." And the high priest tore his garments and said, "What further witnesses do we need? You have heard his blasphemy. What is your decision?" And they all condemned him as deserving death (Mark 14:61–64).

Here the high priest asked Yeshua straight out whether he is the Messiah. He did not ask him whether he is God.§ Yeshua answered him in the affirmative by saying "I am."¶ He then expanded his answer that he is the Messiah by citing messianic prophesies from Psalm 110:1 and Daniel 7:13. The blasphemy was clearly his claim to be the Messiah, not his claim to be God.

According to the *Encyclopaedia Judaica*: "Besides sacrilege of God, vituperation against the king, God's anointed servant, was also considered blasphemy (cf. Ex. 22:27 and I Kings 21:10)."4 This first verse listed in Exodus (English verse 28) states: "You shall not revile God, nor curse a ruler of your people" (Exodus 22:28). The second verse references the false witness that Queen Jezebel (wife of Ahab) brought against Naboth the Jezreelite in order for her to take his vineyard:

> And the two worthless men came in and sat opposite him. And the worthless men brought a charge against Naboth in the presence of the

---

§ "Son of God" was messianic terminology in the first century. (Hershel Shanks, *The Mystery and Meaning of the Dead Sea Scrolls* [New York: Vintage Books, 1999], pp. 69–71).

¶ This "I am" is undoubtedly an answer to the question and does not have the deity implications as the "I am" used in John 8:54–59.

people, saying, "Naboth cursed God and the king." So they took him outside the city and stoned him to death with stones (1Kings 21:13).

Yeshua blasphemed when he made the claim to be the Messiah because "he had no form or majesty that we should look at him, and no beauty that we should desire him" (Isaiah 53:2). In the eyes of the Jewish officials, his claim defiled the name of the King Messiah.

In Matthew, as Yeshua was dying he cried out in a loud voice (in Aramaic), "Eli, Eli, lema sabachthani?" that is, "My God, my God, why have you forsaken me?" (Matthew 27:46). Yeshua seemed to be voicing a clear separation of himself from God at this point as the sins of mankind came upon him.

## For Sha'ul, Yeshua Is Not Coequal with God

In his writing, Sha'ul also frequently distinguishes the one God from Yeshua the Messiah:[5]

> May the God of endurance and encouragement grant you to live in such harmony with one another, in accord with Christ [Messiah] Jesus [Yeshua], that together you may with one voice glorify the God and Father of our Lord Jesus [Yeshua] Christ [Messiah] (Romans 15:5–6).

> To the only wise God be glory forevermore through Jesus [Yeshua] Christ [Messiah]! Amen (Romans 16:27).

> But I want you to understand that the head of every man is Christ [Messiah], the head of a wife is her husband, and the head of Christ [Messiah] is God (1 Corinthians 11:3).

> But thanks be to God, who gives us the victory through our Lord Jesus [Yeshua] Christ [Messiah] (1Corinthians 15:57).

> The God and Father of the Lord Jesus [Yeshua], he who is blessed forever, knows that I am not lying (2 Corinthians 11:31).

> There is one body and one Spirit—just as you were called to the one hope that belongs to your call—one Lord, one faith, one baptism, one God and Father of all, who is over all and through all and in all (Ephesians 4:4–6).

We always thank God, the Father of our Lord Jesus [Yeshua] Christ [Messiah], when we pray for you (Colossians 1:3).

For there is one God, and there is one mediator between God and men, the man Christ [Messiah] Jesus [Yeshua] (1 Timothy 2:5).

Finally, in a fascinating passage, Sha'ul tells us that God the Father places all things in subjection under Yeshua's feet—except Himself, of course:

> Then comes the end, when he delivers the kingdom to God the Father after destroying every rule and every authority and power. For he must reign until he has put all his enemies under his feet. The last enemy to be destroyed is death. For "God has put all things in subjection under his feet." But when it says, "all things are put in subjection," it is plain that he is excepted who put all things in subjection under him. When all things are subjected to him, then the Son himself will also be subjected to him who put all things in subjection under him, that God may be all in all (1 Corinthians 15:24–28).

God gives Yeshua authority over His kingdom similar to Daniel 7:14 (see the previous quote). In the end, however, it will still be God alone who will be "all in all."

The New Testament text shows us that Yeshua is a different "person" from the Father, with his own identity, his own thoughts, his own knowledge, and his own will. Therefore, if we consider Yeshua and the Father (these two different "persons") to be God, we end up with two Gods and not one. Refreshingly, if Yeshua is one hundred percent man and not God, all of these contradictions disappear.

Now to throw a wrench into the works, I have to admit that much of the New Testament does describe Yeshua as God. Christians do not believe in the Trinity without evidence to back up their claim. You will have to wait until chapter 12, though, to hear a discussion about this conundrum.

## A Divine Messiah Also Missing in the Tanach

Finding an accurate picture of the Messiah Yeshua in the messianic prophecies of the Tanach is simple (see chapter 2). Nevertheless, as in the examples given from the New Testament, we also do not see the promised Messiah portrayed as a part of a godhead in the Tanach. The Messiah is portrayed as a man, albeit a unique man.

In Isaiah chapter 11, there is a clear messianic prophecy concerning the Messiah who comes from the line of King David:

> There shall come forth a shoot from the stump of Jesse [King David's father], and a branch from his roots shall bear fruit. And the Spirit of the LORD [YHVH] shall rest upon him, the Spirit of wisdom and understanding, the Spirit of counsel and might, the Spirit of knowledge and the fear of the LORD [YHVH]. And his delight shall be in the fear of the LORD [YHVH]. He shall not judge by what his eyes see, or decide disputes by what his ears hear, but with righteousness he shall judge the poor, and decide with equity for the meek of the earth; and he shall strike the earth with the rod of his mouth, and with the breath of his lips he shall kill the wicked. Righteousness shall be the belt of his waist, and faithfulness the belt of his loins (Isaiah 11:1–5).

Why would the Spirit of YHVH need to rest upon him if he is already God? Why does he need to fear YHVH if he is YHVH?

The Suffering Servant passage in Isaiah 53 seems to be speaking of the Messiah. It describes him as being pierced and crushed for our iniquities. After he completes his work, it says:

> Therefore I will divide him a portion with the many [great], and he shall divide the spoil with the strong, because he poured out his soul to death and was numbered with the transgressors; yet he bore the sin of many, and makes intercession for the transgressors (Isaiah 53:12).

It sounds like he is receiving some reward here for his atoning work. If he were God, would he need a reward for his work or need to earn a reward?

The prophet Daniel speaks of one who is like a son of man coming with the clouds of heaven:

> I saw in the night visions, and behold, with the clouds of heaven there came one like a son of man, and he came to the Ancient of Days and was presented before him. And to him was given dominion and glory and a kingdom, that all peoples, nations, and languages should serve him; his dominion is an everlasting dominion, which shall not

pass away, and his kingdom one that shall not be destroyed (Daniel 7:13–14).

If this is speaking of the Messiah, and he is already God, why would he need to be given dominion, glory, and a kingdom? Would not they already be his?

## Is the Angel of YHVH a Preincarnate Yeshua?

For years, Christian commentators have argued that appearances of God in bodily form throughout the Tanach are actually physical appearances of Yeshua functioning as the second "person" of the Trinity. Most specifically they would say that the angel (*malach*—messenger) of YHVH throughout the text is Yeshua. For instance, they would say that one of the "men" who appeared to Abraham by the oaks of Mamre in Genesis 18 was Yeshua. Likewise, they would say the man who wrestled with Jacob in Genesis 32 was Yeshua; the angel of YHVH who spoke to Moses at the burning bush in Exodus 3 was Yeshua; the appearance of the God of Israel to Moses, Aaron and his sons, and the seventy elders of Israel on Mount Sinai in Exodus 24 was Yeshua; and the appearances of the angel of YHVH to Gideon in Judges 6 and the parents of Samson in Judges 13 were of Yeshua.[6]

There are other arguments made from the Hebrew text that attempt to support the concept of the Trinity. For instance, I have heard that the Hebrew root of the second word of Genesis, "created"—*bet, resh,* and *aleph*—represents *Ben* (Son), *Ruach* (Spirit), and *Elohim* (Father): the Trinity, who existed in the beginning. Again, I have been told that the Trinity can be seen in the three repetitions of God in the *Shema*—"Hear, O Israel: The LORD [YHVH] our God, the LORD [YHVH] is one" (Deuteronomy 6:4) or that the word *echad*—"one"—in this verse means a compound oneness. Some say the Trinity can be seen in the plural name for God—*Elohim*—or the Trinity can be seen in God describing Himself using the word "Us" (Genesis 1:26, 3:22, 11:7, Isaiah 6:8).

These sightings of Yeshua as deity or findings of the Trinity throughout the Hebrew Bible remind me of people who are desperate to see a vision of the Virgin Mary or Elvis. They sometimes create their visions out of random oil spills under a bridge or from patterns of mold in a refrigerator.

Indeed, God was known to make appearances to people in the form of the angel of YHVH or in the likeness of a man (or in the likeness of men, as he appeared to Abraham in Genesis chapter 18). However, the appearance always expressed the mind of the one God. In a simple way, I look at this angel or messenger of YHVH as a loudspeaker that conveys the message of God to this physical world. God is speaking through this angel and, therefore, there is often a blurring between the angel, a separate being, and YHVH speaking through him. Nevertheless, the angel himself is not divine.

The narrative of the burning bush in Exodus is a classic example of this blurring. In Exodus 3:2, we are told that the angel of YHVH appeared to Moses in a flame of fire out of the midst of the bush. A few verses later, in Exodus 3:4, we are told that YHVH saw that Moses turned aside to see this wonder, and God called to him out of the bush. There is a blurring of the angel of YHVH and YHVH Himself. It appears, however, that the voice of God was coming from the loudspeaker, the angel, who was in the bush. God, Himself, was not in the bush.

Moses, like the angel of YHVH but in a less intense way, also became a spokesman for God before Pharaoh. Even in this setting, there was a blurring of the spokesman, Moses, and the speaker YHVH:[7] "Thus says the LORD [YHVH], 'By this you shall know that I am the LORD [YHVH]: behold, with the staff that is in my hand I will strike the water that is in the Nile, and it shall turn into blood'" (Exodus 7:17). Moses did not become divine in this setting.

Since the angel of YHVH represents God, and God's words are coming out of the angel, the one interacting with the angel can get a glimpse of God's glory and can experience a sense of God's presence. In the same way, the face of Moses was shining with a reflection of God's presence when he came down the mountain the second time with the two tablets of the testimony. His face shone because he had been talking with God. He needed to wear a veil so the people would not be afraid to come near him (Exodus 34:29–35).

The entirety of the appearances of the angel of YHVH, from Hagar, to Jacob wrestling with a man (Hosea 12:4 says this man was an angel), to Joshua, to Gideon, to the parents of Samson, can be understood in a very simplified way by this loudspeaker analogy. Often those seeing the angel of YHVH thought that they would die (Genesis 32:30, Exodus 24:11, Judges 6: 23, Judges 13:22–23). At one point, God told Moses, "Man shall not see me and live" (Exodus 33:20). However, in every case no one died, which suggests that he or she did not actually see God.

The appearance of YHVH to Abraham as three men, though more complicated, also has an explanation. In his commentary on Genesis, John Sailhamer suggests that the "appearance" that Abraham had of YHVH in Genesis chapter 18 was the three men jointly, not just one of the three.[8] Sailhamer goes on to say that the three men were three angels. Two of the angels go to the city of Sodom in chapter 19 to investigate the corruption there prior to its destruction. Eventually, however, both Sodom and Gomorrah are destroyed. Sailhamer proposes that the third angel went to investigate Gomorrah before its destruction.[9]

Abraham, who is spiritually attuned, recognized his visitors as coming from God and addressed them as Lords, using the Hebrew form "Adonai," with the vowel *kamatz*, which is reserved only for God in the Tanach. Lot, who was not spiritually attuned, did not at first recognize his two guests as coming from God in Genesis 19. He addressed them initially as lords in Genesis 19:2 using the Hebrew form "adonai," with the vowel *patach*, which is not reserved for God. During his escape from Sodom, however, Lot finally recognized his two guests, and then he also addressed them as Lords, using the Hebrew form "Adonai," with the vowel *kamatz*, in Genesis 19:18. Abraham could not have addressed only one of the three men as Lords (God) in Genesis 18:3 since Lot also addressed the other two as Lords (God) in the next chapter.[10]

Sailhamer summarizes the encounter:

The three men, as such, are to be understood as the physical "appearance" of the Lord to Abraham. In other words, though God himself did not appear to Abraham in physical form, the three men are to be seen as representative of his presence. In much the same way the Burning Bush of Exodus 3:2–3 was a physical representation of God's presence but yet was not actually the physical presence of God.[11]

Did the God of Israel appear physically in the form of Yeshua to Moses, Aaron and his sons, and the seventy elders of Israel on Mount Sinai in Exodus 24:9–11? Curiously, the second word used for "see" in verse 11 comes from the Hebrew root *chet, zion,* and *heh,* and, according to Walter Kaiser, in his commentary on Exodus, "stresses inward, spiritual, or prophetic vision."[12] There appears to be a nonphysical quality to the vision they saw. Rabbi Umberto Cassuto points out that the text does not describe a physical description of God Himself but only what was seen beneath his feet.[13] Not only that, but the passage tells us also that no one died, so each must not have seen God physically.

## The Plural Name Elohim and the Plural Pronoun "Us"

There is no evidence that the plural form of God, *Elohim,* denotes the Trinitarian viewpoint. According to *Gesenius' Hebrew Grammar,* there are a number of words in the plural form in biblical Hebrew called the plural of amplification that seem to intensify the idea of the stem. Examples are *on'im,* "might" (Isaiah 40:26), *de'im,* "thorough knowledge" (Job 37:16), and *rachamim,* "compassion" (Genesis 43:14). The plural form of God, *Elohim,* is closely related to the plurals of amplification, as are the plurals *k'doshim,* "Most Holy" (Proverbs 9:10), and in Aramaic *el'yonin,* "Most High" (Daniel 7:18).[14] The word *Elohim* was also used for the pagan gods Dagon (1 Samuel 5:7) and Chemosh (Judges 11:24).[15]

No one knows the exact reason why God described himself using the plural pronoun "Us" in Genesis 1:26, Genesis 3:22, Genesis 11:7, and Isaiah 6:8. Some suggest this was God speaking to his attendant angels.[16] Addressing the attendant angels is unlikely in Genesis 1:26, since God did not make man in the image of angels, and since we have no other evidence that angels participated in the creation of man.[17] God addressing angels could be a feature of Isaiah 6:1–8, however.

*Gesenius' Hebrew Grammar* suggests that this is a plural of self-de-liberation.[18] Rabbi Cassuto writes, "The best explanation, although rejected by the majority of contemporary commentators, is that we have here the plural of exhortation. When a person exhorts himself to do a given task he uses the plural: 'Let us go!' 'Let us rise up!' 'Let us sit!' and the like."[19]

## Echad as a Compound Unity?

The Hebrew word *echad*—"one"— in the *Shema,* has the numerical value of one, just as in English, and does not suggest a "compound unity."[20] As Buzzard and Hunting write:

> *Echad* is a numerical adjective, and naturally enough is sometimes found modifying a collective noun—one family, one herd, one bunch. But we should observe carefully that the sense of plurality resides in the compound noun and not in the word *echad* (one).[21]

Messianic Jewish debater Michael Brown is probably correct when he says the *Shema* mainly tells us that YHVH is the only God and says nothing about God's essential nature.[22] However, frankly, who would have imagined at the time of Moses that the one God would ever be described as three persons? That was not a concept which anyone was struggling with at that time.

There are other proof texts that have been used over the years in an attempt to demonstrate the deity of Yeshua through the Tanach, but I will address more of these in appendix 2.

## Pre-Christian Jewish Belief in a Plurality of the One God

Liberal historians, as well as conservative Christian historians, have developed complicated theories to explain the origin of high Christology, defined by Daniel Boyarin in *The Jewish Gospels: The Story of the Jewish Christ* as "the theological idea that Jesus actually was God."[23] Liberal scholars in the past, who were not believing Christians, tended to say that Yeshua the man was transformed into a god through the in-fluence of pagan Greek religious thought. Recently, the trend among scholars is to argue that the concept of Yeshua's divinity sprang out of Judaism.

The research suggests that some pre-Christian Jews held views that were similar to Christian views of God. It asserts, for instance, that Jews before the time of Yeshua entertained a plurality of the one God. These Jews took personifications of God's wisdom, or His word, or the angel of the Lord, or the Spirit of the Lord, and made them "intermediary figures" reaching into the physical world.[24] Daniel Boyarin calls this "Logos theology" which "is constituted by several variations of a doctrine that between God and the world, there is a second divine entity, God's word (Logos) or God's wisdom, who mediates between the fully transcendent Godhead and the material world."[25] This Logos theology is one construction some Jews developed to get a handle on the mystery of God. As I pointed out earlier, it is not surprising that Jews had problems understanding how a God who is outside of our physical world (including its space and time) could interact with our physical world. Often, there is that blurring between God and his messenger, whether that messenger is Moses or the angel of YHVH. Logos theology is one way some Jews dealt with this enigma.

## Pre-Christian Jewish Insight or Influence?

Liberal and conservative scholars are in conflict over Yeshua's deity, whether it is truth or fiction. These polar scholars use this Logos theology information in different ways.

Conservative Christian scholars, including Messianic Jewish authors, are excited about this Logos theology research. Some of them argue that this pre-Christian Jewish theology was looking forward to the coming of the divine Yeshua: the divine mediator between God and man. They would say that Yeshua filled the shoes of these intermediary figures that sprang out of the monotheism of Judaism,[26] as John would say, "And the Word became flesh and dwelt among us" (John 1:14).

It is certainly interesting when one finds pre-Christian Jews who hold views of God that nearly match Christian views of Yeshua's deity.

Nevertheless, just because a group of Jews in the past professed or today professes a particular point of view does not make it a viewpoint consistent with the Tanach. For instance, some Orthodox Jews today believe in reincarnation, and some still sacrifice chickens on Yom Kippur. That Logos theology was a slight misunderstanding by pre-Christian Jews of a soon to be revealed reality in a divine Messiah is wishful thinking.

Liberal scholars argue that this Logos theology, in existence before Yeshua, was *influential* on the fictional story about Yeshua. They suggest these pre-Christian Jewish ideas contributed to the transformation of the human Messiah Yeshua into a divine being.

One could also argue that the concept of the virgin birth was a Jewish notion before the time of Yeshua. In *The New Testament and Rabbinic Judaism*, David Daube discusses a rabbinic idea put forth about the miraculous birth of Moses.[27] In Exodus, Pharaoh was putting to death all of the Hebrew, newborn, male infants. A legend arose that the children of Israel stopped having sexual relations at that time. Either this was a command of Pharaoh, an act of atonement, or an action initiated by the people of Israel themselves so as not to supply Pharaoh with any more children to be killed. For the deliverer, Moses, to be born then, a miracle needed to occur. Therefore, God is said to have intervened, and Moses's mother bore Moses without sexual intercourse with her husband. Even though this story was suppressed in later years among the Jews, it remains evident in the Passover Haggadah. In the telling of the Passover story, the Haggadah quotes from Deuteronomy 26:7, "Then we cried to the LORD [YHVH], the God of our fathers, and the LORD [YHVH] heard our voice and saw our affliction, our toil, and our oppression" (Deuteronomy 26:7). The Haggadah goes on to explain this text: "And He saw our affliction: this denotes the separation from their wives as it is said, and[28] God saw the people of Israel and God knew."** "Knowing" in the Torah can

---

** The Haggadah is quoting from Exodus 2:25. In the original context God "knew" about Israel's suffering or "knew" about them in Egypt. There is no sexual connotation.

refer to sexual relations. It sounds as if this Midrash, preserved in the Haggadah, is suggesting just that.[29]

Daube finishes this section about Moses's birth with an interesting comment:

> If the foregoing argument is tenable, it furnishes support for the view—which appears to be increasingly favoured by modern scholars on other grounds—that the narrative of Jesus's birth originated in a properly Jewish rather than Hellenized milieu.[30]

All Jewish beliefs before the time of Yeshua do not necessarily infer truth. It appears that some of these false Jewish notions may have had an *influence* on the "narrative" of Yeshua.

## Monotheism's Inclination toward Polytheism

Liberal theologians who study religion would say that the monotheism of Israel was a result of evolutionary forces over time. Men started out with pagan/polytheistic religions, which eventually were transformed into monotheism.[31] The Bible seems to teach us differently. Men were given the knowledge of God from the beginning. As men moved away from God, their religion always morphed into polytheism. We see this frequently in Israel before the Babylonian exile. I would suggest that this also happened in early Christianity. In the first century, after the appearance of Yeshua the Messiah, the Messianic faith quickly adopted polytheistic features. Polytheistic tendencies in the early Christian movement were most likely a result of the immediate loss of Jewish influence on the new believing communities, the peculiar Jewish beliefs floating around at the time as outlined in this chapter, and the mostly pagan soil from which these communities were growing. We can observe this polytheistic trend early on with the deification of Yeshua and later with Mary worship, the use of icons, and the veneration of the saints. The Protestant church eventually broke away from most of these practices.

The doctrine of the Trinity and the deity of Yeshua cannot be supported by many New Testament passages, the Tanach, or intertestamental Jewish thought. For instance, many passages in the New

Testament contradict a divine Yeshua. Ancient prophecies describing a godly and kingly Messiah never predicted this anointed one would be God himself. The Tanach often blurs God's messenger with the Sender of the message, but Moses and the angel of YHVH are not God. The study of pre-Christian Jewish thought is fascinating, but these notions are not some premonition of a later truth.

If we go back to the very beginning, I think we will find a different theology among the earliest Jewish believers.

## (Endnotes)

1     James R. White, *The Forgotten Trinity: Recovering the Heart of Christian Belief* (Minneapolis: Bethany House Publishers, 1998), p. 26.

2     Ibid., p. 20.

3     Anthony F. Buzzard and Charles F. Hunting, *The Doctrine of the Trinity: Christianity's Self-Inflicted Wound* (New York: International Scholars Publications, 1998), p. 10.

4     "Blasphemy," *Encyclopaedia Judaica*, Vol. 4 (Jerusalem, Israel: Keter Publishing House Ltd., 1971), p. 1074.

5     Geza Vermes, *Christian Beginnings: From Nazareth to Nicaea* (New Haven, CT: Yale University Press, 2013), pp. 106–113.

6     Asher Intrater, *Who Ate Lunch with Abraham: The Appearances of God in the Form of a Man in the Hebrew Scriptures* (Peoria, AZ: Intermedia Publishing Group, 2011). Michael L. Brown, *Answering Jewish Objections to Jesus—Theological Objections*, Vol. 2 (Grand Rapids, MI: Baker Books, 2000), pp. 25–35.

7     Umberto Moshe David Cassuto, *A Commentary on the Book of Exodus*, trans. by Israel Abrahams (Skokie, IL: Varda Books, 2005), p. 97.

8     John H. Sailhamer, "Genesis," Vol. 2 of *The Expositor's Bible Commentary*, ed. by Frank E. Gaebelein, 12 vols. (Grand Rapids, MI: Zondervan Publishing House, 1990), p 142.

9     Ibid., p. 151.

10    Ibid., pp. 142–146.

11    Ibid., p. 145.

12    Walter C. Kaiser Jr., "Exodus," Vol. 2 of *The Expositor's Bible Commentary*, ed. by Frank E. Gaebelein, 12 vols. (Grand Rapids, MI: Zondervan Publishing House, 1990), p 450.

13    Umberto Moshe David Cassuto, *A Commentary on the Book of Exodus*, p. 314.

14    E. Kautzsch and A. E. Cowley, eds., *Gesenius' Hebrew Grammar*, 2nd ed. (Oxford: Clarendon, 1910), BibleWorks, v.9, pp. 397–399.

15    Anthony F. Buzzard and Charles F. Hunting, *The Doctrine of the Trinity: Christianity's Self-Inflicted Wound*, p. 24.

16    E. Kautzsch and A. E. Cowley, eds., *Gesenius' Hebrew Grammar*, p 401.

17    *The ESV Study Bible* (Wheaton, IL: Crossway Bibles, 2008), p. 51.

18    E. Kautzsch and A. E. Cowley, eds., *Gesenius' Hebrew Grammar*, p 401.

19   U. Cassuto, *A Commentary on the Book of Genesis—Part I From Adam to Noah*, trans. by Israel Abrahams (Jerusalem: The Magnes Press, The Hebrew University, 1998), p. 55.

20   Anthony F. Buzzard and Charles F. Hunting, *The Doctrine of the Trinity: Christianity's Self-Inflicted Wound*, pp. 25–28.

21   Ibid., pp. 25–26.

22   Michael L. Brown, *Answering Jewish Objections to Jesus—Theological Objections*, p. 6.

23   Daniel Boyarin, *The Jewish Gospels: The Story of the Jewish Christ* (New York: The New Press, 2012), p. 53.

24   Andrew Chester, "High Christology—Whence, When and Why?" *Early Christianity*, 2 (2011), p. 40–42.

25   Daniel Boyarin, *Border Lines: The Partition of Judaeo-Christianity* (Philadelphia: University of Pennsylvania Press, 2004), p. 30.

26   Daniel C. Juster, "Messianic Theology and a Lost Judaism," in *Who Ate Lunch with Abraham: The Appearances of God in the Form of a Man in the Hebrew Scriptures* by Asher Intrater (Peoria, AZ: Intermedia Publishing Group, Inc., 2011), pp. 174–175. Michael L. Brown, *Answering Jewish Objections to Jesus—Theological Objections*, pp. 14–37.

27   David Daube, *The New Testament and Rabbinic Judaism* (London: School of Oriental and African Studies, The University of London, 1956, Hendrickson Publishers' Edition), pp. 5–9.

28   *Deluxe Edition of the Maxwell House Haggadah* (Kraft General Foods, Inc., 1996), p. 16.

29   David Daube, *The New Testament and Rabbinic Judaism*, pp. 5–9.

30   Ibid., p. 9.

31   Yehezkel Kaufmann, *The Religion of Israel from Its Beginnings to the Babylonian Exile* (New York: Schocken Books, 1960), p. 2.

# Chapter 11: Yeshua and the
# Earliest Jewish Believers

## What if the Earliest Jewish Believers
## Did Not Know a Divine Yeshua?

There seems to be evidence to suggest that most of the earliest Jewish believers in Yeshua did not believe in the deity of Yeshua.[1] If this evidence is correct, it would be a powerful argument against the deity of Yeshua, since the earliest Jewish believers were the first and only believers in the beginning. Unfortunately, inside and outside of the New Testament, we have limited information about what the earliest Jewish believers thought about Yeshua's nature. Moreover, the church fathers, who often were not sympathetic toward Jews, filtered most of the information about the earliest Jewish believers that has come down to us outside of the New Testament.[2]

In the New Testament writings, there should have been evidence of a controversy over the deity of Yeshua, since the coming Messiah was never expected to be God in the first-century Jewish world.* According to Anthony Buzzard and Charles Hunting:

---

\* According to Andrew Chester, if Sha'ul would have explained further about the divine nature of Yeshua in relationship to 1 Corinthians 8:6 or Philippians 2:6–11 (more about these verses in chapter 12), "What he says would certainly be controversial, indeed unacceptable, to his fellow Jews who are not Christians." (Andrew Chester, "High Christology—Whence, When and Why?" *Early Christianity*, 2 (2011), p. 36.)

Belief in the Trinitarian God would have been the most revolutionary and explosive concept ever to have rocked the first-century church. Yet of that revolution, if it ever occurred, the New Testament gives us not one hint.[3]

Controversies over the "Law" are found throughout the New Testament. The problem is explained, and we see the first believers dealing with it. No controversy is evident over the deity of Yeshua, however. Frankly, according to Sha'ul, the major controversy about Yeshua for the Jews was not whether he was God—which it should have been then, as it is for modern Jews today—but whether he, as Messiah, was to be crucified for our sins. The stumbling block was Messiah crucified: "For Jews demand signs and Greeks seek wisdom, but we preach Christ [Messiah] crucified, a stumbling block to Jews and folly to Gentiles" (1 Corinthians 1:22–23). Lack of controversy about the deity of Yeshua among the Jewish people in the New Testament is an obvious clue that the concept had not been developed yet.[4][†]

## The Ebionites: The Direct Descendants of the Jerusalem Community?

Scholars over the years have searched through the writings of the church fathers to try to find the direct offspring of the earliest Jewish believers from the Jerusalem community. According to the church fathers, all of the early Jewish believers after the first century were considered heretics, and this seems to be an accurate assessment of some of the groups they cataloged. Two main groups stand out as being candidates for the descendants of the Jerusalem community—the

---

† Unbelievably, Dean Overman, a conservative Christian, makes the opposite argument from silence: "There is simply no first-century evidence that any members of the Christian circles with which he [Sha'ul] was acquainted refused to honor and worship Jesus in a manner that was normally reserved only for God. No first-century document gives even a hint of an alternative Christology existing among other groups of Christians at this very early time in the life of the church." (Dean L. Overman, *A Case for the Divinity of Jesus* [New York: Rowman & Littlefield Publishers, Inc., 2010], p. 38.)

Ebionites and the Nazarenes.[5] The Ebionites of Irenaeus appear to be the best candidate.[6]

Irenaeus, who wrote around 180 CE, is the first author to mention the Ebionites.[7] We have to keep in mind that this is at least 110 years after the destruction of the Temple in Jerusalem by the Romans in 70 CE. He is also writing after the second Jewish revolt against the Romans that ended in 135 CE with the destruction of the city of Jerusalem. After the second Jewish revolt, the Jewish people were banned from entering Jerusalem.[8] By the time of Irenaeus, many world changing events had transpired since the accounts recorded in the book of Acts.

According to Irenaeus, here is what the Ebionites believed:

Those who are called Ebionites agree that the world was made by God; but their opinions with respect to the Lord are similar to those of Cerinthus and Carpocrates. They use the Gospel according to Matthew only, and repudiate the Apostle Paul, maintaining that he was an apostate from the law. As to the prophetical writings, they endeavour to expound them in a somewhat singular manner: they practice circumcision, persevere in the observance of those customs which are enjoined by the law, and are so Judaic in their style of life, that they even adore Jerusalem as if it were the house of God[9] (*Irenaeus against Heresies*, 1.26.2).

Cerinthus . . . He represented Jesus as having not been born of a virgin, but as being the son of Joseph and Mary according to the ordinary course of human generation, while he nevertheless was more righteous, prudent, and wise than other men. Moreover, after his baptism, Christ descended upon him in the form of a dove from the Supreme Ruler, and that then he proclaimed the unknown Father, and performed miracles[10] (*Irenaeus against Heresies*, 1.26.1).

Vain also are the Ebionites, who do not receive by faith into their soul the union of God and man, but who remain in the old leaven of [the natural] birth, and who do not choose to understand that the Holy Ghost came upon Mary, and the power of the Most High did overshadow her: wherefore also what was generated is a holy thing, and the Son of the Most High God the Father of all, who effected the incarnation of this being, and showed forth a new [kind of] generation; that as by the former generation we inherited death, so by this new generation we might inherit life. Therefore do these men reject the commixture of the heavenly wine, and wish it to be water of the world only[11] (*Irenaeus against Heresies*, 5.1.3).

The book of Acts gives us some limited information about what the earliest Jewish believers in Jerusalem believed. Presumably, what they believed was uncorrupted at this point. This group appears to represent the stream of faith from the beginning. Notice how similar their beliefs were to the Ebionites of Irenaeus. In Acts 21 we are told:

> When we had come to Jerusalem, the brothers received us gladly. On the following day Paul [Sha'ul] went in with us to James [Ya'akov], and all the elders were present. After greeting them, he related one by one the things that God had done among the Gentiles through his ministry. And when they heard it, they glorified God. And they said to him, "You see, brother, how many thousands there are among the Jews of those who have believed. They are all zealous for the law, and they have been told about you that you teach all the Jews who are among the Gentiles to forsake Moses, telling them not to circumcise their children or walk according to our customs. What then is to be done? They will certainly hear that you have come. Do therefore what we tell you. We have four men who are under a vow; take these men and purify yourself along with them and pay their expenses, so that they may shave their heads. Thus all will know that there is nothing in what they have been told about you, but that you yourself also live in observance of the law" (Acts 21:17–24).

> Then Paul [Sha'ul] took the men, and the next day he purified himself along with them and went into the temple, giving notice when the days of purification would be fulfilled and the offering presented for each one of them (Acts 21:26).

Observe the features in common between the Jerusalem community in Acts and the Ebionites. They both practiced the custom of circumcision and were zealous for the Torah. They both adored Jerusalem as if it were the house of God, and the Jerusalem community continued with Temple sacrifices when they were still able. Also, they both had problems with Sha'ul, even though most likely from a misunderstanding. We are not told anything about what the Acts community believed about Yeshua's nature, because maybe it was not an issue at that time.

Justin Martyr, an earlier witness than Irenaeus, writes about the characteristics of some Jewish believers in his day who have some of the same beliefs as the Ebionites, although he does not call them by this name. In his *Dialogue with Trypho*, the Jew, written about 160 CE,[12] he writes about Jewish believers, who understood Yeshua to be "man of men." Justin says to Trypho and his friends:

> "For there are some, my friends," I said, "of our race, [some read "of your race"]‡ who admit that He is Christ, while holding Him to be man of men; with whom I do not agree, nor would I, even though most of those who have [now] the same opinions as myself should say so"[13] (*Dialogue with Trypho*, 48).

> Trypho responds: Those who affirm him to have been a man, and to have been anointed by election, and then to have become Christ, appear to me to speak more plausibly than you who hold those opinions which you express. For we all expect that Christ will be a man [born] of men, and that Elijah when he comes will anoint him[14] (*Dialogue with Trypho*, 49).

Some authors suggest that Justin, at this relatively early date, most likely is describing Ebionites.[15]

Ray Pritz, an early church historian, tries to convince us that Justin acknowledges another group of Jewish believers in his day who believed in the deity of Yeshua but who continued to adhere to the Mosaic Law, unlike the previous group:[16]

> And Trypho again inquired, "But if some one, knowing that this is so, after he recognizes that this man is Christ, and has believed in and obeys Him, wishes, however, to observe these [institutions], will he be saved?" I said, "In my opinion, Trypho, such an one will be saved, if he does not strive in every way to persuade other men—I mean those

---

‡ Oskar Skarsaune suggests this is the more accurate reading. (Oskar Skarsaune, "The Ebionites," in *Jewish Believers in Jesus,* ed. by Oskar Skarsaune and Reidar Hvalvik [Peabody, MA: Hendrickson Publishers, 2007], p. 430.)

Gentiles who have been circumcised from error by Christ, to observe the same things as himself, telling them that they will not be saved unless they do so"[17] (*Dialogue with Trypho*, 47).

Trypho, however, seems to be making a hypothetical statement here. He is asking whether one can be a follower of Yeshua and an observer of the Torah at the same time or if these positions are mutually exclusive. He is not describing a situation he is familiar with himself. Moreover, as in the previous quote from *Dialogue with Trypho*, 48, one can admit that Yeshua is "Christ" and hold him to be "man of men." Admitting that Yeshua is "Christ" or the Messiah does not automatically equate to admitting that Yeshua is God.

Over time, we receive more information about the Ebionites from other early church fathers: Tertullian, Pseudo-Tertullian, Hippolytus, and Origen; and then from the later fathers Eusebius, Epiphanius, and Jerome.[18] In due course, though, the character of this group changes dramatically. Petri Luomenen tells us that by the time of Epiphanius, the Ebionites he describes "differed considerably from the Ebionites known to the earlier church fathers."[19] Luomenen states:

Epiphanius's Ebionites' rejection of the temple and sacrifices as well as the Prophets represents not only, as noted above, a clear break with Jewish traditions; it is also the most significant feature that does not cohere with the Irenaean tradition about the Ebionites.[20]

Skarsaune concludes:

On closer inspection, the apparently very rich patristic material on the Ebionites boils down to the information contained in Irenaeus and Hippolytus, to be supplemented also by evidence in Justin of unnamed Jewish believers who held Ebionite points of view.[21]

After the third century we have no certain firsthand information on them.[22]

## Conservative Scholars Favor the Nazarenes

For conservative authors, the idea that the earliest Jewish believers in Jerusalem did not believe in the deity of Yeshua is unthinkable.

Therefore, for them, it would have been impossible for the Ebionites to be the true heirs of the Jerusalem believing community. Samuele Bacchiocchi[§] writes:

> Another false supposition is that the Ebionites represent or at least can be related to the primitive Jewish Christians. It is true that both stressed the importance of the observance of the law, but they differed radically from each other on their view of the nature of Christ. The Ebionites' Christology was in fact like that of the Gnostics, regarding Christ as a plain and common man "who was the fruit of the intercourse of a man with Mary." Such a Christological error can hardly be attributed to the primitive Jewish Christians.[23]

Ray Pritz is another author who has devoted much effort trying to remove the Ebionites from consideration as the true heirs of the earliest Jewish believers in Jerusalem:

> But Ebionism was not the direct heir of the Jewish apostolic church; it was at best only third generation, and to reconcile its doctrines with those of the New Testament requires no small amount of mental gymnastics.[24]

Pritz is a champion of the Nazarenes, the other most likely candidate for being the descendants of the Jerusalem community. He calls attention to the claim made by Epiphanius that the earliest Jewish believers, identified by Epiphanius as Nazarenes, left Jerusalem for the city Pella, east of the Jordan River in Decapolis, before the first Jewish revolt against Rome and the destruction of the Temple in 70 CE.[25] If this claim is correct, Pritz concludes, the Nazarenes, spoken of by Epiphanius in his day, must be the ancestors of the earliest Jerusalem community. The problem is that Epiphanius is dependent on the Christian historian Eusebius for this information, but Eusebius does not identify these Jewish believers as Nazarenes.[26] It also appears that most scholars today do not believe that Eusebius's historical account of the flight to Pella

---

[§]  Even though I disagree with Dr. Bacchiocchi on this point, he remains one of my heroes.

is based in fact.[27]¶ Therefore, one of Pritz's fundamental assumptions is in doubt.

Pritz points out another major problem with his Nazarene theory. The name Nazarene is used in the book of Acts in 24:5 referring to all of the earliest believers. This name is absent from that point on, however, in the writings of the church fathers in identifying any group of believers until it is used by Epiphanius in 376 CE.[28] This name is not mentioned in any writings for over 300 years. As Pritz laments:

> It might be objected at this point that if it is true that Nazarenes was the earliest name for Christians, then we should expect to find the name more frequently in patristic literature before Epiphanius, more often certainly than the isolated notices of Tertullian and Eusebius. To be sure, it is strange (not to say frustrating) that the name is so universally ignored.[29]

Pritz explains the absence of the name in two ways. The first is that the church fathers were writing in Greek. When they came to any references referring to the early "catholic church" as Nazarene (the Semitic language form of Christian), they changed it to the accepted name *Christianoi* instead.[30] He also says that the sect of the Nazarenes was small after 70 CE and was "not included in the earlier heresy lists because they were simply not considered heretical enough or a threat to 'orthodoxy.'"[31] However, we know from the beginning of the church fathers' writings that Jewish believers who continued to observe the Mosaic Law were considered heretics, as is evident from the previous quotes by Irenaeus and Justin Martyr.

---

¶ Wolfram Kinzig comments that Pritz must not have been aware of the seminal study published by Jozef Verheyden that puts doubt on the "flight to Pella" story. (Wolfram Kinzig, "The Nazoraeans," in *Jewish Believers in Jesus*, ed. by Oskar Skarsaune and Reidar Hvalvik [Peabody, MA: Hendrickson Publishers, 2007], p. 471, footnote 35.) Archaeologist Stephen Bourke summarizes 125 years of exploration at Pella, including his own, by saying, "No one piece of evidence viewed in isolation carries any great weight, but viewed together they form a more coherent whole, suggesting a flight to Pella was possible. More we cannot say." (Stephen Bourke, "The Christian Flight to Pella: True or Tale?," *Biblical Archaeology Review*, vol. 39 [May/June 2013], p. 71.)

Luomenen suggests that Epiphanius made up his description of the Nazarenes:

> The religious profile of Epiphanius's Nazarenes was ingeniously developed by the church father himself because he also needed a category of pure "Jewish Christianity" in his *Panarion*. The Ebionites of his day had too many peculiar beliefs and practices to serve as the only example of a "heresy" that tried to combine Judaism with Christianity.[32]

He also suggests that Jerome was possibly describing as Nazarenes a non-Jewish, Christian, Aramaic-speaking group of Syriac Christians:

> Who perhaps had some sympathy toward Judaism—enough to render them suspicious in the eyes of the overtly anti-Jewish Jerome and his compatriots—but who no doubt felt themselves to be Christian, and thus should be classified as such by modern critics.[33]

Other authors are of the opinion that the Nazarenes and the Ebionites are the same group.[34] Our knowledge is limited here, but connecting the Nazarenes to the earliest Jerusalem community is a stretch.

Even if the Nazarenes were shown to be the direct descendants of the Jerusalem community, what they believed regarding the deity of Yeshua is unclear.[35] According to Epiphanius, speaking of the Nazarenes:

> As to Christ, I cannot say whether they too are captives of the wickedness of Cerinthus and Merinthus, and regard him as a mere man—or whether, as the truth is, they affirm his birth of Mary by the Holy Spirit (*Panarion* 29, 7, 6).[36]

Wolfram Kinzig writes:

> Jerome claims "that they believe in Christ, the Son of God born of Mary the virgin, and they say about him that he suffered and rose again under Pontius Pilate" (*Epist.* 112.13). Yet this may be an extrapolation from a remark made by Epiphanius in a quite different context.[37]

There is convincing evidence to suggest that the earliest orthodox Jewish believers, most likely the Ebionites, did not believe in the deity of Yeshua. Since they were there from the beginning and probably the descendants of the Jerusalem community, one would think that they got the account right. The church fathers regarded the Ebionites as heretics. I suspect the real errors in the Messianic faith originated from a different source.

# (Endnotes)

1    Edward H. Flannery, *The Anguish of the Jews: Twenty-Three Centuries of Antisemitism* (New York: Paulist Press, 1985), p. 43.

2    Samuele Bacchiocchi, *From Sabbath to Sunday: A Historical Investigation of the Rise of Sunday Observance in Early Christianity* (Rome: The Pontifical Gregorian University Press, 1977), pp. 233–234.

3    Anthony F. Buzzard and Charles F. Hunting, *The Doctrine of the Trinity: Christianity's Self-Inflicted Wound* (New York: International Scholars Publications, 1998), p. 7.

4    Ibid., p. 35.

5    Petri Luomenen, "Ebionites and Nazarenes," in *Jewish Christianity Reconsidered*, ed. by Matt Jackson-McCabe (Minneapolis: Fortress Press, 2007), p. 82.

6    Ibid., p. 83.

7    Ibid., p. 81.

8    Paul Johnson, *A History of the Jews* (New York: Harper Perennial, 1988), p. 143.

9    "The Apostolic Fathers, Justin Martyr, Irenaeus," Vol. I in *Ante-Nicene Fathers*, ed. by Alexander Roberts and James Donaldson, revised and arranged by A. Cleveland Coxe, 10 Vols. (Peabody, MA: Hendrickson Publishers, 1994), p. 352.

10    Ibid., pp. 351–352.

11    Ibid., p. 527.

12    Oskar Skarsaune, "The Ebionites," in *Jewish Believers in Jesus*, ed. by Oskar Skarsaune and Reidar Hvalvik (Peabody, MA: Hendrickson Publishers, 2007), p. 384.

13    *The Apostolic Fathers, Justin Martyr, Irenaeus*, p. 219.

14    Ibid., p. 219.

15    Oskar Skarsaune, "The Ebionites," p. 384. *The Apostolic Fathers, Justin Martyr, Irenaeus*, p. 219, note 5.

16    Ray A. Pritz, *Nazarene Jewish Christianity: From the End of the New Testament Period until Its Disappearance in the Fourth Century* (Jerusalem: the Magnes Press, 1992), pp. 19–21.

17    *The Apostolic Fathers, Justin Martyr, Irenaeus*, p. 218.

18    Oskar Skarsaune, "The Ebionites," p. 423.

19    Petri Luomenen, "Ebionites and Nazarenes," p. 102.

20  Ibid., p. 100.

21  Oskar Skarsaune, "The Ebionites," p. 462.

22  Ibid., p. 462.

23  Samuele Bacchiocchi, *From Sabbath to Sunday: A Historical Investigation of the Rise of Sunday Observance in Early Christianity*, p. 154.

24  Ray A. Pritz, *Nazarene Jewish Christianity: From the End of the New Testament Period until Its Disappearance in the Fourth Century*, p. 9.

25  Ray A. Pritz, *Nazarene Jewish Christianity: From the End of the New Testament Period until Its Disappearance in the Fourth Century*, p. 10. Epiphanius, *The Panarion*, 29 7,7–8.

26  Ray A. Pritz, *Nazarene Jewish Christianity: From the End of the New Testament Period until Its Disappearance in the Fourth Century*, p. 10. Eusebius, *Ecclesiastical History*, III.5.3.

27  Wolfram Kinzig, "The Nazoraeans," in *Jewish Believers in Jesus,* ed. by Oskar Skarsaune and Reidar Hvalvik (Peabody, MA: Hendrickson Publishers, 2007), p. 471, footnote 35.

28  Ray A. Pritz, *Nazarene Jewish Christianity: From the End of the New Testament Period until Its Disappearance in the Fourth Century*, p. 15.

29  Ibid., pp.15–16.

30  Ibid., p. 16.

31  Ibid., p. 109.

32  Petri Luomenen, "Ebionites and Nazarenes," p. 116.

33  Ibid., p. 114.

34  Wolfram Kinzig, "The Nazoraeans," p. 481, footnote 97.

35  Ibid., p. 474.

36  *The Panarion of Epiphanius of Salamis*, trans. by Frank Williams (Leiden, The Netherlands: Koninklijke Brill, 1997), p. 118.

37  Wolfram Kinzig, "The Nazoraeans," p. 474.

# Chapter 12: Is the New Testament Scripture?

## Does the New Testament Always Reflect the Earliest Convictions?

The New Testament is a collection of books that are felt to be divinely inspired by the church. Without a doubt, the concept of the deity of Yeshua is derived from many passages in the text. Should all of these chosen books be accepted as Scripture, however? Are the passages that discuss the deity of Yeshua reliably authentic to the earliest believers?

## John's Gospel under the Microscope

The book of John is the premier New Testament book that unmistakably builds the case for the deity of Yeshua. New believers are typically told to begin their reading of the Bible in the book of John for this very reason, so that they can understand from the beginning that Yeshua is God. The book of John has major problems, though, and, as I will try to show with the help of Maurice Casey, author of *Is John's Gospel True?*, it cannot be trusted as a reliable source.

Most scholars believe that the book of John was written between 85–100 CE.* Its creation, therefore, is about sixty years after the death

---

* F. F. Bruce: 90–100 CE. (F. F. Bruce, *The New Testament Documents: Are They Reliable?* [Downers Grove, IL: InterVarsity Press, 1960], p. 12.) Craig Blomberg: late 80s or to the 90s. (Craig L. Blomberg, *The Historical Reliability of John's Gospel: Issues and Commentary* [Downers Grove, IL: InterVarsity Press, 2001], p. 44.) Conservative scholars would date the synoptic gospel books

of Yeshua (a considerable amount of time) and about twenty years after the destruction of the Temple in Jerusalem by the Romans. There was much turmoil in Israel at this time—it was a nation under occupation.[1†] Many modern scholars believe that a Johannine community[2] in Asia Minor[3] produced the book of John and its related books. Some feel that this community had lost its Jewish identity even though it was ethnically Jewish.[4]

Yeshua and all of his disciples were Jewish. Naturally, they should have considered themselves to be Jewish and a part of the people of Israel. Nevertheless, in the book of John we see a clear separation between "the Jews" and Yeshua and his followers.

Maurice Casey notes, "The fourth gospel uses the term 'the Jews' more than sixty times, and in the majority of cases it denotes opponents of Jesus."[5] By contrast, the wording "the Jews" is used only sixteen times altogether in Matthew, Mark, and Luke.[6]

Some argue that "the Jews" should be understood as "the Judeans," meaning those Jews from Judea in contrast to those Jews from Galilee or elsewhere.[7] However, in John 6, in Capernaum, a city in Galilee, Yeshua argued with "the Jews" who knew his family—local Galilean Jews, not "Judeans" (John 6:41, 52, 59).[8]

Some say "the Jews" is referring to "Jewish authorities." However, this opinion does not make sense in a number of places, and there were other terms used by John that could have been used to refer to the Jewish authorities—"rulers," "the Pharisees," "the chief priests."[9] For instance, Nicodemus was referred to as "a man of the Pharisees" and "a ruler of the Jews" (John 3:1). He was not a ruler of the "Jewish

Matthew, Mark, and Luke to the 60s CE. (D. A. Carson, "Matthew," Walter W. Wessel, "Mark," and Walter L. Liefeld, "Luke," Vol. 8 of the *The Expositor's Bible Commentary*, ed. by Frank E. Gaebelein, 12 vols. [Grand Rapids, MI: Zondervan Publishing House, 1990], pp. 21, 608, 809.)

† Paul Johnson says, "The Great Revolt of 66 AD and the siege of Jerusalem constitute one of the most important and horrifying events in Jewish history" (p. 137). "Tacitus said 1,197,000 Jews were killed or sold as slaves in the 66–70 struggle alone" (p. 148). (Paul Johnson, *A History of the Jews* [New York: Harper Perennial, 1987].)

authorities."[10] "Jewish authorities" is also not implied in John 2:13, "The Passover of the Jews was at hand" (John 2:13), since Passover was not the festival of the "Jewish authorities."[11] Finally, in relation to the story of Lazarus, it could not have been many "Jewish authorities" who came to console Martha and Mary (John 11:19). In addition, it could not have been many "Jewish authorities" who witnessed the raising of Lazarus and reported this event to the Pharisees, so that the Pharisees and the chief priests could gather the council (John 11:45–47). Nor could it have been a large crowd of "Jewish authorities" who came to see Lazarus, forcing the chief priests to plot to put Lazarus to death (John 12:9–11).[12]

Unfortunately, I would need to disagree with David Stern and say that the book of John *is* "making statements about 'the Jews' that not only are negative, unfriendly, misleading, and false, but are intended by the authors to induce dislike and hatred of 'the Jews' as a class and as individuals."[13]

Curiously, the book of John also seems to come down hard on certain Jewish believers, such as in John 6:60–71 and John 8:31–59.[14] Raimo Hakola, investigating the Jewishness of the Johannine community, writes:

> In the course of the dialogue in 8:31–59, even the believing Jews are counted among those who try to kill Jesus. Jesus here bunches the believing Jews together with other Jews in such a way that they lose their distinctive characteristics. Jesus's harshest words in the Gospel, "You are from your father the devil" (v.44), are addressed not to those who have been openly hostile to him right from the beginning, but to those Jews who are said to believe in him.[15]

Could it be that this narrative represents a conflict around the year 90 CE between the Johannine believers and descendants of the earliest Jewish believers, rather than reflect the situation at the time of Yeshua sixty years earlier? Maybe the Jewish believers maligned here are those who denied the deity of Yeshua and who continued to observe the Torah.[16]

Another set of curious passages in John concerns the excommunication of Jewish believers in Yeshua from the synagogues:[17]

His parents answered, "We know that this is our son and that he was born blind. But how he now sees we do not know, nor do we know who opened his eyes. Ask him; he is of age. He will speak for himself." (His parents said these things because they feared the Jews, for the Jews had already agreed that if anyone should confess Jesus [Yeshua] to be Christ [Messiah], he was to be put out of the synagogue.) (John 9:20–22).

Nevertheless, many even of the authorities believed in him, but for fear of the Pharisees they did not confess it, so that they would not be put out of the synagogue; for they loved the glory that comes from man more than the glory that comes from God (John 12:42–43).

I have said all these things to you to keep you from falling away. They will put you out of the synagogues. Indeed, the hour is coming when whoever kills you will think he is offering service to God. And they will do these things because they have not known the Father, nor me (John 16:1–3).

The problem here, as Casey tells us, is that during the lifetime of Yeshua, no Jews would have been or were kicked out of the synagogue for believing that Yeshua was the Messiah. If Jewish believers were being excommunicated at that time, the twelve disciples of Yeshua would have been the first to go, but we have no hint of this even being threatened. Jews were not known to be cast out of the synagogue until after the destruction of the Temple in 70 CE.[18]

Excommunication of Jewish believers from the synagogue first became evident in the modification of the daily synagogue prayer called the *Shemoneh-Esreh* (Eighteen Benedictions or *Amidah*—standing prayer) by Samuel the Small, at the request of Rabbi Gamaliel II around 85 CE.[19] This twelfth benediction also named *Birkat haMinim* (Benediction Concerning Heretics) was applied according to Joseph Heinemann "specifically to Jewish heretics. It is generally assumed that this new formulation was meant to force the Judeo-Christians out of the Jewish community; in the Genizah version, the word *Notzerim* ('Christians') actually occurs."[20] Excommunication from the synagogue did not seem to be in effect until about the time of the writing of the book of John. As early Christian scholar Peter Hirschberg tells us, "All three of these texts [in John] make sense only when they are interpreted as addressing the problems of the Johannine community, not when attributed directly to Jesus"[21]

The book of John's conflict with "the Jews" and with some "Jews who had believed," as well as its concern about excommunication from the synagogue, seems to be taking the situation of the Johannine community at the end of the first century and rewriting this into the history of Yeshua's time. Naturally, this causes us to have a concern for the reliability of this book.

Hakola does not think that the separation of the Johannine community from the Jewish community came mainly from Jewish opposition to the Johannine community but stemmed from the Johannine community's loss of Jewish identity.[22] According to Casey, Jewish identity during the first century can be measured with an eight-point identity scale. This scale involves the following identity factors: ethnicity, scripture, monotheism, circumcision, Sabbath observance, dietary laws, purity laws, and major festivals.[23] As seen in the book of John, the Johannine community had lost most of its points on the Jewish identity scale.

1) **Ethnicity:** As outlined earlier in this chapter, the Johannine community seemed to have separated itself from "the Jews."[24]

2) **Scripture:** In John, Yeshua referred to the Tanach as "your Law" when speaking to the Pharisees or "the Jews" (John 8:17, 10:34), and "their Law" when talking about the Jewish community (John 15:25). These verses suggest the Johannine community had little value for the Tanach.[25] According to Hakola, the representative figures of Jewish tradition in the Torah, Abraham and Moses, are found to be lacking in comparison to Yeshua in the Book of John (John 6 and 8).[26] "Jesus' revelation is presented not as a natural continuation of the past but as a superior alternative to the past tradition."[27]

3) **Monotheism:** The Johannine community had clearly elevated the man Yeshua as God, which some would argue is not consistent with monotheism.[28]

4)  **Circumcision:** John 7:22 has Yeshua declare to "the Jews," "Moses has given you circumcision." Circumcision did not also belong to Yeshua.[29]

5)  **Sabbath Observance:** "The Jews" understood that Yeshua was doing away with[‡] the Shabbat in John 5:18.[30]

6)  **Dietary Laws:** The dietary laws are not discussed in John.[31]

7)  **Purity Laws:** At the wedding in Cana, the stone water pots were "for the purification of the Jews" (John 2:6). Purification seemed to be an "alien" custom.[32]

8)  **Major Festivals:** Both Sukkot (Tabernacles) and Passover were "of the Jews" in the book of John (John 7:2 and John 11:55). There was a lack of ownership here.[33]

The Johannine community is getting a failing score when it comes to Jewish identity.[34] This group consisting of Jews by physical descent and Gentiles does have detailed knowledge of Judaism[35] and Israel,[36] but Casey concludes they have a "Gentile self-identification."[37]

The book of John also has some historical problems. Most Christians, when asked how many times the Temple was cleansed by Yeshua, would say one. In the synoptic books (Matthew, Mark, and Luke), the Temple was cleansed at the end of Yeshua's ministry and became the final stimulus for those seeking to kill him (Matthew 21:12–13, Mark 11:15–18, Luke 19:45–46). In the book of John, however, the Temple cleansing came just after the wedding in Cana at the beginning of Yeshua's ministry (John 2:12–22). It was the resurrection of Lazarus in the book of John that was the final event that pushed his enemies to seek his life, not the Temple cleansing (John 11:53).[38]

Another historical problem in John is the dating of the "Last Supper." In the synoptic books, the Last Supper was clearly a Passover meal (Seder) eaten by Yeshua and his disciples before his death. The

‡  According to Thayer's Greek Lexicon, the verb in John 5:18 "is equivalent to annul, subvert; to do away with; to deprive of authority whether by precept or by act." Most English versions say he "was breaking the Sabbath," but more accurately he was "breaking up" the Shabbat. (Joseph Thayer, *A Greek-English Lexicon of the New Testament* [n.p.: n.p., 1889], BibleWorks, v.9.)

Passover lambs had been killed on the 14th of Nisan, and the meal was being eaten after dark. Yeshua died after the Seder.

In the book of John, the Last Supper was not a Passover meal but occurred before Passover. Yeshua then died on the 14th of Nisan with the Passover lambs. Many clues in the text give us this understanding.[39]

First, John the Baptist identified Yeshua specifically as "the Lamb of God, who takes away the sin of the world!" (John 1:29) The Johannine community had Yeshua die with the Passover lambs to prove this point.[40]

John 13:1 tells us that the meal happened before the feast of Passover. We are not given any clues that the disciples were to "prepare" for Yeshua to "eat the Passover," as depicted in the synoptic books (Mark 14:12, Matthew 26:17, Luke 22:7–8).[41]

During the meal, Yeshua identified Y'hudah from K'riot (Judas Iscariot) as his betrayer and sent him out to perform this act. The other disciples, however, who did not understand, began to speculate why Y'hudah left the meal:

> Then after he had taken the morsel, Satan entered into him. Jesus [Yeshua] said to him, "What you are going to do, do quickly." Now no one at the table knew why he said this to him. Some thought that, because Judas [Y'hudah] had the moneybag, Jesus [Yeshua] was telling him, "Buy what we need for the feast," or that he should give something to the poor. So, after receiving the morsel of bread, he immediately went out. And it was night (John 13:27–30).

If this meal were an evening Seder and the beginning of the feast, this first day would have been a holy convocation where ordinary work was not to be done (Leviticus 23:7). It would have been unlikely that the disciples would have thought that Y'hudah was going out to spend money to buy things for the feast. If this meal were held on the day of preparation for the Passover, though, as John suggests, when the lambs were to be killed, spending money to buy things for the feast would make sense.[42]

When Yeshua was arrested after the meal, "the Jews" eventually took him to Pilate. They were unable to enter the praetorium, however, so as not to be defiled. Otherwise, they would have been unable to eat the Passover.

> Then they led Jesus [Yeshua] from the house of Caiaphas [Kayafa] to the governor's headquarters. It was early morning. They themselves did not enter the governor's headquarters, so that they would not be defiled, but could eat the Passover (John 18: 28).

Some conservative scholars argue that this eating of the Passover refers to other sacrifices eaten during the seven days of the feast, such as the *Chagigah* (Numbers 28:18–19).[43] Nevertheless "eating the Passover" undoubtedly always refers to the eating of the Pesach sacrifice—the lamb.[44]

In John 19:14, we are told that Yeshua was being put to death on "the day of preparation of the Passover." This day was always the day that the Passover lambs were slaughtered.[45]

The text seems clear that the Last Supper in the book of John was something other than a Passover meal. Yeshua was made to die with the Passover lambs in John, before the Seder. Larry Hurtado, author of *Lord Jesus Christ: Devotion to Jesus in Earliest Christianity*, agrees. He states "In the Synoptics Jesus eats a Passover meal on the night before his death, but in GJohn he dies on the day the lambs are slain in preparation for the Passover meal."[46]

A multitude of other details in the book of John cause us to question its accuracy and its purpose.

Yochanan (John) the Baptist had a different role to play in the book of John compared to the synoptic books (John 1:19–36, 3:22–36). In the synoptic books, Yochanan the Baptist prepared the way for Yeshua. In the book of John, Yochanan the Baptist bore witness to Yeshua's preexistence and deity. He had no doubts about Yeshua's identity, which is contrary to the synoptic accounts.[47] It is interesting that Yeshua, the God-man in John, was not actually baptized by Yochanan the Baptist. In contrast, in the book of Mark, Yochanan the Baptist baptized Yeshua as he proclaims "a baptism of repentance for the forgiveness of sins" (Mark 1:4).[48] As written by Casey, the purpose of Yochanan the Baptist in the book of John is to be "an unambiguously positive witness to the Johannine Christ."[49]

In the synoptic books, Yeshua took two elements from the Passover Seder, the unleavened bread and wine, and used them as a symbolic remembrance of his soon to be atoning death. In the book of John, these elements were not mentioned in the context of the Last Supper but were included in an extensive discussion of the Eucharist, or communion, in John chapter 6. This early presentation on the body and blood of Yeshua was out of place in the book of John. It most likely represented the practice of the Johannine community toward the end of the first century. It was probably not tied to the Jewish Passover on purpose. Partaking in the Eucharist ceremony appeared to have become an actual requirement in the Johannine community for those seeking salvation and eternal life (John 6:52–58). No wonder many Jewish believers did not accept this theology (John 6:60–66).[50]

There are a number of inconsistencies in the arrest and crucifixion of Yeshua in the book of John compared to the synoptic books.[51] In John, Yeshua the God-man was not in distress over his impending death and continued to be in full control of the situation.[52] In John alone, a band of Roman soldiers was also involved in arresting Yeshua (John 18:3).[53] Yeshua was not betrayed by a kiss from Y'hudah, but, in command of the situation, came up to the arresting party himself and asked them, "Whom do you seek?" When they asked for him by name, he identified himself, saying "I am he," and promptly the arresting party drew back and fell to the ground (John 18:4–6).[54] Only in John did Yeshua tell the Roman governor Pilate, "You would have no authority over me at all unless it had been given you from above" (John 19:11).[55] In John only, three women—including Miryam from Magdala (Mary Magdalene) and Yeshua's mother—and the disciple whom he loved were standing by the cross, close enough to hear Yeshua speak to them (John 19:25–27). In the synoptic books, Miryam from Magdala and some different women looked on, but from a distance with many other women (Mark 15:40–41).[56]

The giving of the Holy Spirit in the synoptic tradition occurred on Shavuot, or Pentecost, fifty days after Yeshua's resurrection (Acts 2:1–4). Yeshua ordered his disciples to stay in Jerusalem and wait for this very event (Acts 1:4–5). In the book of John, the disciples were given the Holy Spirit by Yeshua on the evening of his resurrection: "Jesus [Yeshua] said to them again, 'Peace be with you. As the Father has sent me, even so I am sending you.' And when he had said this, he breathed on them and said to them, 'Receive the Holy Spirit'" (John 20:21–22).

According to Bart Ehrman, in the synoptic books, Yeshua did miracles to help the needy according to their faith. He did not perform miracles to prove who he was.[57] Often Yeshua tried to keep the miracles low key (Mark 1:23–25, Mark 1: 32–34, Mark 1:40–44, Mark 5:35–43, Mark 7:32–36, Mark 8:22–26). In the book of John, however, Yeshua performed miracles ("signs") to prove his divine identity (John 2:6–11, John 6:5–14, John 11:1–44). He also did "signs" for causing people to have faith in him (John 4:46–54, John 11:1–44, John 20:30–31).[58]

In John, there are no parables even though we are told in the synoptic tradition that Yeshua spoke to the crowds in parables:[59] "With many such parables he spoke the word to them, as they were able to hear it. He did not speak to them without a parable, but privately to his own disciples he explained everything" (Mark 4:33–34). In the synoptic books, when Yeshua spoke, he was mainly teaching people how to live. In John, Yeshua was primarily speaking about himself. Any red-letter edition of the New Testament (in which all of Yeshua's words are written in red) will quickly confirm this point. Geza Vermes, Dead Sea Scroll and early Christianity scholar, states of John that "the doctrinal message is expounded in the many rambling, self-descriptive monologues of the Johannine Jesus."[60]

The gospel book of John, and most likely its related books (the three letters of John and the book of Revelation), appear to have been produced by a Johannine community in Asia Minor at the end of the first century. Even from our short review of the book of John, one can see that these texts are unreliable sources of truth concerning the historical figure Yeshua. It appears that this community, with "Gentile self-identification," must have invented the divinity claims made in these texts. This portrayal of the man Yeshua as God could not possibly reflect the understanding of Jewish believers in Jerusalem from the beginning, as I will continue to show.

## Philippians 2:5–11: The Hymn Not Composed by Sha'ul

Many other New Testament texts clearly speak of the preexistence of Yeshua and his deity. As I began to investigate these texts outside of the book of John, I started with the next most famous called Carmen Christi—the "Hymn to Christ as God."[61] This passage is found in Philippians 2:5–11:

> Have this mind among yourselves, which is yours in Christ [Messiah] Jesus [Yeshua], who, though he was in the form of God, did not count equality with God a thing to be grasped, but emptied himself, by taking the form of a servant, being born in the likeness of men. And being found in human form, he humbled himself by becoming obedient to the point of death, even death on a cross. Therefore God has highly exalted him and bestowed on him the name that is above every name, so that at the name of Jesus [Yeshua] every knee should bow, in heaven and on earth and under the earth, and every tongue confess that Jesus [Yeshua] Christ [Messiah] is Lord, to the glory of God the Father.

This passage takes the verse of Isaiah 45:23 and uses it to equate Yeshua with YHVH. Initially, it appeared to me that Sha'ul also believed that Yeshua was God. After I had glanced at some commentaries on these verses, however, I was shocked. In just about every case, the commentators were saying that Sha'ul most likely did not write this passage.[62] They pointed out that the Greek used in these seven verses is not consistent with Sha'ul's Greek.[63]

Carmen Christi's lack of Pauline authorship became an interesting problem to investigate. We could generate about three reasonable hypotheses as to how these atypical verses ended up in Philippians chapter 2. First, Sha'ul could have written these verses using a different writing style. Secondly, Sha'ul could have borrowed these verses from another source and placed them in his letter. Alternatively, maybe a later editor inserted these verses into this letter unbeknownst to Sha'ul.

As I discussed in chapter 1, the historical sciences use the method of multiple competing hypotheses when trying to interpret historical, scientific data.[64] Here we have a similar historical problem. None of us was a witness to the writing and reproduction of Sha'ul's letters. None of these hypotheses can be proven true. With these three competing hypotheses, we need to infer to the best explanation.

Few commentators would argue that Sha'ul changed his writing style to produce this hymn.[65] It is hard to image a contemporary writer of nonfiction who would change his writing style and vocabulary for a brief section when attempting to explain one of his most weighty and complex issues. This hypothesis is the least appealing.

Most conservative scholars insist that these verses were taken from an early hymn, preceding Sha'ul, and sung by the first believers.[66] Some suggest that since the Greek here appears to be translated from Aramaic, this hymn is ancient and suggests a Judeo-Christian psalm.[67] It is proposed that Sha'ul took this well-known hymn and stuck it into his letter. James White tries to explain what he thinks Sha'ul is doing here:

> In our day, it is common for a minister to incorporate a reference to a well-known and well-loved hymn so as to make a strong point. Many close a sermon on the grace of God, for example, by saying, "Amazing grace, how sweet the sound, that saved a wretch like me!"
>
> I believe that is exactly what Paul is doing in the second chapter of his letter to the Philippians.[68]

Maybe there is a loose association in the context of this hymn concerning humility, the context of the beginning of Philippians chapter 2, but Sha'ul was not speaking about the preexistence and deity of Yeshua before or after these interrupting verses. Vermes points out that one could remove these verses from the chapter and not have a clue that something was missing.[69]

I was stunned when I first heard this explanation. It is hard for me to imagine that Sha'ul did not pen one of the main arguments made for the deity of Yeshua in the letter to the Philippians but borrowed from another source. Sha'ul, a man with chutzpah, did not seem afraid to talk about any topic or to confront his own leaders and kings. Here, however, instead of putting forth an argument for the deity of Yeshua himself, it is suggested that Sha'ul borrowed a hymn to explain this complicated concept. What we know about Sha'ul and human nature makes this hypothesis very unlikely also.

Could it be that a later editor inserted these verses into Philippians chapter 2 unbeknownst to Sha'ul? Not only is this hymn inconsistent with Sha'ul's understanding of Yeshua (see chapter 10), but the man Sha'ul was more than capable and willing to explain difficult concepts. He could expound on the nature of God, reveal who Yeshua was, and detail what Yeshua did for us in his own words. Someone trying to incorporate the idea of the deity of Yeshua into the Messianic faith must have inserted these verses later into Sha'ul's letter, unbeknownst to Sha'ul. It must have happened early enough to become a fixed part of the letter to the Philippians. If we are to infer to the best explanation conforming to our present day knowledge, the most obvious conclusion to draw here is that hypothesis three must be correct.

## First-Century Letter Writing

Is it possible that a letter written by Sha'ul could have been changed?§ Bart Ehrman outlines some of the features involved in letter writing by believers in the first century. How confident can we be that we have the exact words of Sha'ul? First, probably less than 10–15 percent of people in the first Christian century could read.[70] The information in such a letter would be conveyed to the community by having the letter

---

§ According to Darrell Bock and Daniel Wallace, most liberal and conservative New Testament scholars have known for over a century that the last section of Mark, verses 16:9–20, and the story of the woman caught in adultery found in John 7:53–8:11 are not found in the earliest New Testament manuscripts. Therefore, they were added to the New Testament later. Most modern Bible translations acknowledge this fact in footnotes. (Darrell L. Bock and Daniel B. Wallace, *Dethroning Jesus: Exposing Popular Culture's Quest to Unseat the Biblical Christ* [Nashville: Thomas Nelson, 2007], pp. 62–64.) A multitude of sermons have been delivered about the woman caught in adultery. However, the Tanach teaches that sin continues to have consequences in this world even after one repents (2 Samuel 12:7–23), and communities, made up of sinners, are entrusted with the responsibility to judge and punish sin as long as they use righteous justice.

read aloud.[71] Most people could not verify the accuracy of a particular letter themselves by reading it. Another fact is that copies of these letters needed to be reproduced by hand. There were no photocopy machines where thousands of reproductions could be made at once. The copyists of these letters were not professionals but the educated members of the Christian communities.[72] Now imagine a letter being dictated to a scribe by Sha'ul and sent to a faraway congregation. Can we assume that the document will remain pure as multiple copies are made over time, especially after the original letter is destroyed by use and time?[73] Can we trust that the letter will continue unadulterated after Sha'ul dies and the original keepers of the letter die?

Using the book of Galatians as an example, Ehrman says the earliest, nearly complete copy of Galatians that we have today is from 200 CE, about 150 years after Paul wrote it.[74] The transmission of the New Testament text from some time in the second century onward has been found to be fairly reliable.[75] Nevertheless, what could have happened to these texts in predominantly Gentile hands outside of the land of Israel between the time of the destruction of the Temple in Jerusalem, in 70 CE, to the end of the Second Jewish Revolt against Rome, in 135 CE, as the Jewish world in Israel came crashing down?[76] The Romans kicked up much dust shortly after the death of Yeshua, and it did not begin to settle until the latter part of the second century.

Could a hymn have been added to Sha'ul's letter to the Philippians after it left his hands? I believe there is no evidence to say that this could not have happened. Robert Hawkins, writing in the 1940s, is one who suggested that Carmen Christi was added to Sha'ul's letter later:

> It is best to interpret the passage for what it is, a meditation upon the humiliation of Christ written by someone at a later time when the emphasis had been shifted more and more to his divinity, so that anything which resembled humanity had been reduced to mere seeming and shadow. The Philippian situation is not even remotely in the mind of its author.[77]

Geza Vermes likewise wrote:

> Both the terminology and the style seem to point to the ideology of early second century AD. Ancient Church tradition connects

the Fourth Gospel, filled with similar ideas, to Ephesus. We also know from Pliny the Younger, governor of Bithynia in AD 110, that Christians from Asia Minor were in the habit of "singing alternately a hymn to Christ as to a god" (Letters 10.96: '*carmenque Christo quasi deodiceresecuminvicem*'). My critics complained that I rejected the authenticity of the passage from Philippians because its Christ picture did not agree with my theory. As a matter of fact, I argue against its Pauline origin on the grounds that it does not fit into *Paul's understanding* of Jesus, as reflected throughout all his genuine letters and in particular in his numerous prayer formulas and doxologies (see pp. 111–12). In consequence, I continue to maintain that the poem was inserted into the Letter to the Philippians by a later editor.[78]

## What Other Passages Did Sha'ul Not Write?

Now, to solidify my argument a little more I need to bring out one additional amazing fact. It seems Sha'ul did not compose any passage discussing the preexistence and deity of Yeshua in his letters. All passages discussing the preexistence and deity of Yeshua in Sha'ul's letters appear to be non-Pauline creations that were embedded into the text. Conservative Christian Dean Overman boldly explains that:

> Paul's letters incorporate earlier traditions, hymns, creeds, and practices so that they constitute extremely important historical evidence of the traditions, practices, devotion, and beliefs of the earliest Jewish Christians in the decades prior to the 50s.[79]

The one major assumption made by Overman is that Sha'ul was the one who did the incorporating.

It does seem true, in at least two places, that Sha'ul borrows sayings that did not originate with himself and sticks them into his letter.[80] In each case, though, he tells us exactly what he is doing:

> For I delivered to you as of first importance what I also received: that Christ [Messiah] died for our sins in accordance with the Scriptures, that he was buried, that he was raised on the third day in accordance with the Scriptures, and that he appeared to Cephas [Kefa], then to the twelve (1 Corinthians 15:3–5).

> For I received from the Lord what I also delivered to you, that the
> Lord Jesus [Yeshua] on the night when he was betrayed took bread,
> and when he had given thanks, he broke it, and said, "This is my body
> which is for you. Do this in remembrance of me." In the same way also
> he took the cup, after supper, saying, "This cup is the new covenant in
> my blood. Do this, as often as you drink it, in remembrance of me."
> For as often as you eat this bread and drink the cup, you proclaim the
> Lord's death until he comes (1 Corinthians 11:23–26).

In these examples, Sha'ul told us he is delivering information that he
received from others. Both of these passages are in the context of the
rest of Sha'ul's message. Both of these teachings can be found in the
synoptic tradition. Neither of these passages speaks to the preexistence
or deity of Yeshua.

When it comes to the other embedded passages in Sha'ul's letters
describing Yeshua's preexistence and deity, however, Sha'ul did not
hint that they were traditions he had received. The passages are usually
out of context with the rest of the letter. Moreover, if these embedded texts were truly pre-Pauline traditions of the early believers in
Jerusalem, we should see these concepts on the preexistence of Yeshua
and his deity clearly recorded in the synoptic tradition written ten to
twenty years after Sha'ul's letters. We do not find them there.

Three other well-known, non-Pauline creations embedded into
the Pauline letters that speak to the preexistence and deity of Yeshua
are 1 Corinthians 8:5–6, Colossians 1:15–20, and 1 Timothy 3:16:[81]

> For although there may be so-called gods in heaven or on earth—as
> indeed there are many "gods" and many "lords"—yet for us there is one
> God, the Father, from whom are all things and for whom we exist, and
> one Lord, Jesus [Yeshua] Christ [Messiah], through whom are all things
> and through whom we exist (1 Corinthians 8:5–6).

> He is the image of the invisible God, the firstborn of all creation. For
> by him all things were created, in heaven and on earth, visible and
> invisible, whether thrones or dominions or rulers or authorities—all
> things were created through him and for him. And he is before all
> things, and in him all things hold together. And he is the head of the
> body, the church. He is the beginning, the firstborn from the dead,

that in everything he might be preeminent. For in him all the fullness of God was pleased to dwell, and through him to reconcile to himself all things, whether on earth or in heaven, making peace by the blood of his cross (Colossians 1:15–20).

Great indeed, we confess, is the mystery of godliness: He was manifested in the flesh, vindicated by the Spirit, seen by angels, proclaimed among the nations, believed on in the world, taken up in glory (1 Timothy 3:16).

## "Something Is Rotten in the State of Denmark!"

Is it possible that Sha'ul could only rely on "ancient hymns, creeds, or confessions" to explain the preexistence and deity of Yeshua and that he was incapable of using his own words when it came to this topic? Something is drastically wrong with this picture. Conservative scholar Andrew Chester is also surprised that Sha'ul does not explain more about Yeshua's deity associated with 1 Corinthians 8:6 or Philippians 2:6–11. However, he feels that Sha'ul did not need to explain further since his audience was already well-versed on this topic:

It is indeed striking that Paul does not, either at 1 Corinthians 8:6 or Philippians 2:6–11, explain at all the Christological significance of what he says. The more obvious conclusion from this, however, is that those he is addressing are already familiar with this kind of claim about Christ, rather than that it has no such significance.[82]

To me, the most obvious conclusion is that no believers at the time of Sha'ul ever entertained the idea that Yeshua could be God.

## The Primitive Confession "Jesus Is Lord"

Many authors also point out a "primitive" confession (*homologia*) of the earliest believers—"Jesus is Lord"—that is found embedded in Sha'ul's writing and found in other New Testament texts.[83] The most prominent of these passages is Philippians 2:5–11, already discussed. Two other classic examples where this "primitive" confession is found are 1 Corinthians 12:3 and Romans 10:9–10:[84]

Because, if you confess with your mouth that Jesus [Yeshua] is Lord and believe in your heart that God raised him from the dead, you will be saved. For with the heart one believes and is justified, and with the mouth one confesses and is saved (Romans 10:9–10).

Therefore I want you to understand that no one speaking in the Spirit of God ever says "Jesus [Yeshua] is accursed!" and no one can say "Jesus [Yeshua] is Lord" except in the Holy Spirit (1 Corinthians 12:3).

The expression "Jesus is Lord" in each case is introduced by the Greek form of a quotation mark—the *hoti recitativum* (found in Codex Vaticanus [B] for Romans 10:9).[85] Romans 10:13, quoting from Joel 2:32 (Joel 3:5 in the Hebrew Bible), equates this "Lord" with YHVH, "For 'everyone who calls on the name of the Lord will be saved'" (Romans 10:13). Curiously, removing verses 9 and 10 from the chapter establishes YHVH as the Lord about whom Sha'ul is speaking and no longer suggests Yeshua. The flow of the full texts surrounding both Romans 10:9–10 and 1 Corinthians 12:3 are also not interrupted by the deletion of these verses. Therefore, I suspect monkey business in these "primitive" confessions also.

New Testament scholars over the years have unearthed many insightful facts. Specifically, superimposed upon the original New Testament writings are a distinct layer of books and passages that were written to force the deity of Yeshua upon the early Messianic faith. Astonishingly, these grafted writings became rapidly fused into the whole. They have changed the nature of the true Messianic faith for the last 1,900 years.

## Did the Earliest Believers Really Understand That Yeshua Was God?

Various conservative authors use the books of the Johannine community and the embedded texts in Paul's letters to prove that the earliest Jewish believers believed in the deity of Yeshua. If the deity of Yeshua was a concept that evolved over time, as more liberal scholars believe, then it was just an idea, not a reality. Conservative scholars, who consider Yeshua's deity to be factual, however, would say that the earliest believers understood that Yeshua was God during his lifetime or shortly afterward, but certainly before the earliest New Testament writings of Sha'ul.

One author, Richard Bauckham, uses these passages to show that Yeshua at the very beginning was included in the "unique divine identity" in sovereignty, in creation (John 1:3, 1 Corinthians 8:6, Colossians 1:16–17, Hebrews 1:3¶), in name (Philippians 2:9), and in worship (Philippians 2: 9–11, Revelation 5).[86] He believes there is a boundary between God and everything else created, and Yeshua is on the side of God as argued from these passages.[87]

Another author, Larry Hurtado, makes another argument from these very same passages saying that the worship of and devotion to Yeshua occurred as a "mutation within Judaism" very early after Yeshua's death. This mutation arose as a "binitarian schema."[88] In addition, incredibly, he makes an argument from silence:

> There is hardly any indication in Paul's letters that he knew of any controversy or serious variance about this exalted place of Jesus among the various other Christian circles with which he was acquainted. In historical terms we may refer to a veritable "big bang," an explosively rapid and impressively substantial Christological development in the earliest stage of the Christian movement.[89]

More likely, there was not controversy or variance, because this concept concerning Yeshua's deity did not come until a later date.

If the embedded hymns and confessions were a later addition to the text, they tell us nothing about the faith of the earliest believers but about the faith of a later group. Without the Johannine books and the embedded non-Pauline texts in Sha'ul's letters, these conservative authors, such as Bauckham and Hurtado, lack the needed evidence to demonstrate that the earliest believers regarded Yeshua as God.

---

¶ Hebrews 1:3 is another verse felt to be a Christological hymn. (Jack T. Sanders, *The New Testament Christological Hymns: Their Historical Religious Background* [New York: Cambridge University Press, 1971], pp. 19–20. Dean L. Overman, *A Case for the Divinity of Jesus: Examining the Earliest Evidence* [New York: Rowman & Littlefield Publishers, Inc., 2010], p. 246.)

## Alterations in the Synoptic Books to Bolster Yeshua's Deity

Before closing, I would like to examine some of the texts in the synoptic books that seem to have been altered to bolster the divinity claims of Yeshua.

Since the book of Mark appears to be a source that the books of Matthew and Luke used to write their books, it is interesting when one finds changes to Mark that make Yeshua out to be God.

Compare the following verses:

> For whoever is ashamed of me and of my words in this adulterous and sinful generation, of him will the Son of Man also be ashamed when he comes in the glory of his Father with the holy angels (Mark 8:38).

> For whoever is ashamed of me and of my words, of him will the Son of Man be ashamed when he comes in his glory and the glory of the Father and of the holy angels (Luke 9:26).

In Mark, Yeshua will return in the glory of his Father. Luke, dissatisfied with that, has him return in his own glory also.

Compare the following verses:

> And as he was setting out on his journey, a man ran up and knelt before him and asked him, "Good Teacher, what must I do to inherit eternal life?" And Jesus [Yeshua] said to him, "Why do you call me good? No one is good except God alone" (Mark 10:17–18).

> And behold, a man came up to him, saying, "Teacher, what good deed must I do to have eternal life?" And he said to him, "Why do you ask me about what is good? There is only one who is good. If you would enter life, keep the commandments" (Matthew 19:16–17).

Yeshua is clearly denying that he is God in the book of Mark. Matthew tweaks the dialogue to remove this denial.

The end of Matthew seems to make a plug for the Trinity,** but

---

** Similar verses supporting the Trinity are found in 1 John 5:7–8. These verses are still included in the King James tradition but are known for over one hundred years by most scholars, including conservatives, to be inauthentic (italicized section): "For there are three that bear witness *in heaven: the Father,* there is some evidence that this may not be the original.

> And Jesus [Yeshua] came and said to them, "All authority in heaven and on earth has been given to me. Go therefore and make disciples of all nations, baptizing them in the name of the Father and of the Son and of the Holy Spirit, teaching them to observe all that I have commanded you. And behold, I am with you always, to the end of the age" (Matthew 28:18–20).

Some authors suggest that Eusebius quotes numerous times from a different form of Matthew 28:19, which does not have the Trinitarian formula:[90]

> Go ye and make disciples of all the nations *in my name*, teaching them to observe all things, whatsoever I commanded you.[91]

An early document called the *Didache*, which is felt to be a product of Jewish believers, quotes Matthew 28:18–20 as found in our current New Testament in *Didache* 7:1. However, *Didache* 9:5 states:

> But let no one eat or drink of your Thanksgiving (Eucharist), but they who have been baptized into the name of the Lord; for concerning this also the Lord hath said, Give not that which is holy to the dogs.[92]

This variation causes Jonathan Draper to suggest that the earlier Trinitarian reference is a later redaction.[93]

Moreover, curiously, a shorter form of Matthew 28:18–20 is located in the Hebrew Matthew found in the fourteenth-century treatise *Even Bohan* produced by Shem-Tob ben-Isaac ben-Shaprut, which could also reflect an earlier tradition of the text.[94]

---

*the Word, and the Holy Spirit; and these three are one. And there are three that bear witness on earth:* the Spirit, the water, and the blood; and these three agree as one (1John 5:7–8, New King James Version). (Daniel B. Wallace, "Lost in Transmission: How Badly Did the Scribes Corrupt the New Testament Text?" in *Revisiting the Corruption of the New Testament: Manuscript, Patristic, and Apocryphal Evidence* ed. by Daniel B. Wallace [Grand Rapids, MI: Kregel Publications, 2011], p. 44.)

## Inconsistencies with the Virgin Birth Narrative

The birth narratives in Matthew and Luke pose another problem. First, as seen in chapter 11, the earliest Jewish believers, the Ebionites of Irenaeus, did not believe in the virgin birth but understood Yoseph (Joseph) and Miryam (Mary) to be the parents of Yeshua. According to Irenaeus: "They [the Ebionites] use the Gospel according to Matthew only" (*Irenaeus against Heresies*, 1.26.2).[95] Now the Ebionites were probably rational folk. They most likely did not use a text that spoke of the virgin birth—a concept they did not accept. Therefore, their "Matthew" must have been different from the one we have today.

Another difficulty with the virgin birth narrative is that it is not found in the book of Mark, a presumed earlier source for Matthew and Luke. If the virgin birth happened, its importance should have also caused it to show up in the earliest record of Yeshua's life, but it is not there.[††]

The birth narrative in Luke sounds more like Greek mythology where Yeshua is a divine human because God is his actual father:[96]

> And the angel said to her, "Do not be afraid, Mary [Miryam], for you have found favor with God. And behold, you will conceive in your womb and bear a son, and you shall call his name Jesus [Yeshua]. He will be great and will be called the Son of the Most High. And the Lord God will give to him the throne of his father David, and he will reign over the house of Jacob forever, and of his kingdom there will be no end." And Mary [Miryam] said to the angel, "How will this be, since I am a virgin?" And the angel answered her, "The Holy Spirit will come upon you, and the power of the Most High will overshadow you; therefore the child to be born will be called holy—the Son of God" (Luke 1:30-35).

---

†† Vermes writes that an earlier author, Sha'ul, also does not mention the virgin birth. Sha'ul says Yeshua was born to an unnamed Jewish woman: "But when the fullness of time had come, God sent forth his son, born of woman, born under the law" (Galatians 4:4). (Geza Vermes, *Christian Beginnings: From Nazareth to Nicaea* [New Haven, CT: Yale University Press, 2013], p. 107.)

Luke misused the phrase "son of God." "Son of God" should be the designation for a human being with a unique relationship with God, ultimately naming the Messiah.[97] Luke is describing a semidivine being with God as his physical father.[‡‡]

The idea of the virgin birth seems to come out of the Greek translation of the Tanach—the Septuagint. To justify the virgin birth, Matthew quotes from Isaiah 7:14: "All this took place to fulfill what the Lord had spoken by the prophet: 'Behold, the virgin shall conceive and bear a son, and they shall call his name Immanuel' (which means, God with us)" (Matthew 1:22–23). Often when the New Testament quotes the Tanach, as in this case, it quotes from the Greek Septuagint rather than from the Hebrew Bible. The Greek word to describe this woman in the Greek Matthew and the Septuagint is *parthenos*, which means "virgin." The Hebrew text of Isaiah 7:14, however, uses the word *almah*, which means "young woman."[§§] Now an *almah* may be a virgin, but the specific word for virgin in Hebrew is *b'tulah*.

If the Hebrew text had been quoted, in this case, the author would have had difficulty making the point that Miryam was a virgin using the Hebrew word *almah*—"young woman." One would think that if Matthew were originally written in Hebrew, all of the quotes from the Tanach would have been taken from the Hebrew Bible rather

---

‡‡    The virgin birth also leads to an enigma. One of the identifying characteristics of the Messiah is that he will be a descendant of King David. The genealogy of a Judean king never ran through a woman, so even if Miryam were descended from King David, this would not place her offspring in line to the throne. Some say that if Yoseph were the descendant of King David, then he could have just adopted Yeshua as his son, and that would place him in line to the throne. However, that would mean that anyone could have become the Messiah—the only requirement would have been adoption by Yoseph.

§§    It is curious that there is an example in the Septuagint where the word *parthenos* or "virgin" is used for someone who is no longer a virgin. In Genesis 34:3, Dinah is referred to twice by Shechem as a *parthenos* after he has raped her. (Rabbi Tovia Singer, "A Christian Defends Matthew by Insisting That the Author of the First Gospel Relied on the Septuagint When He Quoted Isaiah to Support the Virgin Birth," Outreach Judaism, accessed June, 21, 2015, outreachjudaism.org/septuagint-virgin-birth/.)

from the Greek Septuagint. The virgin birth narrative in Matthew might have been a later Greek addition to the original Hebrew text when it was translated into Greek.

## The Altered Text Became the Dominant Manuscript

How much did the early church alter the text of the New Testament to conform to its theology? In 1902, Fred Conybeare suggested that manipulation of the text was a regular occurrence:

> First, it is quite erroneous to assert, as Westcott and Hort have in their introduction asserted, that the text of the gospels bears no trace of having been altered anywhere for dogmatic or doctrinal reasons. And, what is more, the interpolated texts have been regularly appealed to for centuries and centuries in defense of the very doctrines in behalf of which they were inserted.
>
> Secondly, it is useless, as a rule, to look for these old texts in manuscripts, for the Church has exercised too vigilant a censorship for them to survive.[98]

It makes sense that a dominant orthodoxy would preserve its own theology at the expense of its competitors.

Most conservative believers view the New Testament as inerrant Scripture. Unfortunately, as many authors have shown, these books do not faithfully present the absolute truth of the Messianic faith from the very beginning. It appears that the veracity of the text was altered quickly from the start. Specifically, the books from the Johannine community as well as the scattered hymnic passages and confessions seem to be forcing a preexistent and divine Yeshua into the text. The New Testament still conveys information that is reliable, and that is essential for us to know, but we need to weigh the tainted witness that we have received against the Tanach. It is church tradition, not God, which has taught us to regard the current New Testament text as sacred.

# (Endnotes)

1   Paul Johnson, *A History of the Jews* (New York: Harper Perennial, 1987), pp. 137–150.

2   Raimo Hakola, "The Johannine Community as Jewish Christians? Some Problems in Current Scholarly Consensus," in *Jewish Christianity Reconsidered*, ed. by Matt Jackson-McCabe (Minneapolis: Fortress Press, 2007), p. 181.

3   Peter Hirschberg, "Jewish Believers in Asia Minor According to the Book of Revelation and the Gospel of John," in *Jewish Believers in Jesus*, ed. by Oskar Skarsaune and Reidar Hvalvik (Peabody, MA: Hendrickson Publishers, 2007), p. 231.

4   Raimo Hakola, "The Johannine Community as Jewish Christians? Some Problems in Current Scholarly Consensus," p. 199. Maurice Casey, *From Jewish Prophet to Gentile God* (Louisville, KY: Westminster/John Knox Press, 1991), p. 27.

5   Maurice Casey, *Is John's Gospel True?* (New York: Routledge, 1996), p. 85.

6   Ibid., p. 85.

7   David H. Stern, *Jewish New Testament Commentary* (Clarksville, MD: Jewish New Testament Publications, 1992), pp. 157–161.

8   Maurice Casey, *Is John's Gospel True?*, p. 119.

9   Ibid., pp. 120–123.

10  Ibid., p. 120.

11  Ibid., p. 120.

12  Ibid., p. 121.

13  David Stern, *Jewish New Testament Commentary*, p.157.

14  Peter Hirschberg, "Jewish Believers in Asia Minor According to the Book of Revelation and the Gospel of John," pp. 234–235. Raimo Hakola, "The Johannine Community as Jewish Christians? Some Problems in Current Scholarly Consensus," p. 193.

15  Raimo Hakola, "The Johannine Community as Jewish Christians? Some Problems in Current Scholarly Consensus," p. 193.

16  Peter Hirschberg, "Jewish Believers in Asia Minor According to the Book of Revelation and the Gospel of John," p. 235. Raimo Hakola, "The Johannine Community as Jewish Christians? Some Problems in Current Scholarly Consensus," p. 196.

17  Peter Hirschberg, "Jewish Believers in Asia Minor According to the Book of Revelation and the Gospel of John," p. 232.

18   Maurice Casey, *From Jewish Prophet to Gentile God*, p.31.

19   Casey, *From Jewish Prophet to Gentile God*, p. 31. Joseph Heinemann, "Amidah," *Encyclopaedia Judaica*, 1st ed., II, pp. 838–842.

20   Joseph Heinemann, "Amidah," p. 842.

21   Peter Hirschberg, "Jewish Believers in Asia Minor According to the Book of Revelation and the Gospel of John," p. 232.

22   Raimo Hakola, "The Johannine Community as Jewish Christians? Some Problems in Current Scholarly Consensus," pp. 191–192.

23   Maurice Casey, *From Jewish Prophet to Gentile God*, p.12.

24   Ibid., pp. 27–28.

25   Ibid., p. 28.

26   Raimo Hakola, "The Johannine Community as Jewish Christians? Some Problems in Current Scholarly Consensus," p. 186.

27   Ibid., p. 186.

28   Maurice Casey, *From Jewish Prophet to Gentile God*, p. 29.

29   Ibid., p. 29.

30   Ibid., p. 29.

31   Ibid., p. 29.

32   Ibid., p. 29.

33   Ibid., p. 29.

34   Ibid., p. 29.

35   Maurice Casey, *Jesus of Nazareth* (New York: T&T Clark International, 2010), p. 521.

36   Craig L. Blomberg, *The Historical Reliability of John's Gospel* (Downers Grove, IL: InterVarsity Press, 2001), p. 34.

37   Maurice Casey, *From Jewish Prophet to Gentile God*, p. 29.

38   Maurice Casey, *Is John's Gospel True?*, pp. 4–10.

39   Ibid., p. 18.

40   Ibid., p. 49.

41   Ibid., pp. 20–22.

42   David H. Stern, *Jewish New Testament Commentary*, p. 195.

43   Ibid., p. 206.

44   Maurice Casey, *Is John's Gospel True?*, p. 22.

45   Ibid., pp. 22–24.

46    Larry W. Hurtado, *Lord Jesus Christ: Devotion to Jesus in Earliest Christianity* (Grand Rapids, MI: William B. Eerdmans Publishing Company, 2003), p. 355.

47    Maurice Casey, *Is John's Gospel True?*, p. 79.

48    Ibid., p. 67.

49    Ibid., p. 67.

50    Maurice Casey, *Jesus of Nazareth*, p. 515–516.

51    Maurice Casey, *Is John's Gospel True?*, pp. 178–191.

52    Ibid., p. 182.

53    Ibid., pp. 180–181.

54    Ibid., p. 181.

55    Ibid., p. 184.

56    Ibid., p. 188.

57    Bart D. Ehrman, "The New Testament Part I" (Course Guidebook) in *The Great Courses* (Chantilly, VA: The Teaching Company Limited Partnership, 2000), p. 45.

58    Ibid., p. 45.

59    Ibid., p. 44.

60    Geza Vermes, *Christian Beginnings: From Nazareth to Nicaea* (New Haven, CT: Yale University Press, 2013), p. 115.

61    James R. White, *The Forgotten Trinity* (Minneapolis: Bethany House Publishers, 1998), p. 119.

62    David H. Stern, *Jewish New Testament Commentary*, pp. 595–596. Kenneth Barker, general ed., *The NIV Study Bible* (Grand Rapids, MI: Zondervan Bible Publishers, 1985), p. 1805, footnote 2:6–11.

63    Ralph P. Martin, *A Hymn of Christ: Philippians 2:5–11 in Recent Interpretation & in the Setting of Early Christian Worship* (Downers Grove, IL: InterVarsity Press, 1997), pp. 42–45.

64    Stephen Meyer, "On Not Reading Signature in the Cell: A Response to Francisco Ayala" in *Signature of Controversy*, ed. by David Klinghoffer (Seattle: Discovery Institute Press, 2010), p. 18.

65    Ralph P. Martin, *A Hymn of Christ: Philippians 2:5–11 in Recent Interpretation & in the Setting of Early Christian Worship*, p. 55.

66    David H. Stern, *Jewish New Testament Commentary*, pp. 595–596.

67    Ralph P. Martin, *A Hymn of Christ: Philippians 2:5–11 in Recent Interpretation & in the Setting of Early Christian Worship*, p. 27.

68    James R. White, *The Forgotten Trinity*, p. 120.

69    Geza Vermes, *Christian Beginnings: From Nazareth to Nicaea*, p. 109.

70    Bart D. Ehrman, *Misquoting Jesus: The Story Behind Who Changed the Bible and Why* (New York: HarperSanFrancisco, 2005), pp. 37–38.

71    Ibid. pp. 41–42.

72    Ibid. pp. 50–51.

73    Ibid. p. 59.

74    Ibid., pp. 58–60.

75    Daniel B. Wallace, "Lost in Transmission: How Badly Did the Scribes Corrupt the New Testament Text?" in *Revisiting the Corruption of the New Testament: Manuscript, Patristic, and Apocryphal Evidence*, ed. by Daniel B. Wallace (Grand Rapids, MI: Kregel Publications, 2011), pp. 26–30.

76    Paul Johnson, *A History of the Jews,* pp. 137–150.

77    Robert Martyr Hawkins, *The Recovery of the Historical Paul*, (Nashville: Vanderbilt University Press, 1943), p. 253.

78    Geza Vermes, *Christian Beginnings: From Nazareth to Nicaea*, p. 109.

79    Dean L. Overman, *A Case for the Divinity of Jesus* (New York: Rowman & Littlefield Publishers, Inc., 2010), p. 47.

80    Ibid., pp. 29–35.

81    Ibid., pp.35–40.

82    Andrew Chester, "High Christology—Whence, When and Why?," *Early Christianity*, 2 (2011), p. 36.

83    Vernon H. Neufeld, *The Earliest Christian Confessions* (Grand Rapids, MI: Wm. B. Eerdmans, 1963), pp. 42–68. Dean L. Overman, *A Case for the Divinity of Jesus*, pp.23–29. Larry W. Hurtado, *Lord Jesus Christ: Devotion to Jesus in Earliest Christianity*, pp.108–118.

84    Vernon H. Neufeld, *The Earliest Christian Confessions*, pp. 43–44. Larry W. Hurtado, *Lord Jesus Christ: Devotion to Jesus in Earliest Christianity*, pp. 113–114.

85    Vernon H. Neufeld, *The Earliest Christian Confessions*, pp. 43–44.

86    Richard Bauckham, *Jesus and the God of Israel: God Crucified and Other Studies on the New Testament's Christology of Divine Identity* (Grand Rapids, MI: William B. Eerdmans Publishing Company, 2008), pp. 18–30.

87    Andrew Chester, "High Christology—Whence, When and Why?", p.

30.

88  Larry W. Hurtado, *Lord Jesus Christ: Devotion to Jesus in Earliest Christianity* (Grand Rapids, MI: William B. Eerdmans Publishing Company, 2003). Andrew Chester, "High Christology—Whence, When and Why?," pp. 28–29.

89  Larry W. Hurtado, *Lord Jesus Christ: Devotion to Jesus in Earliest Christianity*, p. 135.

90  Jonathan A. Draper, "The Holy Vine of David Made Known to the Gentiles through God's Servant Jesus: 'Christian Judaism' in the Didache," in *Jewish Christianity Reconsidered*, ed. by Matt Jackson-McCabe (Minneapolis: Fortress Press, 2007), p. 270.

91  Fred C. Conybeare, "A Doctrinal Modification of a Text of the Gospel," *The Hibbert Journal*, Vol. 1, No. 1, October 1902, pp. 102–108, prepared by Randall D. Hughes, God Glorified, accessed June 21, 2015, www.godglorified.com/F.C.%20Conybeare.htm.

92  "The Teaching of the Twelve Apostles," Vol. 7 in *Ante-Nicene Fathers*, ed. by Alexander Roberts and James Donaldson, revised and arranged by A. Cleveland Coxe, 10 Vols. (Peabody, MA: Hendrickson Publishers, 1994), p. 380.

93  Jonathan A. Draper, "The Holy Vine of David Made Known to the Gentiles through God's Servant Jesus: 'Christian Judaism' in the Didache," p. 270.

94  George Howard, *Hebrew Gospel of Matthew* (Macon, GA: Mercer University Press, 1995), pp. 192–194.

95  "The Apostolic Fathers, Justin Martyr, Irenaeus," Vol. I in *Ante-Nicene Fathers*, ed. by Alexander Roberts and James Donaldson, revised and arranged by A. Cleveland Coxe, 10 Vols. (Peabody, MA: Hendrickson Publishers, 1994), p. 352.

96  Bart D. Ehrman, "The Historical Jesus Part I" (Course Guidebook) in *The Great Courses* (Chantilly, VA: The Teaching Company Limited Partnership, 2000), p. 10.

97  Geza Vermes, *Christian Beginnings: From Nazareth to Nicaea*, pp.48–49.

98  Fred C. Conybeare, "A Doctrinal Modification of a Text of the Gospel," *The Hibbert Journal*, Vol. 1, No. 1, October 1902, pp. 102–108, prepared by Randall D. Hughes, God Glorified, accessed June 21, 2015, www.godglorified.com/F.C.%20Conybeare.htm.

# Chapter 13: The Real God, Messiah, and Messianic Faith

## Don't Throw out the Baby with the Bathwater

The goal of this book is not to cause anyone to fall away from God but to bring individuals closer to God. I have found a number of errors in my faith positions over the years requiring correction. I suspect there are others who have also had their convictions challenged. What shall we say then? Are we to chuck faith in God and the worldview that goes with it overboard? May it never be!

The ultimate mystery of the biblical faith is the amazing tendency for God's truth to be rapidly inverted, turned upside down, at every stage along the way up to our day. What is true becomes false, and falsehood becomes the new truth. Right becomes wrong, and wrong becomes the new right. Good becomes evil, and evil becomes the new good. Who would have thought that the nation of Israel, recently brought out of Egypt "by a mighty hand and an outstretched arm" (Deuteronomy 4:34), would quickly violate their newly given, divine instructions and change the reality of YHVH into a manufactured golden calf? Who would have thought that the early church, growing out of the roots of the patriarchs Abraham, Isaac, and Jacob, would almost immediately reject the Jewish people, the Torah, God's Holy Days, and the Shabbat, and replace the Father with the "Son"? Who would have thought that the Jewish people would reject and grow to loathe their own Messiah?

## Three Lines of Evidence against Yeshua's Deity

I have spent much time countering many of the church's established dogmas concerning the nature of God and the person Yeshua. Evidence against the deity of Yeshua is three-pronged.

First, a divine Yeshua is not found in much of the New Testament, nor is this concept supported by the Tanach or by intertestamental opinions. The synoptic texts and the writings from Sha'ul's own hand contradict a divine Yeshua in multiple examples. Messianic prophecies, godly messengers, and pre-Christian intermediary figures also do not validate Yeshua's deity.

The second line of evidence against Yeshua's deity is the lack of acceptance of this position by the earliest Jewish believers from Jerusalem—the first believers.

The third prong of evidence is the apparent fact that every text which affirms the preexistence and deity of Yeshua in the New Testament is from the unreliable Johannine community, or from "hymns" or "confessions" that were inserted into the text at a later time.

## Who Is Yeshua?

If Yeshua is not a divine "person" of the Trinity, then who is he and why does it matter?

Yeshua was not just some poor first-century Jewish prophet without any significance, whose real life story was altered by various circumstances of history causing him to be transformed into the Gentile god, Jesus Christ. He is *the* real Messiah or the anointed one—the one chosen by the King of the universe, YHVH. YHVH did not adopt him into this position because he was more righteous than any other man. He is the one, revealed through prophecy, who would come to reestablish the broken relationship between God and man (see chapter 2). He is a descendant of Abraham, Isaac, Jacob, Judah, and ultimately King David. He is the son of Yoseph (Joseph) and Miryam (Mary), which confirms his Davidic descent and his humanity. He is a man and not God. He is not an ordinary man, however. God chose him as His special "son" from the beginning because God knew in advance that men would fall.

Most believers say that only a divine Messiah could live a sin-less life and become the perfect sacrifice for our sins. They often get hung up on the theology of original sin that states all men born in this world automatically carry the guilt and pollution of our ancestor Adam (see my discussion of this problem in chapter 3). However, there is an example in the Torah of Enoch, a "type" of Yeshua, who "walked with God" and appeared to have lived a sinless life. According to John Sailhamer, the Torah gives the suggestion that Enoch did not die because he was a righteous man (Genesis 5:24).[1]

We are told through prophecy that the peerless Messiah, similarly, would live a perfect, righteous life because God's power and influence would rest upon him:

> There shall come forth a shoot from the stump of Jesse [the father of King David], and a branch from his roots shall bear fruit. And the Spirit of the LORD [YHVH] shall rest upon him, the Spirit of wisdom and understanding, the Spirit of counsel and might, the Spirit of knowledge and the fear of the LORD [YHVH]. And his delight shall be in the fear of the LORD [YHVH]. He shall not judge by what his eyes see, or decide disputes by what his ears hear, but with righteousness he shall judge the poor, and decide with equity for the meek of the earth; and he shall strike the earth with the rod of his mouth, and with the breath of his lips he shall kill the wicked. Righteousness shall be the belt of his waist, and faithfulness the belt of his loins. The wolf shall dwell with the lamb, and the leopard shall lie down with the young goat, and the calf and the lion and the fattened calf together; and a little child shall lead them. The cow and the bear shall graze; their young shall lie down together; and the lion shall eat straw like the ox. The nursing child shall play over the hole of the cobra, and the weaned child shall put his hand on the adder's den. They shall not hurt or destroy in all my holy mountain; for the earth shall be full of the knowledge of the LORD [YHVH] as the waters cover the sea. In that day the root of Jesse, who shall stand as a signal for the peoples—of him shall the nations inquire, and his resting place shall be glorious (Isaiah 11:1–10).

We know that in the messianic age, men will be living sinless lives through the power of God's Spirit. Is it not reasonable to conceive that God could have kept His special "son," the Messiah, pure and sinless all of his life? In fact, those who accept Yeshua's atonement and walk with God will eventually become perfect "sons" of God just like Yeshua (Romans 8:14–17, Galatians 3:26, 4:4–7), because God's Spirit will also change them. Nevertheless, they will not become divine.

Since Yeshua was a man, his suffering and death are extremely meaningful to us. As men, we know what it is like to suffer and to experience mental and physical pain. We can understand and appreciate what the man Yeshua went through to atone for our sins. On top of this, Yeshua, being an entirely righteous man, did not need to suffer death. However, he chose to suffer a horrible death on our behalf:

> For he grew up before him like a young plant, and like a root out of dry ground; he had no form or majesty that we should look at him, and no beauty that we should desire him. He was despised and rejected by men; a man of sorrows, and acquainted with grief; and as one from whom men hide their faces he was despised, and we esteemed him not. Surely he has borne our griefs and carried our sorrows; yet we esteemed him stricken, smitten by God, and afflicted. But he was pierced for our transgressions; he was crushed for our iniquities; upon him was the chastisement that brought us peace, and with his wounds we are healed. All we like sheep have gone astray; we have turned—every one—to his own way; and the LORD [YHVH] has laid on him the iniquity of us all. He was oppressed, and he was afflicted, yet he opened not his mouth; like a lamb that is led to the slaughter, and like a sheep that before its shearers is silent, so he opened not his mouth. By oppression and judgment he was taken away; and as for his generation, who considered that he was cut off out of the land of the living, stricken for the transgression of my people? And they made his grave with the wicked and with a rich man in his death, although he had done no violence, and there was no deceit in his mouth. Yet it was the will of the LORD [YHVH] to crush him; he has put him to grief; when his soul makes an offering for guilt, he shall see his offspring; he shall prolong his days; the will of the LORD [YHVH] shall prosper in his hand. Out of the anguish of his soul he shall see and be satisfied; by his knowledge shall the righteous one, my servant, make many to be accounted righteous, and he shall bear their iniquities. Therefore I will divide him a portion with the many, and he shall divide the spoil with the strong, because he poured out his soul to death and

was numbered with the transgressors; yet he bore the sin of many, and makes intercession for the transgressors (Isaiah 53:2–12).

He died for our sins according to the Scriptures.

The Messiah was never expected to be God or to be equal with God. According to the book of Daniel, the Ancient of Days would give the Messiah:

> Dominion and glory and a kingdom, that all peoples, nations, and languages should serve him; his dominion is an everlasting dominion, which shall not pass away, and his kingdom one that shall not be destroyed (Daniel 7:14).

The Messiah would receive dominion from God.

The transfer of godly authority to Yeshua is mirrored to us from the story of Joseph. As was discussed previously (at the end of chapter 2), Joseph is a "type" of Yeshua. Developing this theme further, one could say that the Pharaoh in the narrative represents God, and Joseph represents the Messiah Yeshua. Look what the narrative reveals to us:

> And Pharaoh said to his servants, "Can we find a man like this, in whom is the Spirit of God?" Then Pharaoh said to Joseph, "Since God has shown you all this, there is none so discerning and wise as you are. You shall be over my house, and all my people shall order themselves as you command. Only as regards the throne will I be greater than you." And Pharaoh said to Joseph, "See, I have set you over all the land of Egypt." Then Pharaoh took his signet ring from his hand and put it on Joseph's hand, and clothed him in garments of fine linen and put a gold chain about his neck. And he made him ride in his second chariot. And they called out before him, "Bow the knee!" Thus he set him over all the land of Egypt. Moreover, Pharaoh said to Joseph, "I am Pharaoh, and without your consent no one shall lift up hand or foot in all the land of Egypt" (Genesis 41:38–44).

Joseph was a man in whom was the Spirit of God. Notice that he was given "dominion and glory and a kingdom, that all peoples, nations, and languages should serve him." Even though Joseph was given great power throughout the land, there was never any hint in the narrative that Joseph's position ever rivaled that of the Pharaoh. The Pharaoh and Joseph were not on the same plane. Yeshua is similar to Joseph. Yeshua is the superior, unique man who is given great power and responsibility to carry out the plan of God. Because of his kingship and service to us, he is given honor. However, he does not rival God.

Sha'ul confirms this truth about Yeshua:

> Then comes the end, when he delivers the kingdom to God the Father after destroying every rule and every authority and power. For he must reign until he has put all his enemies under his feet. The last enemy to be destroyed is death. For "God has put all things in subjection under his feet." But when it says "all things are put in subjection," it is plain that he is excepted who put all things in subjection under him. When all things are subjected to him, then the Son himself will also be subjected to him who put all things in subjection under him, that God may be all in all (1Corinthians 15:24–28).

As believers recognize Yeshua to be a man of men, they can then elevate YHVH, the God of Yeshua and the Father of us all, back to His supreme, awe-inspiring position in the universe: "Know therefore today, and lay it to your heart, that the LORD [YHVH] is God in heaven above and on the earth beneath; there is no other" (Deuteronomy 4:39).

I am not trying to diminish Yeshua the Messiah, my lord and my king, or trivialize his selfless atonement for my sins or his future reign over God's creation. Instead, I am trying to raise up YHVH, my Lord and my God, the righteous Holy One, the King of the universe.

Does this actually change what most Christians believe? Listening to Christian radio, I hear such things as: "The Lord Jesus loves us. The Lord Jesus watches over us. The Lord Jesus knows our futures." Is there a change if we say that it is YHVH who does all of these things? When songs are sung to Yeshua as God, would there be a change if we only sang songs to our Father? Can Yeshua still be our Messiah who died for our sins without being our God? Most believers are not far from this understanding.*

---

\* I have not written anything about the third "person" of the Trinity to this point—the Holy Spirit—since the argument supporting this concept is

## Reviving the Reformation: Restoring Truth

Those who would say that we do not need to revive the Reformation need to take a closer look at the early years of the Messianic faith—this faith later known as Christianity. The Messianic faith started clearly within the boundaries of Judaism. All of the participants were Jewish, living in a Jewish cultural setting, but under Roman occupation. After coming out of the first and second Jewish revolts against Rome, about one hundred years after Yeshua's death, the picture had changed dramatically. Now the Messianic faith is devoid of Jews, and the leaders of the faith tend to have low opinions about Jews and Judaism. Could truth be reliably transmitted under such circumstances?

When we revive the Reformation and begin to peel back the layers of mistruth that have been laid down over the past two thousand years, we find a Messianic faith that is the continuation of the true faith of Israel, as outlined in the Tanach. In this faith Jews, and yes, Gentiles also, find atonement, healing, rejuvenation, and relationship with the God of the universe. Jews and Gentiles also form a bond with each other. May YHVH, the God of Abraham, Isaac, and Jacob, give us the wisdom and motivation to discern His truth in these matters.

---

unconvincing. An exact understanding of the Spirit of YHVH is difficult to grasp. Often one needs to glean through various biblical passages to get a flavor for what the Spirit is. Sometimes the Spirit of YHVH is personified in Scripture in a literary-poetic device (Genesis 1:2). In general, as described by Buzzard and Hunting, the Spirit of YHVH is not a "person" of the godhead but "God in action . . . His energy . . . His outreach . . . His power and personality extended to His creation." (Anthony F. Buzzard and Charles F. Hunting, *The Doctrine of the Trinity: Christianity's Self-Inflicted Wound* [New York: International Scholars Publications, 1998], pp. 216–217.) A somewhat related Jewish concept is the *Shechinah*: "dwelling" or "Divine Presence." (Alan Unterman, "Ru'ah HaKodesh," *Encyclopaedia Judaica*, Vol. 14 [Jerusalem, Israel: Keter Publishing House Ltd., 1971], p. 366.)

# Appendix 1: Appointed Seasons of YHVH

## The Seven Moadim

Even though the traditional church has rejected the biblical Holy Days, these appointed times/seasons were established by God and continue to be relevant for the followers of YHVH. The appointed times/seasons (*moed* in Hebrew) of YHVH are described in Leviticus 23:

> The LORD [YHVH] spoke to Moses, saying, "Speak to the people of Israel and say to them, These are the appointed feasts of the LORD [*moaday* YHVH] that you shall proclaim as holy convocations [*mik'ra kodesh*]; they are my appointed feasts [*moadai*]" (Leviticus 23:1–2).

They are not the seasons of the Jews or Moses but the seasons of YHVH. God instituted them.

Even before Abraham and the Jewish people, God separated out special days for men to observe. On the fourth day in Genesis chapter 1:14–19, God announces one of His purposes for creating the sun, the moon, and the stars some time after they had been created in the beginning:

> And God said, "Let there be lights in the expanse of the heavens to separate the day from the night. And let them be for signs and for seasons [moadim], and for days and years, and let them be lights in the expanse of the heavens to give light upon the earth" (Genesis 1:14–15).

As John Sailhamer discussed regarding Genesis 1:14, *y'hee*—"let there be"—is associated with an infinitive "to separate." It is better translated "Let the lights be for separating." The work of God on the fourth day is not making the lights again, but giving purpose to the lights that have already been made. The lights mark the appointed times/ seasons (moadim) in which men were instructed to worship God.[2]

The Tanach describes a lunar calendar. The Jews use a bound lunar calendar with added months in leap years to keep the moadim in their respective seasons, unlike the Muslim lunar calendar:[3] "He made the moon to mark the seasons [moadim]" (Psalm 104:19).

The people of Israel were given the responsibility of proclaiming these moadim as holy convocations (*mik'ra kodesh*) (Leviticus 23:2). To convoke is to call together to a meeting, which translates the Hebrew root *koof, resh*, and *aleph*—"to call, proclaim, read," but also "to summon or invite." The community is summoned for common worship at these holy (set apart) convocations or sacred assemblies. Observance of the moadim is not something that is done alone.

There are seven moadim. Seven is God's number of completeness. Most of the moadim point to a historical or agricultural event. They all have a prophetic meaning, specifically depicting God's plan of salvation. Except for Shabbat, these moadim occur yearly. There are three in the spring and three in the fall.

The moadim in the spring (Pesach/Passover, First Fruits, and Shavuot/Pentecost) are tied to events surrounding Yeshua's first coming, and those in the fall (*Yom Teruah*/The Feast of Trumpets, Yom Kippur/Day of Atonement, and Sukkot/Tabernacles), his second coming. The spring moadim begin in the first month, Nisan, after a symbolic winter of death. The second group occurs in the seventh month, Tishri, after a long summer.[4]

Most in the traditional church assume the observance of these moadim ended after Yeshua died and the Temple was destroyed, but Leviticus 23 tells us, "It is a statute forever throughout your generations in all your dwellings" (Leviticus 23:14). This permanence is also confirmed in Leviticus 23:3, 23:21, 23:31, and 23:41. These moadim are never ending. The past once-and-for-all sacrifice of Yeshua still fulfills the sacrificial requirement of each moadim for us today (Hebrews 9 and 10).[5] They should be observed even when living outside of Jerusalem.

## Shabbat/Sabbath

Shabbat or Sabbath is the first moadim listed in Leviticus 23:3 (see also Genesis 2:1–3, Exodus 16:21, Exodus 20:8–11, Exodus 23:12, Exodus 31:12, Exodus 34:21, Exodus 35:1–3, Leviticus 19:1–3, Leviticus 19:30, Numbers 15:32–36, Numbers 28:9–10, Deuteronomy 5:12–15, Isaiah 58:13–14, Jeremiah 17:19–27). Since it is listed first, it may be the most important.

Shabbat causes us to remember the rest that God took after preparing the Land—"For in six days the LORD [YHVH] made heaven and earth, the sea, and all that is in them, and rested on the seventh day. Therefore the LORD [YHVH] blessed the Sabbath day and made it holy" (Exodus 20:11). God intended man to experience a similar rest.

Sailhamer shows us that in Genesis there is no "And there was evening and there was morning, the seventh day." The Shabbat rest was to have continued indefinitely. Since the Shabbat occurs weekly, it has a continuous quality to it. In Shabbat, we look forward to our future rest in the messianic age (for further discussion on Shabbat, see chapter 5):[6]

> So then, there remains a Sabbath rest for the people of God, for whoever has entered God's rest has also rested from his works as God did from his. Let us therefore strive to enter that rest, so that no one may fall by the same sort of disobedience (Hebrews 4:9–11).[7]

The other six moadim prophetically proclaim how God will restore our relationship with Him so that we can enter His rest.

## Pesach/Passover

Pesach or Passover and the Feast of Unleavened Bread is described in Leviticus 23:5–8 (see also Exodus 12:2–39, Exodus 12:43–51, Exodus 34:18, Numbers 28:16–25, Deuteronomy 16: 1–8). It is one of the three pilgrimage moadim (along with Shavuot/Pentecost and Sukkot/Tabernacles)—as told in Deuteronomy 16:16–17. Jews were required to observe the festival in Jerusalem.

Pesach historically remembers Israel's deliverance from Egypt. God brought the children of Israel out of Egypt "by a mighty hand

and an outstretched arm" (Deuteronomy 4:34). At the tenth plague, the blood on the doors prevented the death of the Israelite firstborn sons. Egyptians, also, who applied the blood, would have been saved.

Prophetically, Pesach pointed to Yeshua's sacrificial death for us. It was not a coincidence that Yeshua died at Pesach. He is the Passover lamb whose blood causes the angel of death to pass over us. Leaven, representing sin, is to be removed from our houses for seven days.

> Your boasting is not good. Do you not know that a little leaven leavens the whole lump? Cleanse out the old leaven that you may be a new lump, as you really are unleavened. For Christ [Messiah], our Passover lamb, has been sacrificed. Let us therefore celebrate the festival, not with the old leaven, the leaven of malice and evil, but with the unleavened bread of sincerity and truth (1 Corinthians 5:6–8).

Since Pesach was one of the pilgrimage festivals, Jews from all over the world were present in Jerusalem during Yeshua's death and resurrection.

## First Fruits

First Fruits occurs during the week of Pesach/Feast of Unleavened Bread described in Leviticus 23:10–14. It is the day of waving the sheaf (omer) of new barley. The barley harvest happened at Passover time and the wheat harvest at the time of Shavuot/Pentecost.

The agricultural significance of First Fruits is the presenting of the first fruits of the barley harvest before YHVH. The counting of the omer for calculating the beginning of Shavuot/Pentecost begins on this day. First Fruits should start the day after the weekly Shabbat during the week of Passover. Therefore, First Fruits should always fall on the first day of the week (see the controversy in the discussion about Shavuot/Pentecost).

First Fruits has prophetic significance in that it is the day that Yeshua rose from the dead. Yeshua was the first fruits to be raised from the dead. Since Yeshua was raised from the dead, so also will those of us who believe. First Fruits should have been the true Resurrection

Day observed by believers, instead of Easter:

> But in fact Christ [Messiah] has been raised from the dead, the first fruits of those who have fallen asleep. For as by a man came death, by a man has come also the resurrection of the dead. For as in Adam all die, so also in Christ [Messiah] shall all be made alive. But each in his own order: Christ [Messiah] the first fruits, then at his coming those who belong to Christ [Messiah] (1 Corinthians 15:20–23).

## Shavuot/Pentecost

Shavuot is outlined in Leviticus 23:15–22 (see also Exodus 34:22, Numbers 28:26–31, Deuteronomy 16:9–12). It is also called the Feast of Weeks or Pentecost. This festival begins seven weeks or fifty days from First Fruits, thus the names given to it. One "counts the omer" for fifty days to calculate the starting date.

There is a controversy over of the commencement of the feast. When should one start counting the omer? The Encyclopedia Judaica states in the article "Shavuot":

> The Sadducees (and later the Karaites) understood the term "Sabbath" in these verses literally, hence, for them Shavuot always falls on a Sunday. The Pharisees, however, interpreted "Sabbath" as the first day of Passover (which was a Sabbath, "day of rest") so that, for them, Shavuot always falls on the 51st day from the first day of Passover.[8]

The Torah seems to say that the counting of the omer should commence the day after the weekly Shabbat during the week of Pesach (Leviticus 23:11, 15). It would always begin on the first day of the week or Sunday. The designated days of rest during the moadim are always called *Shabbaton* rather than Shabbat, except during Yom Kippur (Leviticus 23:24, 23:32, 23:39). Leviticus 23:15–16, however, uses the word Shabbat rather than *Shabbaton*. One is to count off seven Sabbaths (*Shabbatot*) to calculate the day of Shavuot, not seven weeks. Shavuot falls on the day after the seventh Shabbat. If counting always began on the second day of Passover, the day of Shavuot would always fall on Sivan 6 on the calendar. There would be no need to calculate the day by counting every year.

Shavuot is one of the three pilgrimage moadim (along with Pesach/Passover and Sukkot/Tabernacles)— as told in Deuteronomy 16: 16–17. Acts 2:5–13 tells us that on Shavuot there were Jews from every country staying in Jerusalem. They had traveled to Jerusalem for the festival and spoke in many different languages.

Agriculturally, Shavuot celebrates the first fruits of the wheat harvest (the first fruits of the barley harvest occur at the time of Pesach).

Historically, Moses received the Ten Commandments (representing the Torah) on Mount Sinai on Shavuot. Exodus 19:1 tells us, "On the third new moon after the people of Israel had gone out of the land of Egypt, on that day they came into the wilderness of Sinai" (Exodus 19:1). Since they left in the middle of the first month—Nisan—the beginning of the third month when they arrived at Sinai would place them some forty days after the first Passover.

Prophetically, Shavuot is the day that God's Holy Spirit would come upon believers for the first time in Jerusalem. The first believers were like the first of the wheat harvest, with much more to come. God's Holy Spirit coming upon these believers was seen as tongues of fire coming upon them:

> When the day of Pentecost arrived, they were all together in one place. And suddenly there came from heaven a sound like a mighty rushing wind, and it filled the entire house where they were sitting. And divided tongues as of fire appeared to them and rested on each one of them. And they were all filled with the Holy Spirit and began to speak in other tongues as the Spirit gave them utterance (Acts 2:1–4).

Dedication of the Tabernacle and Temple also involved fire from YHVH:

> And Moses and Aaron went into the tent of meeting, and when they came out they blessed the people, and the glory of the LORD [YHVH] appeared to all the people. And fire came out from before the LORD [YHVH] and consumed the burnt offering and the pieces of fat on the altar, and when all the people saw it, they shouted and fell on their faces

(Leviticus 9:23–24).

As soon as Solomon finished his prayer, fire came down from heaven and consumed the burnt offering and the sacrifices, and the glory of the LORD [YHVH] filled the temple. And the priests could not enter the house of the LORD [YHVH], because the glory of the LORD [YHVH] filled the LORD's [YHVH's] house. When all the people of Israel saw the fire come down and the glory of the LORD [YHVH] on the temple, they bowed down with their faces to the ground on the pavement and worshiped and gave thanks to the LORD {YHVH], saying, "For he is good, for his steadfast love endures forever" (2 Chronicles 7:1–3).

Since the physical Temple was soon to be destroyed in 70 CE, believers gathered at God's house on Shavuot in Acts chapter 2 had tongues of fire rest on them, designating them as the new Temple for God's presence to dwell.[9]

Do you not know that you are God's temple and that God's Spirit dwells in you? (1 Corinthians 3:16).

So then you are no longer strangers and aliens, but you are fellow citizens with the saints and members of the household of God, built on the foundation of the apostles and prophets, Christ [Messiah] Jesus [Yeshua] himself being the cornerstone, in whom the whole structure, being joined together, grows into a holy temple in the Lord. In him you also are being built together into a dwelling place for God by the Spirit (Ephesians 2:19–22).

## Yom Teruah/Feast of Trumpets

*Yom Teruah* or the Feast of Trumpets is summarized in Leviticus 23:23–25 (see also Numbers 29:1–6). The modern name—Rosh Hashanah—Head of the Year or New Year, is not the biblical New Year, which would be the first of Nisan. Calling this festival the New Year could be a result of designating the final harvest as the end of the old agricultural year and the beginning of the new agricultural year (Exodus 23:16).[10] Jewish tradition also called this day *Yom HaDin*—Day of Judgment.[11]

Prophetically, this day seems to be related to the final judgment and the return of Yeshua for the second time.

As I looked, thrones were placed, and the Ancient of Days took his seat; his clothing was white as snow, and the hair of his head like pure wool; his throne was fiery flames; its wheels were burning fire. A stream of fire issued and came out from before him; a thousand thousands served him, and ten thousand times ten thousand stood before him; the court sat in judgment, and the books were opened. I looked then because of the sound of the great words that the horn was speaking. And as I looked, the beast was killed, and its body destroyed and given over to be burned with fire. As for the rest of the beasts, their dominion was taken away, but their lives were prolonged for a season and a time. I saw in the night visions, and behold, with the clouds of heaven there came one like a son of man, and he came to the Ancient of Days and was presented before him. And to him was given dominion and glory and a kingdom, that all peoples, nations, and languages should serve him; his dominion is an everlasting dominion, which shall not pass away, and his kingdom one that shall not be destroyed (Daniel 7:9–14).

Immediately after the tribulation of those days the sun will be darkened, and the moon will not give its light, and the stars will fall from heaven, and the powers of the heavens will be shaken. Then will appear in heaven the sign of the Son of Man, and then all the tribes of the earth will mourn, and they will see the Son of Man coming on the clouds of heaven with power and great glory. And he will send out his angels with a loud trumpet call, and they will gather his elect from the four winds, from one end of heaven to the other (Matthew 24:29–31).

Behold! I tell you a mystery. We shall not all sleep, but we shall all be changed, in a moment, in the twinkling of an eye, at the last trumpet. For the trumpet will sound, and the dead will be raised imperishable, and we shall be changed (1 Corinthians 15:51–52).

But we do not want you to be uninformed, brothers, about those who are asleep, that you may not grieve as others do who have no hope. For since we believe that Jesus [Yeshua] died and rose again, even so, through Jesus [Yeshua], God will bring with him those who have fallen asleep. For this we declare to you by a word from the Lord, that we who are alive, who are left until the coming of the Lord, will not precede those who have fallen asleep. For the Lord himself will descend from heaven with a cry of command, with the voice of an archangel, and with the sound of the trumpet of God. And the dead in Christ [Messiah] will rise first (1 Thessalonians 4:13–16).

## Yom Kippur/Day of Atonement

Yom Kippur or the Day of Atonement is detailed in Leviticus 23:26–32 (see also Leviticus 16, 25:8–12, Numbers 29:7–11).

Prophetically, Yom Kippur points to a future, final day of atonement for Israel—a day of cleansing. Yeshua is the "perfect" Yom Kippur sacrifice (Hebrews 9).[12] This coming day of atonement will commence the permanent Jubilee year (Leviticus 25:8–12). Liberty will be proclaimed throughout the land:

> I will take you from the nations and gather you from all the countries and bring you into your own land. I will sprinkle clean water on you, and you shall be clean from all your uncleannesses, and from all your idols I will cleanse you. And I will give you a new heart, and a new spirit I will put within you. And I will remove the heart of stone from your flesh and give you a heart of flesh. And I will put my Spirit within you, and cause you to walk in my statutes and be careful to obey my rules. You shall dwell in the land that I gave to your fathers, and you shall be my people, and I will be your God. And I will deliver you from all your uncleannesses. And I will summon the grain and make it abundant and lay no famine upon you. I will make the fruit of the tree and the increase of the field abundant, that you may never again suffer the disgrace of famine among the nations. Then you will remember your evil ways, and your deeds that were not good, and you will loathe yourselves for your iniquities and your abominations. It is not for your sake that I will act, declares the Lord GOD [YHVH]; let that be known to you. Be ashamed and confounded for your ways, O house of Israel. Thus says the Lord GOD [YHVH]: On the day that I cleanse you from all your iniquities, I will cause the cities to be inhabited, and the waste places shall be rebuilt. And the land that was desolate shall be tilled, instead of being the desolation that it was in the sight of all who passed by. And they will say, "This land that was desolate has become like

the garden of Eden, and the waste and desolate and ruined cities are now fortified and inhabited." Then the nations that are left all around you shall know that I am the LORD [YHVH]; I have rebuilt the ruined places and replanted that which was desolate. I am the LORD [YHVH]; I have spoken, and I will do it (Ezekiel 36:24–36).

## Sukkot/Tabernacles

Sukkot or the Feast of Booths or Tabernacles is detailed in Leviticus 23:34–43 (see also Exodus 34:22, Numbers 29: 12–38, Deuteronomy 16:13–15). Sukkot is also called the Feast of Ingathering or just "The Feast."[13] Sukkot is also one of the three pilgrimage moadim (along with Pesach/Passover and Shavuot/Pentecost)—as told in Deuteronomy 16: 16–17.

Agriculturally, Sukkot celebrates the final harvest of the year.

Historically, Sukkot recalls Israel's wilderness wanderings, living in booths.

Prophetically, Sukkot looks forward to the messianic age when we will finally enter God's rest. It looks forward to the ingathering of believers. All nations will come to Jerusalem at that time:

> Then everyone who survives of all the nations that have come against Jerusalem shall go up year after year to worship the King, the LORD [YHVH] of hosts, and to keep the Feast of Booths. And if any of the families of the earth do not go up to Jerusalem to worship the King, the LORD [YHVH] of hosts, there will be no rain on them. And if the family of Egypt does not go up and present themselves, then on them there shall be no rain; there shall be the plague with which the LORD [YHVH] afflicts the nations that do not go up to keep the Feast of Booths. This shall be the punishment to Egypt and the punishment to all the nations that do not go up to keep the Feast of Booths (Zechariah 14:16–19).

Thanksgiving was the American Pilgrims' attempt to observe Sukkot.[14]

# (Endnotes)

1    John H. Sailhamer, "Genesis," Vol. 2 in *The Expositor's Bible Commentary*, ed. by Frank E. Gaebelein (Grand Rapids, MI: Zondervan Publishing House, 1990), pp. 74.

2    John Sailhamer, *Genesis Unbound: A Provocative New Look at the Creation Account* (Sisters, OR: Multnomah Books, 1996), pp. 129–135.

3    "Calendar," *The Standard Jewish Encyclopedia*, ed. by Cecil Roth (Garden City, NY: Doubleday & Company, Inc., 1966), p. 388.

4    Lawrence Rich, *The Feasts of Israel: A Picture of God's Eternal Plan in Messiah* (Unpublished one-page table).

5    Daniel Juster, *Jewish Roots: A Foundation of Biblical Theology* (Rockville, MD: Davar Publishing Company, 1986), p. 202.

6    John Sailhamer, "Genesis," vol. 2 in *The Expositor's Bible Commentary*, ed. by Frank E. Gaebelein, 12 vols. (Grand Rapids, MI: Zondervan Publishing House, 1990), p 39.

7    Ariel and D'vorah Berkowitz, *Torah Rediscovered: Challenging Centuries of Misinterpretation and Neglect* (Littleton, CO: First Fruits of Zion, 1996), pp. 44–45.

8    Louis Jacobs, "Shavuot," *Encyclopaedia Judaica*, Vol. 14 (Jerusalem, Israel: Keter Publishing House Ltd., 1971), p. 1319.

9    Ariel and D'vorah Berkowitz, *Take Hold: Embracing Our Divine Inheritance with Israel* (Littleton, CO: First Fruits of Zion, 1998), pp. 160–166.

10    Mitch and Zhava Glaser, *The Fall Feasts of Israel* (Chicago: Moody Press, 1987), pp. 30–31.

11    Shirley Stern, *Exploring the Jewish Holidays and Customs* (Hoboken, NJ: Ktav Publishing House Inc., 1981), pp. 66–67.

12    Lawrence Rich, *The Feasts of Israel: A Picture of God's Eternal Plan in Messiah* (Unpublished one page table).

13    Mitch and Zhava Glaser, *The Fall Feasts of Israel*, pp. 157–159.

14    Shirley Stern, *Exploring the Jewish Holidays and Customs*, p. 54.

# Appendix 2: The Deity of Yeshua in the Tanach

A number of "proof texts" from the Tanach are used to defend the deity of Yeshua. Many of these were reviewed in chapter 10. In this appendix, I will examine other examples.

## Genesis 3:14–15

Genesis 3:14–15 seems to be a prophecy about the future Messiah. Some say it is also a prophecy of the virgin birth: "The Lord [YHVH] God said to the serpent, 'Because you have done this, cursed are you above all livestock and above all beasts of the field; on your belly you shall go, and dust you shall eat all the days of your life. I will put enmity between you and the woman, and between your offspring [seed] and her offspring [seed]; he shall bruise your head, and you shall bruise his heel.'" Here we have an odd designation: "the seed of the woman." Usually, the Tanach speaks about the seed of a man. Maybe the woman is linked with the serpent because she was the one interacting with him. In the next verse, God tells the woman that she will have great pain in childbirth, which is bringing forth seed. It is problematic to make a case for the virgin birth through these verses. Maybe this is poetic language, such as in Job 14:1, "Man who is born of a woman is few of days and full of trouble (Job 14:1)."

## Isaiah 9:6–7 and Jeremiah 23:5–6

Both Isaiah 9:6–7 and Jeremiah 23:5–6 are clearly messianic prophecies. Each gives a name for the Messiah. Trinitarians say these names are titles for God alone: "Wonderful Counselor, Mighty God, Everlasting Father, Prince of Peace" and "YHVH Our Righteousness." Sometimes in the Torah, names characterized the person being named, such as Abraham, Sarah, Jacob, and Esau, but this was not typically the case in the rest of the Tanach. For instance, God tells Isaiah to name one of his sons "The Spoil Speeds, The Prey Hastens" (Isaiah 8:3). This name does not tell us anything about Isaiah's son, but his name is relaying a prophetic truth. The same could be said about these names of the Messiah. They are conveying to us truths about God but not labeling the Messiah as God: "Wonderful in counsel is God the Mighty, the everlasting Father, the Ruler of peace" (Jewish Publication Society, 1917) and "YHVH is our righteousness." In addition, nowhere is Yeshua ever called "the everlasting Father."

## Isaiah 7:14

It is not clear that Isaiah 7:14 is a messianic prophecy, but even if this prophecy were naming the Messiah "Immanuel," it would mean "God is with us" as used later in Isaiah 8:8 and 8:10 and not "God with us." The name here gives us a truth about God rather than characterizing the person named. This argument would be the same given for Isaiah 9:6–7 and Jeremiah 23:5–6.

## Micah 5:2 (5:1 in the Hebrew)

Micah 5:2 tells us that the Messiah's "coming forth is from of old, from ancient days." This verse is a claim for the preexistence of the Messiah and, therefore, his deity. One could say, however, that God always knew that the Messiah would come. In a sense, he preexisted in the mind of God. Raphael Patai, in *The Messiah Texts*, tells us how this type of thinking was widespread in various forms in rabbinic literature.[1]

## Zechariah 12:10

Zechariah 12:10 is a rather complicated passage to translate. The opening speaker, YHVH, seems to state that the inhabitants of

Jerusalem will look to "Me." The Hebrew *et asher* is the sticking point. Those who believe in the deity of Yeshua would say that *et asher* means whom. They would favor the translation, "They will look on Me whom they pierced" (New King James). It then would be YHVH who would be pierced as the person Yeshua. Probably a more accurate translation would be, "They will look to Me concerning him whom they pierced."[2] This translation would be more consistent with the second section, "They shall mourn for him, as one mourns for an only child, and weep bitterly over him, as one weeps over a firstborn." I believe this prophecy is referring to the future recognition of Yeshua as Messiah by his brethren similar to the reunion of Joseph and his brothers.

## Psalm 110:1

Psalm 110:1 seems to be suggesting that King David is calling the Messiah God: "A Psalm of David. The LORD [YHVH] says to my Lord: 'Sit at my right hand, until I make your enemies your footstool.'" In Hebrew, the first "Lord" here is YHVH. The second mentioned "Lord" in Hebrew is *adonee*. *Adonee* means "my lord" or "my master" and is never used to refer to God in the Hebrew Bible. If the verse wanted to say "Lord," referring to God, it would have used "Adonai." King David is identifying a person greater than himself, but he is not calling this figure God. To sit at the right hand is probably signifying a position of honor. There are other passages in Scripture where certain men are given honor by others bowing to them and calling them "lord' or "master": "And as Obadiah was on the way, behold, Elijah met him. And Obadiah recognized him and fell on his face and said, 'Is it you, my lord Elijah?'" (1 Kings 18:7). Honor given to men is not foreign to the Hebrew Bible.

## (Endnotes)

1   Raphael Patai, *The Messiah Texts: Jewish Legends of Three Thousand Years* (Detroit: Wayne State University Press, 1979), pp. 16–20.

2   Francis Brown, S. R. Driver, and Charles A. Briggs, *The Brown-Driver-Briggs Hebrew and English Lexicon: With an appendix containing Biblical Aramaic* (Oxford: Clarendon, 1907), BibleWorks, v.9, p. 82.

# Bibliography

Albright, William F. "Toward a More Conservative View." *Christianity Today*, vol. 7, January 18, 1963.

Alter, Robert. *The Art of Biblical Narrative*. New York: Basic Books, 1981.

*The American Heritage High School Dictionary*. 4th ed. New York, NY: Houghton Mifflin Company, 2004.

*Aramaic English New Testament*. Compiled, edited, and translated by Andrew Gabriel Roth. Sedro-Woolley, WA: Netzari Press LLC, 2008.

Archer, Gleason L. "Is the Sabbath Saturday or Sunday According to the Bible?" Taped message in 1991 at a John Ankerberg apologetics conference.

"Atonement." *Encyclopaedia Judaica*. Vol. 3. Jerusalem, Israel: Keter Publishing House Ltd., 1971.

*Authorized Daily Prayer Book*. Translated by Joseph H. Hertz. Revised ed. New York: Bloch Publishing Company, 1975.

Bacchiocchi, Samuele. *From Sabbath to Sunday: A Historical Investigation of the Rise of Sunday Observance in Early Christianity*. Rome: The Pontifical Gregorian University Press, 1977.

Bauckham, Richard. *Jesus and the God of Israel: God Crucified and Other Studies on the New Testament's Christology of Divine Identity*. Grand Rapids, MI: William B. Eerdmans Publishing Company, 2008.

Behe, Michel J. *Darwin's Black Box: The Biochemical Challenge to Evolution*. New York: Free Press, 2006.

Behe, Michael J. *The Edge of Evolution: The Search for the Limits of Darwinism*. New York: Free Press, 2007.

Ben Natan, Menashe. *Come, Let Us Reason Together*. Tucson, AZ: Desert Ulpan, 1983.

Berkowitz, Ariel and D'vorah Berkowitz. *Take Hold: Embracing Our Divine Inheritance with Israel*. Littleton, CO: First Fruits of Zion, 1998.

Berkowitz, Ariel and D'vorah Berkowitz. *Torah Rediscovered: Challenging Centuries of Misinterpretation and Neglect.* Littleton, CO: First Fruits of Zion, Inc., 1996.

Berlinski, David. *The Devil's Delusion: Atheism and Its Scientific Pretensions.* New York: Basic Books, 2009.

"Blasphemy." *Encyclopaedia Judaica.* Vol. 4. Jerusalem, Israel: Keter Publishing House Ltd., 1971.

Blidstein, Gerald J. "Messiah." *Encyclopaedia Judaica.* Vol. 11. Jerusalem, Israel: Keter Publishing House Ltd., 1971.

Blomberg, Craig L. *The Historical Reliability of John's Gospel: Issues and Commentary.* Downers Grove, IL: InterVarsity Press, 2001.

Bock, Darrell L and Daniel B. Wallace. *Dethroning Jesus: Exposing Popular Culture's Quest to Unseat the Biblical Christ.* Nashville: Thomas Nelson, 2007.

Bourke, Stephen. "The Christian Flight to Pella: True or Tale?" *Biblical Archaeology Review* 39 (May/June 2013).

Boyarin, Daniel. *Border Lines: The Partition of Judaeo-Christianity.* Philadelphia: University of Pennsylvania Press, 2004.

Boyarin, Daniel. *The Jewish Gospels: The Story of the Jewish Christ.* New York: The New Press, 2012.

Brown, Francis, S. R. Driver, and Charles A. Briggs. *The Brown-Driver-Briggs Hebrew and English Lexicon: With an appendix containing Biblical Aramaic.* Oxford: Clarendon, 1907. BibleWorks, v.9.

Brown, Michel L. *Answering Jewish Objections to Jesus—Theological Objections.* Vol. 2. Grand Rapids, MI: Baker Books, 2000.

Bruce, F. F. *The New Testament Documents: Are They Reliable?* Downers Grove, IL: InterVarsity Press, 1960.

Buksbazen, Victor. *The Prophet Isaiah.* Vol. II. West Collingswood, NJ: The Spearhead Press, 1971.

Buzzard, Anthony F, and Charles F. Hunting. *The Doctrine of the Trinity—Christianity's Self-Inflicted Wound.* New York: International Scholars Publications, 1998.

"Calendar." *The Standard Jewish Encyclopedia.* Edited by Cecil Roth. Garden City, NY: Doubleday & Company, Inc., 1966.

Carson, D. A., Walter W. Wessel, and Walter L. Liefeld. *The Expositor's Bible Commentary: Matthew, Mark, Luke.* Edited by Frank E. Gaebelein. Vol. 8. Grand Rapids, MI: Zondervan Publishing House, 1990.

Carson, David A., ed. *From Sabbath to Lord's Day: A Biblical, Historical, and Theological Investigation.* Grand Rapids, MI: Zondervan Publishing House, 1982.

Casey, Maurice. *From Jewish Prophet to Gentile God*. Louisville, KY: Westminster/John Knox Press, 1991.

Casey, Maurice. *Is John's Gospel True?* New York: Routledge, 1996.

Casey, Maurice. *Jesus of Nazareth*. New York: T&T Clark International, 2010.

Cassuto, U. *A Commentary on the Book of Genesis—Part I From Adam to Noah*. Translated by Israel Abrahams. Jerusalem: The Magnes Press, The Hebrew University, 1998.

Cassuto, Umberto Moshe David. *A Commentary on the Book of Exodus*. Translated by Israel Abrahams. Skokie, IL: Varda Books, 2005.

Chester, Andrew. "High Christology—Whence, When and Why?" *Early Christianity* 2 (2011).

*Complete ArtScroll Machzor: Rosh Hashanah*. Translated and with commentary by Rabbi Nosson Scherman. Brooklyn, NY: Mesorah Publications, Ltd., 1985.

Conybeare, Fred C. "A Doctrinal Modification of a Text of the Gospel." *The Hibbert Journal* 1, no. 1 (October 1902). Prepared by Randall D. Hughes, God Glorified. Accessed June 21, 2015. http://www.godglorified.com/F.C.%20Conybeare.htm.

Cooper, David L. *The 70 Weeks of Daniel*. Los Angeles: Biblical Research Society, 1941.

Cranfield, C. E. B. *A Critical and Exegetical Commentary of the Epistle to the Romans*. Vol. 2. New York: T & T Clark Ltd., 1979.

*Daily Prayer Book—Ha-Siddur Ha-Shalem*. Translated by Philip Birnbaum. New York: Hebrew Publishing Company, 1997.

Darwin, Charles. *The Origin of Species*. New York: Signet Classics, 2003.

Daube, David. *The New Testament and Rabbinic Judaism*. London: School of Oriental and African Studies, The University of London, 1956.

Davies, Paul. *Cosmic Jackpot: Why Our Universe Is Just Right for Life*. Boston: Houghton Mifflin Company, 2007.

Dawkins, Richard. *The Blind Watchmaker: Why the Evidence of Evolution Reveals a Universe without Design*. New York: W. W. Norton & Company, Inc., 1996.

Dawkins, Richard. *The Greatest Show on Earth*. New York: Free Press, 2009.

Dawkins, Richard and John Lennox. *The God Delusion Debate*. Birmingham, AL: Fixed Point Foundation, 2007.

*Deluxe Edition of the Maxwell House Haggadah*. Kraft General Foods, Inc., 1996.

Dembski, William A. and Jonathan Wells. *The Design of Life: Discovering Signs of Intelligence in Biological Systems*. Dallas: The Foundation for Thought and Ethics, 2008.

Devine, Daniel James. "Debunking Junk." *World Magazine* (October 6, 2012): 34–39.

Dimont, Max I. *The Indestructible Jews*. New York: The New American Library, Inc., 1971.

Ehrman, Bart D. "The Historical Jesus Part I" (Course Guidebook). In *The Great Courses*. Chantilly, VA: The Teaching Company Limited Partnership, 2000.

Ehrman, Bart D. *Misquoting Jesus: The Story Behind Who Changed the Bible and Why*. San Francisco: Harper Collins Publishers, 2005.

Ehrman, Bart D. "The New Testament Part I" (Course Guidebook). In *The Great Courses*. Chantilly, VA: The Teaching Company Limited Partnership, 2000.

Elazar, Daniel J. "How Strong is Orthodox Judaism—Really? The Demographics of Jewish Religious Identification." Jerusalem Center for Public Affairs. Accessed May 30, 2015. http://www.jcpa.org/dje/articles2/demographics.htm.

Esping, Amber. "Does Birth Order Affect Intelligence?" Human Intelligence. Accessed March 13, 2016. http://www.intelltheory.com/birthOrder.shtml.

*ESV Study Bible*. Wheaton, IL: Crossway Bibles, 2008.

*Eusebius' Ecclesiastical History*. Translated by C. F. Cruse. Peabody, MA: Hendrickson Publishers, 1998.

Feinberg, Charles Lee. *The Prophecy of Ezekiel: The Glory of the Lord*. Chicago: Moody Press, 1969.

Feldman, Louis Harry. "Hellenism." *Encyclopaedia Judaica*. Vol. 8. Jerusalem, Israel: Keter Publishing House Ltd., 1971.

*Fiddler on the Roof*. DVD. Directed by Norman Jewison. Beverly Hills, CA: Metro-Goldwyn-Mayer Studios, Inc., 1971, 2007.

Fischer, John. *Sharing Israel's Messiah*. Highland Park, IL: The Watchman Association, 1978.

Flannery, Edward H. *The Anguish of the Jews: Twenty-Three Centuries of Antisemitism*. New York: Paulist Press, 1985.

Fohrman, David. "Passover: What Does It Mean to Be Chosen?" 8 videos. AlephBeta. Accessed June 14, 2015. https://www.alephbeta.org/course/lecture/setting-the-stage.

Freedman, Harry. "Akiva." *Encyclopaedia Judaica*. Vol. 2. Jerusalem, Israel: Keter Publishing House Ltd., 1971.

Fruchtenbaum, Arnold G. *Hebrew Christianity: Its Theology, History, and Philosophy*. Washington, DC: Canon Press, 1974.

Fruchtenbaum, Arnold G. *Israelology: The Missing Link in Systematic Theology*. Tustin, CA: Ariel Ministries Press, 1993.

Gauger, Ann, Douglas Axe, and Casey Luskin. *Science & Human Origins*. Seattle: Discovery Institute Press, 2013.

Glaser, Mitch and Zhava Glaser. *The Fall Feasts of Israel*. Chicago: Moody Press, 1987.

Gonzalez, Guillermo and Jay W. Richards. *The Privileged Planet: How Our Place in the Cosmos Is Designed for Discovery*. Washington, DC: Regnery Publishing, Inc., 2004.

Hawkins, Robert Martyr. *The Recovery of the Historical Paul*. Nashville: Vanderbilt University Press, 1943.

Heinemann, Joseph. "Amidah." *Encyclopaedia Judaica*. Vol. 2. Jerusalem, Israel: Keter Publishing House Ltd., 1971.

*The Hiding Place*. Videocassette. Directed by James F. Collier. Minneapolis: World Wide Pictures, Inc., 1975, 1990.

House, H. Wayne, ed. *Intelligent Design 101*. Grand Rapids, MI: Kregel Publications, 2008.

Howard, George. *Hebrew Gospel of Matthew*. Macon, GA: Mercer University Press, 1995.

Hurtado, Larry W. *Lord Jesus Christ: Devotion to Jesus in Earliest Christianity*. Grand Rapids, MI: William B. Eerdmans Publishing Company, 2003.

Intrater, Asher. *Who Ate Lunch with Abraham: The Appearances of God in the Form of a Man in the Hebrew Scriptures*. Peoria, AZ: Intermedia Publishing Group, 2011.

Irenaeus. "The Apostolic Fathers with Justin Martyr and Irenaeus." Vol. 1 in *Ante-Nicene Fathers*. Edited by Alexander Roberts and James Donaldson. Revised and arranged by A. Cleveland Coxe. 10 Vols. Peabody, MA: Hendrickson Publishers, 1994.

Jackson-McCabe, Matt, ed. *Jewish Christianity Reconsidered*. Minneapolis: Fortress Press, 2007.

Jacobs, Louis. "Shavuot." *Encyclopaedia Judaica*. Vol. 14. Jerusalem, Israel: Keter Publishing House Ltd., 1971.

Jacobs, Louis. "Sin." *Encyclopaedia Judaica*. Vol. 14. Jerusalem, Israel: Keter Publishing House Ltd., 1971.

Jocz, Jakob. *The Jewish People and Jesus Christ: The Relationship between Church and Synagogue*. 3rd ed. Grand Rapids, MI: Baker Book House, 1979.

"Johanan ben Zakkai." *Encyclopaedia Judaica*. Vol. 10. Jerusalem, Israel: Keter Publishing House Ltd., 1971.

Johnson, Paul. *A History of the Jews*. New York: Harper Perennial, 1987.

Johnson, Phillip E. *Darwin on Trial*. Downers Grove, IL: InterVarsity Press, 1993.

Johnson, Phillip E. *Defeating Darwinism by Opening Minds*. Downers Grove, IL: InterVarsity Press, 1997.

Johnson, Phillip E. *Reason in the Balance: The Case against Naturalism in Science, Law, & Education*. Downers Grove, IL: InterVarsity Press, 1995.

Juster, Daniel C. *Growing to Maturity (A Messianic Jewish Guide)*. Gaithersburg, MD: UMJC, 1982.

Juster, Daniel C. *Jewish Roots: A Foundation of Biblical Theology*. Gaithersburg, MD: DAVAR Publishing Co., 1986.

Juster, Daniel C. "Letter to a Rabbi," *The American Messianic Jew* (Spring 1980).

Kac, Arthur, W. *The Messianic Hope*. Baltimore: Reese Press, Inc., 1975.

Kac, Arthur W. *The Rebirth of the State of Israel: Is it of God or of Men?* Revised ed. Grand Rapids, MI: Baker Book House, 1976.

Kaiser, Walter C. "Exodus." In *The Expositor's Bible Commentary*. Edited by Frank E. Gaebelein. Vol. 2. 12 vols. Grand Rapids, MI: Zondervan Publishing House, 1990.

Kaplan, Aryeh. *The Real Messiah?: A Jewish Response to Missionaries*. New York: National Conference of Synagogue Youth/Union of Orthodox Jewish Congregations of America, 1976.

Kaufmann, Yehezkel. *The Religion of Israel from Its Beginnings to the Babylonian Exile*. Translated and abridged by Moshe Greenberg. New York: Schocken Books, 1972.

Kautzsch, E., and A. E. Cowley, eds. *Gesenius' Hebrew Grammar*. 2nd ed. Oxford: Clarendon, 1910. BibleWorks, v.9.

Kertzer, Morris N. *What Is a Jew?* New York: Collier Books, 1978.

*The Kingfisher Science Encyclopedia*. New York: Kingfisher, 2000.

Klinghoffer, David, ed. *Signature of Controversy*. Seattle: Discovery Institute Press, 2010.

Lapide, Pinchas. *The Resurrection of Jesus: A Jewish Perspective*. Minneapolis: Augsburg Publishing House, 1983.

Lehninger, Albert L. *Biochemistry*. New York: WorthPublishers, Inc., 1975.

Lennox, John C. *God's Undertaker: Has Science Buried God?* Oxford, UK: Lion Books, 2009.

Levine, Samuel. *You Take Jesus, I'll Take God: How to Refute Christian Missionaries*. Los Angeles: Hamoroh Press, 1980.

*The Life of Pi*. Directed by Ang Lee. Produced by Gil Netter, Ang Lee, and David Womark. Screenplay by David Magee. Based on *Life of Pi* by Yann Martel. Los Angeles: 20th Century Fox, 2012.

Martin, Ralph P. *A Hymn of Christ: Philippians 2:5–11 in Recent Interpretation and in the Setting of Early Christian Worship*. Downers Grove, IL: InterVarsity Press, 1997.

Martyr, Justin. "The Apostolic Fathers with Justin Martyr and Irenaeus." Vol. 1 in *Ante-Nicene Fathers*. Edited by Alexander Roberts and James Donaldson. Revised and arranged by A. Cleveland Coxe. 10 Vols. Peabody, MA: Hendrickson Publishers, 1994.

Meyer, Stephen C. *Darwin's Doubt: The Explosive Origin of Animal Life and the Case for Intelligent Design*. New York: Harper One, 2013.

Meyer, Stephen C., Paul A. Nelson, Jonathan Moneymaker, Scott Minnich, and Ralph Seelke. *Explore Evolution: The Arguments For and Against Neo-Darwinism*. London: Hill House Publishers, 2007.

Meyer,Stephen C. *Signature in the Cell: DNA and the Evidence for Intelligent Design*. New York: HarperCollins Publishers, 2009.

Moseley, Ron. *Yeshua: A Guide to the Real Jesus and the Original Church*. Hagerstown, MD: Ebed Publications, 1996.

Neufeld, Vernon H. *The Earliest Christian Confessions*. Grand Rapids, MI: Wm. B. Eerdmans, 1963.

*The NIV Study Bible*. Grand Rapids, MI: Zondervan Bible Publishers, 1985.

Notley, Steven R. "The Sabbath Was Made for Man." Jerusalem Perspective: Exploring the Jewish Background to the Life and Words of Jesus. Accessed March 13, 2016. http://www.jerusalemperspective.com/4616/.

Overman, Dean L. *A Case for the Divinity of Jesus: Examining the Earliest Evidence*. New York: Rowman & Littlefield Publishers, Inc., 2010.

*The Panarion of Epiphanius of Salamis*. Translated by Frank Williams. New York: Brill, 1997.

Patai, Raphael. *The Messiah Texts*. Detroit: Wayne State University Press, 1988.

Pritz, Ray A. *Nazarene Jewish Christianity: From the End of the New Testament Period until Its Disappearance in the Fourth Century*. Jerusalem: The Magnes Press, 1992.

Rausch, David A. *Messianic Judaism: Its History, Theology, and Polity*. New York: The Edwin Mellen Press, 1982.

Rich, Lawrence. *The Feasts of Israel: A Picture of God's Eternal Plan in Messiah*. Unpublished one page table.

Richards, Jay W. *God and Evolution: Protestants, Catholics, and Jews Explore Darwin's Challenge to Faith*. Seattle: Discovery Institute Press, 2010.

Rosenblatt, Samuel. "Inclination, Good and Evil." *Encyclopaedia Judaica.* Vol. 8. Jerusalem, Israel: Keter Publishing House Ltd., 1971.

Ross, Hugh. *Creation and Time: A Biblical and Scientific Perspective on the Creation-Date Controversy.* Colorado Springs, CO: NavPress, 1994.

Sailhamer, John H. "Genesis." In *The Expositor's Bible Commentary.* Edited by Frank E. Gaebelein. Vol. 2. 12 vols. Grand Rapids, MI: Zondervan Publishing House, 1990.

Sailhamer, John H. *Genesis Unbound: A Provocative New Look at the Creation Account.* Sisters, OR: Multnomah Books, 1996.

Sailhamer, John H. *The Pentateuch as Narrative.* Grand Rapids, MI: Zondervan Publishing House, 1992.

Sanders, Jack T. *The New Testament Christological Hymns: Their Historical Religious Background.* New York: Cambridge University Press, 1971.

Sandmel, Samuel. *Anti-Semitism in the New Testament?* Philadelphia: Fortress Press, 1978.

Sarna, Nahum M. *The JPS Torah Commentary: Exodus.* Philadelphia: The Jewish Publication Society, 1991.

Sarna, Nahum M. *The JPS Torah Commentary: Genesis.* Philadelphia: The Jewish Publication Society, 1989.

Schonfield, Hugh J. *The History of Jewish Christianity: From the First to the Twentieth Century.* London: Duckworth, 1936.

Schonfield, Hugh J. *The Passover Plot.* New York: Bantam Books, 1967.

"A Scientific Dissent from Darwinism." *Dissent from Darwin.* Accessed August 16, 2015. http://www.dissentfromdarwin.org/index.php.

Shanks, Hershel. *The Mystery and Meaning of the Dead Sea Scrolls.* New York: Vintage Books, 1999.

Singer, Tovia. "A Christian Defends Matthew by Insisting That the Author of the First Gospel Relied on the Septuagint When He Quoted Isaiah to Support the Virgin Birth." Outreach Judaism. Accessed June, 21, 2015. http://outreachjudaism.org/septuagint-virgin-birth/.

Skarsaune, Oskar and Reidar Hvalvik, eds. *Jewish Believers in Jesus: The Early Centuries.* Peabody, MA: Hendrickson Publishers, 2007.

Smalley, Gary and John Trent. *The Language of Love: A Powerful Way to Maximize Insight, Intimacy and Understanding.* New York: Pocket Books, 1991.

Stern, David H. *Jewish New Testament Commentary.* Clarksville, MD: Jewish New Testament Publications, 1992.

Stern, David H. *Messianic Jewish Manifesto.* Jerusalem: Jewish New Testament Publications, 1988.

Stern, Menahem. "History." *Encyclopaedia Judaica*. Vol. 8. Jerusalem, Israel: Keter Publishing House Ltd., 1971.

Stern, Shirely. *Exploring the Jewish Holidays and Customs*. Hoboken, NJ: Ktav Publishing House Inc., 1981.

Stevenson, Robert Louis. *Dr. Jekyll and Mr. Hyde*. New York: Oxford University Press, 1998.

"Stranger." *The New International Dictionary of the Bible*. Edited by J. D. Douglas and Merrill C. Tenney. Grand Rapids, MI: Zondervan Publishing House, 1987.

Strong, James. "A Concise Dictionary of the Words in the Greek Testament; with Their Renderings in the Authorized English Version" in *The New Strong's Exhaustive Concordance of the Bible*. Nashville: Thomas Nelson Publishers, 1984.

"The Teaching of the Twelve Apostles." Vol. 7 in *Ante-Nicene Fathers*. Edited by Alexander Roberts and James Donaldson. Revised and arranged by A. Cleveland Coxe. 10 Vols. Peabody, MA: Hendrickson Publishers, 1994.

Ten Boom, Corrie. *The Hiding Place*. With John Sherrill and Elizabeth Sherrill. Washington Depot, CT: Chosen Books, 1971.

Thayer, Joseph. *A Greek-English Lexicon of the New Testament*. n.p.: n.p., 1889. BibleWorks, v.9.

United Church of God. "Names for Saturday in Many Languages Prove Which Day Is the True Sabbath." In *Sunset to Sunset: God's Sabbath Rest*. Beyond Today. Accessed March 13, 2016. http://www.ucg.org/bible-study-tools/booklets/sunset-to-sunset-gods-sabbath-rest/names-for-saturday-in-many-languages.

Unterman, Alan. "Ru'ah HaKodesh." *Encyclopaedia Judaica*. Vol. 14. Jerusalem, Israel: Keter Publishing House Ltd., 1971.

Vermes, Geza. *Christian Beginnings: From Nazareth to Nicaea*. New Haven, CT: Yale University Press, 2013.

Wallace, Daniel B., ed. *Revisiting the Corruption of the New Testament: Manuscript, Patristic, and Apocryphal Evidence*. Grand Rapids, MI: Kregel Publications, 2011.

Weidner, Richard T. and Robert L. Sells. *Elementary Classical Physics*, Vol. 1. Boston: Allyn and Bacon, Inc., 1973.

White, James R. *The Forgotten Trinity: Recovering the Heart of Christian Belief*. Minneapolis: Bethany House Publishers, 1998.

# Subject and Author Index

# Scripture Index

# The Author's Biography

*Reviving the Reformation* is written by an author who is conservative but sees Christianity and Judaism through a different lens than most. Daniel Lang is the son of a nominally religious Jewish father and a devout Gentile Christian mother—a surgeon and nurse who met at Cook County Hospital in Chicago. His mother was a graduate of Moody Bible Institute and had hoped to be a missionary in a third world country before love and World War II redirected her life.

The author was raised in a small Midwestern town. He attended Hebrew school and was bar mitzvahed in the town's only (conservative) synagogue. Dan could never understand his mother's Gentile Christian presentation of the Messianic faith even though she did help to instill in him a strong faith in the God of the Tanach (Hebrew Bible). Growing up, Dan would cringe when he heard the name "Jesus," and "Christ" would send shivers up his spine. After being introduced to the messianic prophecies in high school, he saw that Yeshua filled the shoes of the expected Jewish Messiah.

Dan is a physician who has been actively working as a primary care internist for over twenty-eight years.